THE GENIUS OF THE PEOPLE

For Kathleen

CONTENTS

ACKNOWLEDGMENTS

I AM INDEBTED to James Hutson at the Library of Congress for good initial guidance to the right sources on the convention; to Richard Morris and James MacGregor Burns for similar advice; to Jerome Stoker of the New York Public Library for his bibliographic help; to David Kimball especially and to Robert Sutton and Anna Coxe Toogood of Independence National Historical Park, not only for their opening up to me the archives they have been assembling over the past years, but also for their meticulous readings of my manuscript; to Michael Hill for research help that was thorough, tireless, and resourceful; to Walter Karp, whose advice on political questions was as clear and invigorating as ever; to my wife, Kathleen Tolan, whose spirit of understanding and respect for all has been my model in this work; and to my editor, Ted Solotaroff, whose counsel from the first thought to the last sentence was always excellent.

"Well, doctor," Mrs. Powel asked Benjamin Franklin, "what have we got—a republic or a monarchy?"
"A republic," Franklin replied, "if you can keep it."

THE GENIUS OF THE PEOPLE

PROLOGUE

Two HUNDRED YEARS AGO, in May of 1787, several dozen delegates—all of them men, all of them white, all members in good
standing of the American political establishment, all of them
men of property—slave owners, plantation owners, gentlemen
farmers, businessmen, lawyers, bankers, and shippers—gathered at the State House in Philadelphia, where, in the next
several months, they wrote the Constitution of the United States,
which has served as the foundation of the country ever since.

They were attacked at once, and they continue to be attacked, for being counterrevolutionaries who took a radical
democratic revolution and turned it into a society dominated
by the rich and powerful; who took thirteen fine sovereign states
with good local governments and transformed them into one
big nation governed by a remote, overbearing central government.

They were attacked immediately by such radical leaders
of the revolution as Patrick Henry, and by farmers and others
on the edge, or outside, of the settled society of the eastern
seaboard. And they are being attacked still, both by critics of
the left who argue that ordinary people are excluded from real
power in the government and do not live under a just system,
and by critics of the right who argue that strong central government has stifled liberty.

To be sure, the framers of the Constitution have not only
been attacked. In the late nineteenth century, they—or those

1

among them, at least, who had been the champions of a strong central government—were regarded almost as demigods, who had foreseen the future and provided it with a form of government that was the envy of mankind. Histories of the Constitutional Convention and biographies of the framers could not find a rhetoric warm enough to praise the founding fathers.

Those among the framers who had opposed a strong central government and argued for the sanctity of the states did not fare quite so well in those years: Before the Civil War they were generally regarded with respect; but after the war they were seen as ignorant, bigoted, demagogic states' rights men, and they were treated with suitable disdain by George Bancroft, Edward Smith, Woodrow Wilson, and most others who wrote about the Constitution then.

In the early twentieth century, during the Progressive Era, the perspective shifted again. The men who had promoted a strong central government came under attack as big-money capitalists who had subverted a democratic revolution. The states' rights men who had opposed them were seen as good democrats. Or, on the other hand, as Charles Beard argued in an influential study of the convention, all the framers could be seen as capitalists: The centrists were those whose money was in investments, manufacturing, and trade; the states' rights men owned land; the convention was a struggle between two kinds of property to find the best sort of protection. Historians rewrote the biographies of the framers and found even the best of them wanting in public virtue and personal integrity.

Since Beard, most historians have written of the convention as a struggle among men with different sorts of economic interests. Merrill Jensen, Cecilia Kenyon, Forrest McDonald, and others have all gone over Beard's work and found fault with it—they demonstrate, for example, that the central-power men did not own more in the way of government securities than the local-power men, that the local-power men were not all democrats, that the small farmers overwhelmingly supported ratification of the constitution, which was said to go against their interests. And yet, even if Beard is found wrong in most of his evidence, his fundamental view is still accepted: that the framers of the constitution were motivated by economic interest. And most of us find ourselves taking such a

view largely for granted. We are all instinctive Marxists in the
twentieth century; we all believe men are most deeply motivated by class interest and by economic appetites.

Indeed, these analyses of the convention from the point of
view of interest have been especially illuminating. They have
dispelled the founding fathers' aura of public virtue to reveal
quite human men, pursuing their fortunes as well as their fame,
looking for the main chance in a land investment, the interest
on public loans, a bit of an edge in the navigation laws—interests the delegates sometimes shared as a class, sometimes had
as their own personal angle. The story of the convention has
become much more complex and interesting and persuasive as
it has passed through the hands of all these historians.

Even so, these schools of interpretation fail in the end to
be convincing, it seems to me, in one common respect: They
all tend to simplify away the particularities in search of gen-
eralizations—and, in the process, miss the essence of what occurred at the convention. They all come down to a view that
the framers of the constitution belonged more or less to one
class, and had more or less one common set of intentions, or
one set of biases or goals or interests, and that their labors in
the summer of 1787 can be seen as the careful codifying of that
set of common intentions into a body of laws.

And yet when one actually looks at the day-to-day debates
during that hot, humid, insect-ridden summer in Philadelphia,
such a view simply won't hold up. Far from there being one
set of intentions, there were as many intentions as there were
framers. What one sees, in fact, is a group of men who, despite
their common background and broad class interests, had myriad diverging appetites, ideals, and interests, and set about
disputing with one another, wrangling, losing patience, lashing out, attacking one another, accusing one another of ignorance and inconsistency, or worse, of lack of principle and even
of treasonous intent; erupting in anger or simply packing up
and leaving town altogether, never to return; warning that
certain provisions could only lead eventually to civil war or
bring down upon the country some even more calamitous
judgment of heaven. By the end of the convention, none of the
delegates, not one, was entirely happy with the constitution
they had written. Some refused entirely to sign the completed

work; and those who did sign signed in varying degrees of reluctance, dismay, anguish, and disgust.

What one sees, indeed, is a group of men forced by all their differences into a succession of vexing or detestable compromises, a group of men forced, in one argument after another, to fall back to general principles in order to buttress their positions—to embrace general principles that finally, by the sheer force of logic, would have to promise liberty and justice for all.

To be sure, these compromises did not at once eliminate slavery or give the vote to women or embrace the destitute. But the principles to which the delegates forced one another to resort placed the country on a course from which—so long as it adhered to the constitution—there could never be a turning back: a course to an increasingly open form of government, open to both sexes, to all races, to the poor and the politically oppressed of other countries; to the free exercise of speech and press and religion (including the freedom to believe in no God); to the guarantee of due process equally to all; to ensuring that the system not be distorted by too great concentrations of power in large business concerns, or in the military, or in the office of the president; to an extreme caution about engaging in foreign adventures; to a due regard for the good opinion of mankind. No wonder these men of property, hoping (in their least pure moments) to give themselves some advantage in the new government, left the convention in such deep anguish.

These days, of course, we are all less enamored of the nineteenth-century great-man interpretation of history, less chagrined when human beings turn out to be merely human. The men who framed the constitution may indeed have been great men, but we tend to find them even more interesting these days as recognizably human beings who were shaped by history as much as they shaped it, as examplars of their class and of their history, as men representative of what they themselves often referred to as the genius of the people—that cumulative body of knowledge and intuition formed by living for centuries under the legacy of the Magna Carta and the rule of common law.

How such a group of privileged eighteenth-century aristocrats, oligarchs, monarchists, lawyers and businessmen and bankers were led by reason and experience to understand that their lives and interests were best protected in a democracy is the story of this book.

PART I

1

THE MAN OF HISTORY

MADISON WAS THE FIRST to arrive—as usual. He was a small man, no bigger, it was said, than half a piece of soap—frail, fearful to travel for what it might do to his health. Shy, pale, reticent, a bookish man, with a small, high-pitched voice, awkward in debate, he always depended, in meetings of the sort he was about to attend, on thorough preparation, and his baggage was stuffed with books and notes.

Jounced painfully over the cobblestones of the city streets, he had just arrived from New York aboard the Philadelphia Flier—an open coach that rode high on its bowed springs like a great teetering soup tureen with leather side curtains flapping down to keep out sun or rain or chill, its dozen passengers jammed in three to a hard backless bench, their luggage shoved under the benches or lashed to the back of the coach. Travelers had a choice of schedule: They could go straight through from New York to Philadelphia, from one o'clock in the morning till late that same night, or they could make the trip in two days, as Madison had done, with an overnight stay at an inn along the way. Either way, travelers arrived in pain.

Madison, just thirty-six years old, combed his powdered hair low on his forehead to hide the beginnings of baldness, and a ribbon held the rest of his hair back in a small queue. Although he was already beginning to show a taste for the somber black clothes that would eventually become his only form of dress, for this particular occasion he had packed a positively sprightly blue-and-buff suit with a long single-breasted coat and breeches that met his stockings at the knee, shirts with billowing ruffles at chest and wrist, shoes with large silver buckles—so that, despite his natural tendency to disappear in a crowd, he could expect to make an impressive showing in Philadelphia.

The business that had brought him to Philadelphia was, in its origins, a vexing little local spat over the oyster fisheries of Chesapeake Bay. It had begun more than 150 years before, in 1632, when King Charles I had made a fateful blunder. As a favor to his friend Lord Baltimore, the king had designated as the southern border of Baltimore's province of Maryland the *far* bank—that is to say, the high-water mark on the Virginia side—of the Potomac River, down to Chesapeake Bay. It was a most unusual gesture, to reach all the way across a river for a border; and beginning at once, the crab and oyster fishermen of Virginia and Maryland fought with one another over fishing rights in the river. The Virginians refused to recognize the unusual border; the Marylanders insisted they must.

By the mid-1780s, with the royal government gone, and a new, independent nation established in America under the Articles of Confederation, the little disagreement over oyster fisheries had grown to include certain rights of navigation and commerce along the river; and Pennsylvania and Delaware, because they used the river for shipping, were dragged into the dispute. The wrangling among the four states called into question whether the new government of America was strong enough to maintain peace and order among the states, to settle even a paltry little "oyster war."

In 1785, the Virginians and Marylanders, who had been particularly plagued by the difficulties over fishing and commerce in the Potomac River, finally determined to take matters in their own hands. They got together, extralegally, completely ignoring the supposed central authority of the Continental Congress, for a meeting at General Washington's Mount Vernon. But because commerce among the midatlantic states involved not only Virginia and Maryland but also their neighboring states, the Mount Vernon meeting could not resolve all issues. The men who met at Mount Vernon arranged to have the Virginia legislature invite the other state legislatures to send delegations to a meeting at Annapolis in September of the following year, 1786, to "take into consideration the trade of the states," and to look into the possibility of a "uniform system in their commercial regulations."

The Annapolis meeting was a failure too: Not enough delegates showed up to make a quorum. But the delegates who did attend passed another resolution, under the bold leadership of Madison and of Alexander Hamilton of New York: to call upon the legislatures of all the states to send delegations to Philadelphia on the second Monday of May 1787, to consider "the situation of the United States" and to "devise such further provisions as shall appear to them necessary to render the constitution of the federal government adequate to the exigencies of the Union." To the gratification of some men—Madison among them—the little aggravation of the "oyster war" was about to become an occasion to transform the nature of the United States profoundly and forever.

The stagecoach pulled in, late in the evening, at its regular terminus, the Indian Queen Tavern at Market and Fourth streets, a block from the boardinghouse where Madison had booked a room, and in the center of Philadelphia's markets and shops. There, during the day, one could buy books, spyglasses, theater tickets, Windsor chairs, wooden tubs, teas from Canton, shoes of local leather, boots of English leather, little baskets, buckets, wines from Provençal, snapping turtles, ice cream, coaches, horses, dueling pistols, tallow candles, loaves of sugar, slaves both male and female, and, just at the time Madison arrived in town, on Thursday, May 3, hyacinths, lilies, and the early spring asparagus.

This city, with a mere 40,000 inhabitants and only a few score old established blocks at its center, was the largest city in America, settled in the very midst of the eastern seaboard, with excellent docks and wharves and a good road heading out to the west. William Penn had laid out the city himself in 1682, and his policy of freedom of religion had attracted a large and cosmopolitan lot of immigrants from England and Wales, Germany, France, and Holland, Sweden and Finland. New York had only 33,000 inhabitants, Boston 18,000, Charleston 10,000. None of these cities compared for sheer sprawl with such cities as Paris (population 600,000) or London (950,000); but Philadelphia withal was a sophisticated place, a prosperous port, in constant touch with the world at large. It was sufficiently civilized and vigorous to support ten newspapers, thirty-three houses of worship, a Philosophical Society, a public library, a university, two theaters, a museum, a poorhouse, a model jail, a model hospital, and a dispensary for the poor, many of the institutions having been inspired by the austere and public-spirited Quaker character of the town. There were 304 blocks between the two rivers, 7,000 houses, 662 streetlamps, outhouses set back from each house, and pumps for water at regular intervals along the street. The city was, according to a traveler from South America, "one of the most pleasant and well-ordered cities in the world."

Brissot de Warville, a Frenchman who was journeying around America at about this time, declared that Philadelphia "may be considered the metropolis of the United States. It is certainly the most beautiful and best built city in the nation, and also the wealthiest, though not the most ostentatious. Here you will find more well-educated men, more knowledge of politics and literature, more political and learned societies than anywhere else in the United States."

To be sure, New York was not a negligible town; but it could not be described as salubrious. Packed with the very rich and the very poor, with aristocrats who still loved England and with slum-dwelling dockhands, day laborers, and free Negroes, with unassimilated communities of Irish, Jews, Scots, and Germans, with the well-entrenched Dutch and an emerging group of members of the establishment who worshiped on Sundays at the Anglican churches of Trinity and St. Paul's, New York was even then a city of scrapping ethnic blocs and warring interests, even then a city that Americans felt they knew and hated.

Boston, already a self-satisfied city, its prominence an established historical fact, or artifact, remained an important port, first among the New England coastal cities of shipbuilders, traders, fishermen, whalers, and smugglers. It was, too, the center of New England democracy, where nearly every adult male had the vote, and despite some differences in wealth and social standing, the principles of simple, egalitarian self-government were deeply embedded in the culture.

To the south, Virginia had no major city to speak of—notwithstanding the distinction of Williamsburg and the pretension of Richmond—and it cultivated yet another political culture: The "first families," agrarians all, lived along the Potomac and James rivers; they met with one another in their homes, or at the occasional sessions of the legislature; they conducted their business directly from their own wharves, and they had no great affection for big urban centers of commercial and political dealmaking.

Farther south, Charleston was a tightly knit little world of intermarried families, an oligarchy whose would-be-English aristocracy managed the vast plantations in the neighboring countryside and made their fortunes from rice and indigo, and from "black gold," or slaves, for which Charleston was the principal port and market in America.

Between these cities of the coast was a countryside surprisingly well settled. Admittedly, much of the land had been cleared only recently. Tree stumps were almost everywhere in evidence. And when Madison made his way down from New York to Philadelphia, crossing the Hudson River by ferry, traveling through the mosquito-ridden swamps of New Jersey, along the muddy, rutted road past the little settlement of Bergen and on toward Snake Hill (so named because it had been infested with rattlesnakes until the local citizenry had set wild pigs loose to devour them—so that now Snake Hill was infested with wild pigs), on down the sticky, narrow, jolting road beyond Passaic and past the unusual new establishments at Newark (spinning mills and a shoe factory, which very few people recognized as harbingers of the industrial future), he might have felt the countryside was not quite as domesticated as that of England.

But beyond Newark, a traveler began to enter a land of small, well-kept farms and little villages, each with a church or two. Elizabethtown was a charming village of about two hundred houses, set on a creek. Just beyond, the stagecoach crossed three bridges over the winding Rahway River, as it made its circuitous way through the town of Rahway, a pleasant village with many little gardens. Past Princeton (where Madison had gone to college), the countryside dissolved into woods and farms, valleys and gentle slopes, a range of low mountains in the distance, field after field of wheat and flax. In this part of the country, the observant traveler could see history before his very eyes in the structure of the farmhouses. When the land had first been settled, a farmer would put up a small hut of heavy planks or logs as his sole dwelling. If he prospered, he would build a second house, of clapboards, twice as large as the first, and the first became his kitchen. If he prospered still, he built a third house, often of stone, and the second house became his kitchen, the first house his cow barn.

New England, with its small farms and tidy villages, its traditions of sturdily independent farmers, was similar to this stretch of New Jersey, though one saw more brick in New England towns, more stone in New Jersey and Pennsylvania. In New York, the great estates of the old Dutch families gave a distinctive character to the landscape. The area farther south, around Chesapeake Bay, with its roads kept dry (and soft for the passing carriages) by layers of gravel and sand, was distinguished by large cultivated plantations, crowned with mansions of Palladian dimensions and refinement, owned by the same families for generations. The plantations even farther south were connected by less dependable roads, worked by hundreds of slaves. They were owned by silk- and satin-wearing men who looked like exotic tropical birds next to the plainly turned out Puritans of the northeast, and gave the seacoast a touch of splendid variety.

The most dramatic contrast to this fringe of settled land along the east coast occurred a hundred or so miles to the west, where the villages and plantations and farms gave way suddenly to forest, to the Appalachian Mountains, to utterly untamed wilderness; and the men of the latest fashion from London and Paris, with their felt hats and laces and velvets, their white wigs and ceremonial swords, gave way to outrageously self-reliant, rude, musket-toting, buckskin-clad frontiersmen who cherished the values not so much of social order and accumulated capital or land as of individualism and of freedom from all authority but their own.

The rush to the west was astonishing. In the seven months just before Madison arrived in Philadelphia, one station on the way west counted "177 boats containing 2,689 souls, 1,333 horses, 766 cattle, 102 wagons and one phaeton; besides a number which passed in the night unobserved." According to one report, in 1775 there were 150 men in Kentucky, but no women. By 1790 there would be 73,677 people, including 12,430 slaves and 114 free Negroes. Almost half the population of South Carolina lived in the backcountry, four-fifths of all the whites. They shared their country less with European diplomats, bankers, young Charlestonians who had been educated at the London courts of law, members of the Philosophical Society, and political theorists than with cattle, horse thieves, social outcasts, and a population of native Americans whom they persisted in seeing as brutish, thieving, treacherous, and nasty savages. Intermingled with these savages on the border of the fragile new nation were the forts and other outposts of former or future enemies: to the south the Spanish, to the west and north the British.

Altogether, not counting Indians, the Americans numbered three and a half million, of whom about one-sixth were black slaves, most of them living in states south of Pennsylvania. (Spain had a population at the time of about ten million, the British Isles of fifteen million, France of twenty-five million.) Although the greatest number of these Americans were of English descent, a wide range of nationalities and religions and languages could already be found among them, and a wide variety of experiences of daily life.

To say, then, that all these different sorts of Americans shared, with Madison, a common ideology or even political mood in the summer of 1787 would be misleading. Some families had been settled in their homes for several generations, and had acquired a great affection for the status quo, for a firmly structured society; others were accustomed to the wide open spaces, to a world without recognized boundaries or customs, to a liberty that was all but absolute; still others—small tradesmen and merchants, immigrants with aspirations—hoped for both order and opportunity to pursue their fortunes. Some were radical egalitarians, some believed the public business was best left in the hands of the leading families. Yet all these Americans had just come through the experience of political revolution together, whether they had approved or resisted it;

they had nearly all hazarded, or been forced to hazard, their towns and farms and livestock and lives on the making of a new nation; they had just rid themselves of a distant and coercive government; they had taken their government more directly into their own hands; they had thrown off the century-old bondage to Europe.

Their revolution had been one for independence, for self-government, in the sense of freedom from the government of England; as such, the self-rule that was won was restricted to men, to white men, and, among white men, to property owners, farmers, shopkeepers, or to those who were at least respectably employed. But even such self-government was all but unique in the world, and the revolution had necessarily been accompanied by a spreading enthusiasm for the ideal of self-rule, an ideal that was hard to keep from spreading and from reaching its logical end, a democratic government. Such an ideal, even when it struck fear into some men, was invigorating; and, whether with abandon or with caution or resistance, Americans were exhilarated, as only those people who govern themselves can be—and they tended to see themselves as the hope of the world, the harbinger of the future.

Some of the world agreed. The French travelers, at least, who flocked to America in the years just after its revolution could not say enough good about the new country. Brissot de Warville, for instance, was delighted even with the sort of rude stagecoach in which Madison traveled to Philadelphia: "you meet people of all walks of life," said Brissot of American public transportation, "a man who is going only fifteen miles yields his seat to another who is going farther; a mother with her daughter takes a ten mile trip to dine with friends . . . you make a new acquaintance every fifteen minutes. . . . A member of Congress sits side by side with the shoemaker who elected him and fraternizes with him. . . . No one puts on important airs as they do only too frequently in France. . . . American stagecoaches are truly political vehicles"—filled with the spirit of liberty and egalitarianism that marked the new world.

One of Brissot's fellow countrymen, a man named Barbe-Marbois, was endlessly amazed by what he saw on his tour of America. "We often meet Senators," wrote this man who came from a continent in which such an august figure as a senator was a frilled demigod, "respected magistrates, coming back from the market carrying green stuffs, or"—would his countrymen believe it?—"fish." In Boston, he paid a call on the president of the Massachusetts Senate, who was, Barbé-Marbois carefully explained, "the head of a body in which resides the exercise of the sovereign power, and he is the most important person in the district." When Barbe-Marbois knocked at his door, "he came himself to open it and"—as if that were not enough—"received us in a clean room, but Spartan in its simplicity. When the call was over he showed us out himself, his candle in his hand, and since it was late, I judge that he put the key in his pocket and went to bed." Such was life in a republic.

The United States was a society pledged to the representative rule of republicanism or even, in some towns, to the direct rule of democracy, in a world otherwise ruled by monarchs and emperors. The eighteenth century was an age in which parliaments struggled to contain the power of their rulers with varying degrees of success or failure. Spain was a monarchy; Austria and Poland were ruled by Joseph II, a "benevolent despot"; Catherine the Great ruled Russia; Frederick William II, nephew of Frederick the Great, ruled Prussia.

France, ruled by Louis XVI, who had tried to ruin the British by helping the Americans in their revolution, now found itself deeply in debt because of the costs of the war. By 1786, debt service in France consumed fully one-half of all revenues; Louis's government was in dreadful financial condition—and America, and all it stood for (represented in Paris at the moment by a minister who had been an illustrious revolutionary, Thomas Jefferson), was becoming wildly fashionable.

England, ruled by King George III, and managed by Prime Minister William Pitt the younger, had by this time recovered from the American Revolution. Contrary to the expectations of many, the loss of colonial America did not destroy British commerce; trade had revived and would soon surpass its prewar volume. And American political ideals were no threat to the British government. Some British politicians were impressed by the American experiment; many looked confidently forward to its early failure.

John Adams was the minister in London, and he fit in

comfortably with British society. He was no revolutionary fire-brand. In fact, he had been watching the British Parliament closely, and he admired it. He had even written a book about the virtues of the British bicameral legislature, and portions of his book were appearing regularly in a Philadelphia news-paper, and would continue to appear for several months—steady summer reading for Philadelphians and their visitors.

Not all Americans would consider their ambassador's writing the last word on the subject. As one letter to the editor said: "The sentiment of our Ambassador Adams, that a person ought to be WELL BORN to be of any consequence in a common-wealth, seems to be rapidly gaining ground in this country. Hardly any person is at present in want of employ but his ad-vertisement gives a plain intimation . . . of his or her being in some one sense or another WELL BORN. As for example: 'A *Gentleman* having about two or three months leisure time, would be happy to employ it in transcribing &c.' . . . Now I would ask these gentlemen and ladies, what are their *good families* and *gentility* to the republicans of America? We ac-complished the late Revolution without being *Well Born* . . . In the late war . . . I remember it was not demanded, Who are the *Nobles* and *Well Born* of the land; but, Who is able and willing to carry his musquet and knapsack through the snows of Canada or the sands of Carolina and Georgia, and repel the invaders of his rights and country?"

Adams liked to think he was enormously influential at least on the delegates who gathered for the convention in Philadel-phia, but in fact there is not a single recorded reference to him in the debates of the convention. As Madison wrote to Jeffer-son about Adams's book: "Men of learning find nothing new in it. Men of taste many things to criticize. And men without either not a few things which they will not understand."

Madison's baggage was thrown to the sidewalk in front of the Indian Queen Tavern, where gentlemen and those of the middling sort mingled in the public rooms over Madeira, beer, and brandy, clay pipes and games of cards and backgammon. Madison did not pause here at the tavern when he first got to town—as he later would—but set out at once toward his room-ing house, his baggage brought along behind him. And he must have cut an odd figure as he made his way along Market Street that late-spring evening. For all his frailty and the diminutiveness of his figure, he walked customarily with a lively step that could only be called bouncing.

The streets were straight as strings. Philadelphia was laid out on a grid pattern. To the east was the broad Delaware River; to the west was the narrow Schuylkill. Between the two rivers Philadelphia lay, as though pressed out by a waffle iron. The private wharves and public docks and ferry landings were all along the Delaware. The street just at the water was called Water Street. Then came Front Street, Second, Third, Fourth, and so on to the Schuylkill, although the paving ran out at about Sixth Street, and quagmire took over soon after on a rainy day. The streets running across the grid from east to west were named mostly for trees: Cherry, Mulberry, Chestnut, Walnut, Locust. But running through the center of these streets, just above Chestnut, was Market Street, the central thoroughfare of the city. It came right out from the docks on the Delaware—with the big public market running along its middle from Front to Fourth—on past the Indian Queen Tavern to some of the finer residential blocks of the city. Nothing of consequence was more than a few blocks walk from anything else.

By ten o'clock in the evening, Philadelphia was quiet, its stillness broken only by the cries of the night watchmen who called out the hours and the weather through the night. The brick sidewalks were marked at intervals by large, solid posts that were designed to keep carriages from coming up over the sidewalk, and glass-enclosed oil lamps lit the way.

Madison had booked a room at Mrs. House's, on Market Street just above Fifth. Like the other residences nearby, it was built of red brick, with white-painted trim around its guillotine windows—and it was large enough to accommodate a household composed of Mrs. Mary House, a widow (like so many proprietors of boardinghouses); her daughter Eliza Trist, just recently widowed; Eliza's young son, Hore Browse; and as many as ten boarders, one or two to a room.

Boardinghouses such as this one were less expensive than a tavern like the Indian Queen, more comfortable and private, quieter, not so exposed to "the Rudeness of the Mobb," as one southern traveler said. Proprietors of boardinghouses could be more selective about their clientele than tavernkeepers could, and a boarder could be assured of sharing a room with a well-behaved roommate, have his own closet with a lock on it, and enjoy the privilege of receiving guests in the front parlor. To be sure, some gentlemen liked a little raucousness when they traveled, an easy access to drink and tobacco and cards and a general relaxation of standards, and they enjoyed the feeling they got in the public rooms of the taverns, where, as one of them said, "you have only to put your hand in your pocket and hall [sic] out some money and everything is at your service"—but the lodgings at Mrs. House's had long been a favorite with Virginia politicians, and Madison always stayed there when he was in town.

James was the eldest of ten children, from a comfortable, though not rich, plantation-owning family, the son of a doting and admiring father, who wrote him often (he would write all summer with thoughts about the work Madison was engaged in). He was sent to Princeton, at a time when the college con-sisted of a single stone building, three floors high, twenty win-dows wide, its front yard covered with sheep droppings and decorated with an old cannon, and surrounded by a crumbling wall from which decorative urns had fallen to the ground. There he studied with one of America's greatest teachers, the presi-dent of the college, John Witherspoon, who held forth to a gen-eration of young Americans about the tenets of the Scottish Enlightenment, extolling "the spirit of liberty" and excoriat-ing tyranny—leaping about in his pulpit and, because of some nervous disorder, twitching violently, fainting, and even, once, falling right out of the pulpit. Of Witherspoon's charges, fifty-six would become state legislators, thirty-three would become judges (three on the Supreme Court), twelve would become state governors, twenty-nine would become members of the House of Representatives, twenty-one would become senators, one would become vice-president, and Madison would become president.

Madison had an extremely sensitive mind, which seemed at times a too delicate instrument. It must have been that sense of delicacy, as much as any real physical reason, that caused him to believe he could not "expect a long or healthy life" (in fact he lived to the age of eighty-five, always fretting about his health), and so he saw no point to studying anything that would be "useless in possessing after one has exchanged time for eternity." He studied Hebrew and ethics, and after he left Princeton, he sank into something of a depression, evidently discontented with the career of plantation management that was most obviously before him. But soon enough he got caught up in a controversy about religious liberty that aroused his passions and his sense of the important. He became embroiled in politics, and in 1776 he was elected to the Virginia convention and to the committee that framed a constitution and a declaration of rights for the newly independent state of Virginia. He was quickly noted for an extraordinarily sharp analytical mind—what one of his political opponents in later years would call "a logic box" that was capable of an almost startling lucidity.

By 1780, he had been elected to the Continental Congress, which was then meeting in Philadelphia; but not everyone was entirely taken with him in Congress. Thomas Rodney, a delegate from Delaware, said that Madison "possesses all the self-conceit that is common to youth and inexperience . . . but it is unattended with that gracefulness and ease which sometimes makes even the impertinence of youth and inexperience agreeable or at least not offensive." A French diplomat, Louis Otto, saw more easily through this awkward youth: he was "well educated," said Otto, "wise, temperate, gentle, studious."

Madison fell in love while he was in Philadelphia, with a young woman named Kitty Floyd, courted her, and became engaged to her. And then, for some unknown reason, she broke off the engagement. Madison was very deeply disappointed, and he wrote to his friend Jefferson of his sorrow. In his old age, however, he went back over the letters and tried to obliterate his confession of feelings for Kitty, so that only a few lines can still be deciphered: ". . . one of those incidents to which such affairs are liable . . . The necessity of my visiting . . . New Jersey no longer exists . . . profession of indifference . . . more propitious turn of fate." The hurt was deep: It was the end of romantic attempts on Madison's part for ten years, until he met, and married, Dolley Todd.

He served in Congress through the remainder of the Revolutionary War, until 1783. Then, in December of that year, he returned home to his father's plantation, to study the law. Although Madison's financial support had always depended on slavery, coming as it did from his father's plantation, he was not comfortable with the institution of slavery. Like Jefferson and Washington and other of his fellow Virginians, he had come to believe that slavery was immoral. He could think of no realistic way to bring it to an end; he believed in the long run that it was uneconomic and destined to disappear of its own accord; but in the meantime he was supported by it and felt a perpetual unease. So it was, toward the end of 1783, that he took up the study of law, in order that, as he wrote to Edmund Randolph, he might at least have a profession in which he could "depend as little as possible on the labour of slaves."

All the while, his health had been delicate, and he had worried about it incessantly. Eliza Trist, Mrs. House's daughter, who fussed over him all the while he had been at the rooming house during the sessions of Congress in Philadelphia, feared constantly that he would be thrust into some public role that would prove too much for him. "He has a soul replete with gentleness, humanity, and every social virtue," she said in a letter to Jefferson, another frequent boarder, "and yet I am certain that some wretch or other will write against him. . . . Mr. Madison is too amiable in his disposition, to bear up against a torrent of abuse. It will hurt his feelings and injure his health, take my word."

During the past several months, however, presumably in preparation for the convention in Philadelphia, which he had sensed might be a unique opportunity to achieve something important, he had undertaken a program of horseback riding and hiking to build his strength. (Ordinarily he detested horseback riding; he much preferred to travel by coach. His only recreation, it was said, was to change the character of his work.) And the training regime had worked. Although he was still, by any ordinary standards, a man of uncertain physical stamina, by his own standards he was quite fit, and even showed a hint of ruddiness in his cheeks, ready once again to throw his keen, delicate, analytical scholar's mind into the midst of the practical world.

What sort of conversation he had with the House family on his arrival we cannot know, although, after the exchange of pleasantries, it seems possible that Madison talked a bit of business with Samuel House, Mrs. House's son, who lived nearby and who handled the merchandising of the tobacco crop for the Madison plantation. Whatever Madison and Samuel House talked about, however, they cannot have talked long. While Madison could manage a certain amount of socializing, long sessions of conversation exhausted him, particularly when they degenerated to small talk, and he liked to get off to his own room, where he could be alone with his thoughts and his books.

At home on his father's plantation, he usually rose early in the morning, ate a sparing breakfast, and then retired to his room to study until dinnertime. After dinner he joined the evening festivities—talk and whist when the company was small, dancing when the company was large. In large groups, it was said, Madison was usually uncomfortable, stiff, and ill at ease, although in small groups he could relax and become quite informal, and even funny. Yet he could not long keep his mind from his books. He was most content when he was reading and writing, where his mind was entirely absorbed and free to move at its own terrific speed.

Mrs. Trist had prepared Madison's usual room for him—a second-floor front room—and he must have retired soon after he arrived. Typically, Philadelphia fashion called for a mahogany bureau for clothes, a mahogany bedstead (with blue-and-white chintz curtains), a small writing table with a brass candlestick and a couple of mahogany Windsor chairs, a washstand, an oval looking glass, and a fireplace—not something Madison would use in May.

He rarely slept more than three or four hours a night. As an adult he never had. He always kept a candle burning by his bed through the night so that he could get up—as he usually did, throughout his life, at least several times in the course of a night—to read, to write, and in the event a new thought occurred to him, to make notes.

Three years before, in 1784, when Jefferson had gone off to Paris as minister to France from the newly independent United States, he and Madison had agreed to correspond with one another, and to send whatever precious things one or the other might require. Madison sent Jefferson all sorts of newspaper clippings, legislative papers, pamphlets, and such objects as Jefferson requested for gifts or objects to display in order to amaze the French: pippin apples, cranberries, pecan nuts, grafts from American fruit trees, Virginia redbirds, opossums. And Jefferson sent Madison such miraculous objects as a pocket telescope, a pedometer, a "chemical box," an umbrella, a packet of matches ("Great care must be taken in extracting the taper that none of the phosphorus drips on your hand, because it is inextinguishable and will therefore burn to the bone if there be matter enough. It is said that urine will extinguish it"), and books.

Madison had particularly asked Jefferson to send any books that might "throw light on the general constitution and *droit public* of the several confederacies which have existed." The books arrived not singly or in pairs but by the score: Fortune Barthélemy de Felice's *Code de l'Humanité, ou La Legislation Universelle, Naturelle, Civile et Politique* in thirteen volumes; Diderot's extraordinary new *Encyclopédie Méthodique;* Abbé Millot's *Éléments d'Histoire Générale* in eleven volumes; Abbé de Mably's *De l'Étude de l'Histoire;* Jacques-Auguste de Thou's *Histoire Universelle*, along with other current French work, and Plutarch's *Lives*, the orations of Demosthenes, and the histories of Polybius.

These books, particularly the books of history, would inform Madison for the meetings that summer in Philadelphia. Like most of his peers, despite his sound education in political theory with Witherspoon, Madison had a great deal less respect for theory, or "reason," than he had for experience. And for Madison, as for his colleagues, experience began with history—in particular with history since 1215, when the nobles of great Britain forced King John to grant them the Magna Carta, which limited the arbitrary power of the king. This history was still very much alive, still shaping daily life in America, and Madison made it his business to understand it.

The feudal lords who forced John to put his hand to the great charter was interested first and foremost in preventing the king from incessantly demanding money and services from them, from arbitrarily depriving them of their property. It was on the basis of their property that all else depended; it was on their property that they established their castles, supported their families and retainers, and defended their lives and whatever liberties they had. Thus it was that property, and its protection, was at the very foundation of all their other political rights. It was not simply an end in itself; it was the means to guarantee life and liberty.

On that foundation the barons laid other agreements, a set of laws by which the king was bound—creating a society of laws, if not yet a perfectly just one. These laws took as their implicit assumption that there was a higher law to which even the king must submit, a higher law that all Englishmen shared and that they might impose on their ruler.

From this sense of a supreme common law derived such specific laws as these: that "no freeman shall be taken or imprisoned . . . or outlawed, or exiled, or in any way destroyed . . . except by the lawful judgment of his peers or by the law of the land"; at the same time, "to no one will we sell, deny, or delay right or justice." In the following centuries, succeeding kings were confronted with demands to recognize other common principles: that a man could not be forced to testify against himself (which, among other things, reduced the usefulness of torture or beatings by a policeman to force confessions), that a standing army must be avoided in peacetime since it was dangerous to liberty, and that in all cases the military must be subordinate to the civil power. By 1787, the virtue of these laws had been tested by the experience of many generations, living through many tumults and under many different conditions, and they were accepted as proved.

They made their way to America with the voyagers in the *Mayflower*, who, before they set foot on shore, drew up a compact among themselves by which they pledged to submit to such "just and equal laws" as the government they organized might pass. Thus, with the movement of a pen, the Pilgrims converted the business arrangement they had for settling a tract of land into a foundation for self-government. (When the English political philosopher John Locke later said that all societies are based upon a contract, that man originally lived in a "state of nature" and entered society by acceptance of this contract, many Americans of Madison's time understood his words not so much as political theory but as historical experience.)

Thus, while all the colonies started off with different founders with different motivations, all—whether they were inhabited by the godly Puritans of New England, the settlers of John Smith's Virginia, the followers of William Penn or of Lord Baltimore—shared a common heritage, and all had some sort of constitution that described how they were to be governed. All assumed the primacy of the British common law, of the rights contained in the Magna Carta and subsequent additions to its fundamental list of liberties. It was such hallowed laws as these, almost six hundred years old by the summer of 1787, that would become part of the American Bill of Rights: The Fourth Amendment would state that every citizen has the right "to be secure . . . against unreasonable searches and seizures"; the Fifth Amendment would state that no citizen could be "deprived of life, liberty, or property, without due process of law"; the Sixth Amendment would state that every citizen has the right "to a speedy and public trial, by an impartial jury."

The sense of a common political heritage could also be seen in the similarity of the state governments. All colonies had a governor, in all but two cases appointed by the king: In Pennsylvania, the Penn family appointed the governor; in Connecticut, he was elected. All colonies had a legislature. All the legislatures were bicameral, or two-house, except in Pennsylvania, which had a unicameral legislature. All colonies had an independent judiciary. In general, the governor was the toady of the king, the members of the upper house were the toadies of the governor, and the lower house was the popularly elected house of the people. This was essentially the British system of government transplanted to American soil—"this beautiful system," as Baron Charles-Louis de Secondat Montesquieu of France said enviously—and the Americans cherished it.

Only when King George III violated the Magna Carta, in Madison's lifetime, and attempted to take money from the pockets of the Americans without their consent, did the Americans rebel—or, rather, as they insisted, did they refuse to accept the king's rebellion against the common law. History was not thought to be bunk; it informed and animated the present.

The Americans threw off British rule, because—so they said, at least—it violated the law, and it violated the social contract by which all were bound, and it violated the immutable rights of man. The Revolution was meant to overthrow nothing; it was meant to preserve the common law against the onslaught of the British government.

And when the Revolution was over, there was no bloodshed, as would soon follow the one in France: there was a government, already in place, and functioning well enough. The royal governors had fled back to Britain, and the lower houses of the provincial legislature had simply taken over the running of the states, though many of them were writing or reviewing their constitutions. Thus, an established mode of government and a set of generally accepted laws were already more or less in effect.

It is often said that the American Revolution was not a social revolution: it did not mean to replace the established ruling class with some other group, or simply with a larger, more democratic franchise. And yet, to some extent, it could not stop itself. The arguments that it had used to justify itself led by an inescapable logic to a democratic conclusion—eventually, if not at once. The special privileges that the church had enjoyed, for instance, were seen as inconsistent with the Revolution; and in the new constitutions that the states drew up at the time of the war, a number of them drafted articles that emphatically separated church and state. Laws of entail and primogeniture, which buttressed a system of large estates, were abolished, so that the ownership of land was democratized and concentrations of large wealth reduced. Several states reduced or abolished property qualifications for suffrage: In Pennsylvania and North Carolina, all taxpayers could vote; in Vermont, there were no such qualifications at all. Slavery, which had long evoked the most passionate denunciations, was denounced anew as inconsistent with revolutionary principles; and as a result the slave trade was either discouraged or abolished by new laws passed in Connecticut, Delaware, Virginia, Maryland, South Carolina, and North Carolina. Massachusetts abolished slavery itself in its constitution of 1780, whose first article declared, "All men are born free and equal."

In the course of the Revolution, seventeen new constitutions were written (some states had to try more than once before they got it right; Connecticut and Rhode Island did not try; they simply used their old colonial charters and removed any references to the king and his ministers). In Virginia, where Madison helped write the constitution, remembrance of the royal governor led to supreme power being given to the legislature. And a bill of rights specified that "all power is vested in . . . the people; that magistrates are their trustees and servants, and at all times amenable to them"; that all men had the right to trial by jury, that no man could be compelled to testify against himself, that no man was subject to unreasonable search or seizure, that the freedom of the press could never be restrained by the government, that standing armies in time of peace should be avoided—along with other rights familiar to those who knew the Magna Carta.

The constitution Madison had helped to write was not the only one that he carried in his mind. Of all the former colonies, Pennsylvania had come up with the most democratic constitution—hailed by the European intelligentsia as nearly perfect. It provided that power be vested primarily in the legislature, which was to be elected by virtually universal male suffrage (the most democratic anywhere): Every freeman over the age of twenty-one who had resided in the state for a year and paid taxes (and his sons, whether they paid taxes or not) was entitled to vote. Legislative elections were held every year (annual elections were held to be the absolute requirement of accountable representatives in a democracy); no man could serve more than two consecutive terms; after two terms he had to stand out for three years before running again. There were to be no professional politicians. To get around the idea that popular legislative houses might pass laws in the heat of the moment (and so there ought to be an upper house to "check" popular passions), the Pennsylvania constitution provided that all laws, after an initial hearing, should be printed and circulated among the people for their consultation, and not passed into law until the next meeting of the assembly. There was no governor. Instead there was an executive council with a presiding officer, or president, who did the bidding of the legislature.

Massachusetts devised a "mixed" constitution, framed

largely by John Adams, which was more to Madison's taste than that of Pennsylvania. Working on the theory that any "pure" government—whether purely democratic or purely aristocratic or purely monarchical—inevitably degenerated into anarchy or oligarchy or absolutism, Adams designed a government with checks and balances to keep it from degenerating: a popularly elected house of representatives, an aristocratic upper house apportioned according to taxable wealth, and a governor given the power to veto legislation, to appoint most officials, and to be himself indefinitely eligible for reelection. (Because the governor was to be invested with independent authority, he was elected by popular vote.)

Altogether, most states provided one-year terms for governors and for most legislators. Judges were appointed for long terms. Membership in the upper house most often had a stiff property qualification attached to it, but in seven states, all male taxpayers could vote. Elsewhere, the property qualifications for voting were moderate. In New Jersey, women could vote if they met the property requirement.

In order to orchestrate their increasingly hostile dealings with Britain, these states—or colonies, as they then were—had first gathered in Philadelphia in 1774 and instituted what was no more than an informal committee, the Continental Congress. Its members had been chosen by committees in a dozen of the colonies; and they gathered without set rules or procedures but with the habit of each colony considering itself a separate entity, with a single voice and a single vote.

At the same time that the Congress drew up the Declaration of Independence in 1776, it appointed a committee (one delegate from each state) to draft a constitution, and that committee produced the Articles of Confederation. Not until five years later, while the war went on apace, were those Articles finally ratified by the states; but they had served, nonetheless, to form the only central government America had known.

The Articles established a "firm league of friendship," not a single nation but an alliance of independent sovereign states, in which each state had one vote, and all states pledged to assist one another in their common defense. They had no powerful executive; they had only a president of Congress, who was charged with seeing to it that the decrees of Congress were carried out. The states agreed in the Articles not to send any independent embassies to any foreign nations without the consent of the Continental Congress, not to make alliances or treaties with any foreign power, not to enter into treaties with any other state without the consent of all the states, not to levy taxes or duties that would interfere with treaties entered into by the United States, not to keep any vessel of war except as agreed to by the Congress, not to engage in any act of war without the consent of Congress, and to pay taxes in support of war "or general welfare." On most important matters, nine states had to vote in favor of a provision for it to pass (though the remaining states could fairly well ignore any law, since there was nothing to coerce them to obey it). To amend the Articles, all the states had to agree, unanimously, to an amendment. In short, the Articles created an alliance, bound together by the exigencies of war, with very little to do except to see to the common defense and let the states otherwise manage their own affairs. The powers of the Congress were remarkably limited—an unusual, and exemplary, practice for a revolutionary body.

The Articles worked well enough so long as the pressures of war kept the states working together. But once the war ended, in 1783, the urgent need for the confederation was no longer felt so keenly, and the former colonies tended to dissolve finally into thirteen sovereign nations. Unhappily, their common problems did not disappear at the same time.

As usual, war had disrupted the economy. Many farmers had depended on the export of their crops to foreign markets for their livelihoods, and exports to foreign markets had been upset. The farmers were in debt, and going more deeply into debt. Inflation had struck. The paper money that had been printed to finance the war was nearly worthless. Merchants pressed by foreign creditors to pay their debts insisted that debts to them be paid not in paper but in gold or other specie. But most of the specie had been drained from the states to pay for imports. Some states, in response to demands of the farmers, printed more paper money. Other states did not. In some places, denied paper money, farmers rose in armed rebellion.

Congress, meanwhile, was sometimes unable to get a quorum to conduct business. When it could get a quorum, it found it could not always enforce the laws it passed. When it tried to improve its situation by amending the Articles, a single state could block an amendment. Some states failed to pay taxes; some states failed to live up to the treaty of 1783 that ended the war with Britain; states that had international ports taxed the exports of states that did not. Whereas the British could coordinate a trade policy to punish American commercial interests, the Americans could not coordinate a retaliatory policy to force the British to reverse the their practices. In sum, the United States government could not reliably levy taxes, could not ensure that its laws would be obeyed, could not repay its debts, could not ensure that it would honor its treaty obligations. It was not clear, in fact, that it could be called a government at all, and some feared that the Revolution, for which so many had fought so hard, could still be lost in the turbulence of this postwar disorder.

So it was that Madison arrived in town with his baggage filled with notes on the history of republics and of confederacies. He carried, in particular, one little notebook that he had filled with a list of the "Vices of the Political System of the United States," and a little forty-one page notebook in which he had preserved his observations "Of Ancient and Modern Confederacies." Among those observations he had jotted down notes about the world's other great attempts at confederate governments, their structures, strengths, and weaknesses: the Lycian, Amphictyonic, and Achaean confederacies of ancient Greece; the government of the Holy Roman Empire; the Swiss Confederation; and the United Provinces of the Netherlands. He noted their histories, what bonds held these confederacies together, ånd what tore them apart.

The fear of disorder usually drove men to seek a strong central government. The fear of tyranny usually drove them to seek local government. The wish for a uniform system of laws usually spurred men to prefer a central government. The wish for liberty spurred them to prefer local government, particularly direct self-government. It was the conflict between those two inherently contradictory impulses that had often torn apart even the best-intentioned of governments in the past, or caused them, in the pursuit of one or the other of the impulses, to degenerate into tyranny on the one hand or anarchy on the other. How to avoid these fateful historical errors was the quandary that occupied Madison's notes and mind.

2

THE MAN OF ORDER

SHORTLY AFTER SUNRISE on Wednesday, May 9, Washington descended the front steps at Mount Vernon to the serpentine gravel drive and got into his elegant windowed coach—or chariot, as such little coaches were called—for the five-day trip to Philadelphia. A team of two horses pulled the chariot; Washington's saddle horse was tied on behind; the driver was perched on a seat high up on the front of the carriage; and Washington himself was settled back into the finely stitched upholstered cushions, the leather-lined doors having been pulled to and closed with a precision-crafted click.

He was a big man, and strong. Indeed, he was a giant for his time—six feet two inches tall, 175 pounds, big-boned, with big hands and feet, and solid, well-developed muscles. His body was clumsily shaped—his shoulders were substantial, his chest was narrow, and his hips were broad—but he was astonishingly graceful and quick, splendid on horseback, a good dancer and athlete, even still, at the age of fifty-five. Once when some young men at Mount Vernon had been on the lawn in their shirtsleeves throwing weights, Washington happened to come out the front door, and without removing his coat, he threw the weight far beyond their best mark. He was a man who tended instinctively to act. When he traveled, if he happened to be crossing a river by raft and the current became dangerous, he was quick to take the steering pole. He had an extraordinary, volcanic temper, over which he exercised extraordi-

33

nary control. Indeed, he was a self-made man in the deepest sense. He had made for himself a controlled and balanced character.

He loved fox hunting and horse races and spectacles of all sorts, whether the theater or puppet shows or parties or cock-fights. He understood dramatic effect, and enjoyed it. He loved a good-looking uniform. He arranged not only his flower gardens but his vegetable gardens with decorative paths and hedges, and he took care to space a piece of correspondence pleasingly on a page. He hated to attend meetings, but he loved to have company at home, and in the decade just before the outbreak of the Revolution he received almost two thousand guests at Mount Vernon. He loved cardplaying, billiards, fishing, shooting, boat racing, oysters, watermelons, and Madeira wine.

He was a social man, not a bookish man. He liked newspapers, and he consumed as many as ten a day; but he was not a great reader of books; his tastes ran to such popular novels as *Peregrine Pickle, Humphrey Clinker,* and *Tom Jones,* and to books of history, biography, military affairs, and, of course, agriculture.

He was not feeling well as he settled into the coach. He had been suffering the past couple of weeks from "fever and ague," as he said—which may have been a recurrence of an old bout with malaria—and his rheumatism had been acting up as well, so badly in fact that he had recently, for ten days, been carrying one arm in a sling and had barely been able to turn over in bed at night.

Washington's current expense were exceeding his income, and he was concerned about it. Just before he left Mount Vernon, he wrote a hurried note to his cousin Lund, who had pressed him for some money: "there is no source from which I derive more than a sufficiency for the daily calls of my family, except what flows from the collection of old debts, and scantly and precarious enough, God knows this is. My estate for the last 11 years has not been able to make both ends meet. I am encumbered now with the deficiency. . . . I am not able to pay debts unless I could sell land, which I have publicly advertised without finding bidders."

He was worried about his family. Only a few days before

his departure for Philadelphia, he had received an urgent message that both his sister and his seventy-nine-year-old mother were dying. The message proved to be untrue, as he discovered after a fast journey in his disordered state of mind and body to his mother's home in Fredericksburg. But the thought of her age and fragile condition weighed still on his mind.

And he had lied. He had told the Society of the Cincinnati, the fraternal organization of the officers of the Revolution, of which he was the honorary president, that he was not well enough to attend their meeting in Philadelphia. In truth, Washington did not want to be seen with the Cincinnati. Although he was fond of his old companions in arms, the Cincinnati had come to appear, to many Americans, somewhat threatening—a group of soldiers who seemed to refuse to entirely disband, who might, if political conditions became serious, decide to take over the government, who might conduct a coup, with Washington at their head. None of this, in Washington's mind, was remotely possible, but he did not want to be seen keeping the company of the Cincinnati. And so he had told them he was ill. And now it turned out that he was on his way to Philadelphia after all, to meet with another group of prominent men.

Nor was he at all happy to be drawing away from his farm at just this time of year, for he was, first and last, a farmer. He had left his nephew George Augustine Washington in charge, and he commenced to compose letters of instruction to the young man at once—already, in early May, anticipating the results of the first harvests: "Inform me . . . how your Grain, particularly the Barley and Oats, stand on the ground, that is, the height of them, whether thick or thin, how branched, how headed, and what the farmer (who ought to be a judge) thinks of their yield, provided no accident happens. I wish also to be particularly informed of the various kinds of grass seeds which have been Sown, as well in the fields as the smaller spots, and what prospect there is of their coming to any thing."

Washington was able to summon a maddening attention to detail. It was the foundation of his intelligence—his ability to observe minutely and particularly, and to learn by experience. It was his observations as a farmer that had first led him to understand the economics of colonialism. He had grown tobacco at Mount Vernon and shipped it to a factor in England, who sold the tobacco and used the proceeds to buy farm machinery, clothes, shoes, and other supplies which he sent back to Mount Vernon. But no matter how hard Washington worked, not matter how efficiently his farm was organized, no matter how clever he was, his debt to his English factor grew. At the same time, although he sent the most careful measurements abroad, his clothes never fit. The goods provided him were invariably inferior. Machinery arrived with parts missing. In this way, Washington learned the lesson of all colonials: So long as he supplied raw materials to the imperial nation and bought manufactured goods in return, he could do nothing but exchange good value for bad and sink further and further into debt. The colonial system itself, he found, was by its nature "disastrous." And so, as early as the 1760s, he turned from tobacco to wheat and corn, which could be sold on the American market. He built a commercial mill to grind his grain, and he tried to buy more and more of his goods from merchants in Philadelphia. Thus, his own sense of independence from England grew naturally out of the experience of his daily life.

The rest of his career grew, too, from this ability to learn from experience. As a young man making his way up as a surveyor and military officer, he had not been a distinguished— he had not even been a competent—commander. Even as commander in chief of the Continental Army, he bungled his early battles. He had told Congress, when they appointed him head of the army, "I do not think myself equal to the command I am honored with"—and his saying so was always thought an example of unparalleled modesty; but it was simply the truth. And yet he did have the invaluable capacity to stay unruffled, not to let his ego get tangled up with his disappointments, to look with even-tempered clarity at his mistakes, to watch his men, and to consider the circumstances under which he had to conduct the war, and learn from his men what sort of military strategy was possible, and so, in time, to develop a victorious strategy. He became, in short, a great guerrilla general. During the war he had not failed to drink and gamble and swap stories with his comrades (with his officers, that is, not with his men.) Indeed, he loved the soldier's life, and if the soldiers did not quite love him, they held him in great respect and even awe, for the fact that he stayed with them through-out the sufferings of the war, and for the dignity that he dis-played on behalf of them all. He was the symbol of the Amer-ican victory, the embodiment of the Revolution, and so the most deeply respected man in America. When Americans cel-ebrated Washington they celebrated themselves and their own achievement.

His route to Philadelphia took him across the Potomac River and up its eastern bank, through what was to become the District of Columbia, past Bladensburg, and toward Elk-ridge Landing and Baltimore—just the reverse, as it happened, of the route he had traveled on his way to final victory at York-town. As he traveled he was able to check the fields of his fel-low farmers, who grew wheat, flax, corn, maize, potatoes, and (still) tobacco. The soil was heavy, with a large clay content. The trees were oaks and walnuts. Turtle doves brightened the drive, and occasionally the road was lined with hedges of white thorn, whose flowers are among the local splendors of May.

He spent this first night about twenty miles south of Bal-timore, at the home of Major Thomas Snowden, and because he was still suffering from the illness with which he had begun his journey, he retired earlier than his customary ten o'clock bedtime, "feeling," as he noted punctiliously in his diary, "very severely a violent hd. ach and sick stomach."

Some have suggested that Washington's stomach troubles were caused by the anxieties he felt about attending the Phil-adelphia convention. He disliked large meetings under any cir-cumstances; they were not suited to his talents or tempera-ment, and he could modestly (and honestly) have said that he was not equal to the duty to which he was being called.

Furthermore, he had given his farewell address to his sol-diers at the end of the war in 1783 and retired permanently, as he said, from public life—and he had meant it. And, as he set out for Philadelphia, Martha reminded him that she had based all her plans for future happiness on the belief that he had meant what he had said.

At the same time, he was not convinced that this Philadel-phia meeting offered the best chance of solving what he took to be the country's problems in a definitive way, and he was worried that a failed attempt would be worse than no attempt at all, that it would create such confusion as to make a later attempt impossible. He fretted, too, about how his return from retirement would be taken. On the one hand, his joining the convention might be construed as an indication that his word could not be depended on; on the other hand, a refusal to help shore up the government might be interpreted (there were rumors to this effect) as a wish on Washington's part to see the collapse of the government so that he could take over—many hoped he would—as king.

Madison was especially aware of the delicacy of the situation. Washington's prestige was one of the greatest treasures the new nation had. The act of coming out of retirement was a momentous one. His prestige needed to be held in reserve, to be used only for something crucial, and then only with the certainty of success. Madision had written Washington that perhaps the general should not come to Philadelphia at once, that it might be best for him to hold back and see whether the early meetings portended success; if it looked as though the convention might fail, then Washington need not attend at all. Nonetheless, once Washington made up his mind to attend, he threw his reputation into the balance at once, and with his misgivings still gnawing at him, he set out in time to be at the opening sessions in Philadelphia.

The next morning, because it was raining, and out of consideration for his coachman and horses, Washington put off his departure until after eight o'clock. He made Baltimore by one o'clock, and dined at the Fountain Inn, one of the best-known public houses in America, boasting six public parlors, twenty-four bedrooms, eight garrets for servants, a barber's shop, four brick stables with eight-four stalls for horses, three kitchens, and excellent food. After dinner he went directly along to the home of James McHenry.

McHenry—an Irishman, a hater of the English by birthright—had signed up with the Continental Army at the outbreak of the Revolution, had served as a surgeon for a time, and then, at Valley Forge, had been a secretary to Washington. Like most others who had been through the crucible of Valley Forge, he had formed a powerful bond with the general.

McHenry was himself a Maryland delegate to the Philadelphia convention and was about to set out north on his own.

If Washington had any convictions about what the country needed, they had come from the experience he had shared with McHenry and his other companions at Valley Forge—that it had been almost mortally difficult to get the Continental Congress to give his troops the food and clothing and ammunition they had needed to conduct the war. What was needed, based on Washington's experience, was a central government with more authority to conduct the nation's necessary business and bring order to its affairs.

Washington had been particularly impressed—even alarmed—by an event that had occurred in Massachusetts only six months earlier. Farmers there, hard pressed by debt, and bedeviled by the courts that hauled them in and sent them off to debtors' prision, resorted to a simple expedient: They got a mob together and prevented the courts from sitting. Their idea was to continue to do so until the date of the annual legislative elections, when they would be able to elect representatives who would issue paper money or grant some other form of relief (such as a reduction of taxes, an easing of payment schedules, or even an easing of onerous lawyers' fees). But the governor, James Bowdoin, called out the militia to disperse them. The farmers, even more desperate now, thrust one of their number forward to lead them, Daniel Shays, who had distinguished himself as a captain during the Revolutionary War. But none of the farmers were dedicated to an armed uprising: After a single volley of fire from the militia, Shays' men turned and ran; and Shays' Rebellion, as it was called, was over.

The concern that Shays' Rebellion aroused, however, was enormous. Men of means saw it at once as the opening of a war of poor against rich, of dreadful disorder, even of a new revolution. "Our affairs seem to lead to some crisis," wrote John Jay to Washington, "some revolution—something I cannot foresee or conjecture. I am uneasy and apprehensive; more so than during the war."

Some said the Saysites were seeking some sort of alliance with Britain. A diplomat from France suggested that the ultimate program of the Shaysites was to establish "a perfect democracy" after the example of the Pennsylvania constitution. The Continental Congress issued a call for troops to put down an Indian threat—though everyone knew that the "Indians" were none other than American farmers.

Washington was deeply shaken by the rebellion. "Good God!" exclaimed the normally imperturbable general. "Who besides a Tory could have foreseen, or a Briton have predicted," such disorders. And the rebellion was only a symptom, Washington felt, of a more general anarchy possible throughout the country. There were, he said, "combustibles in every state." The need for a strong central government, capable of maintaining order, was, in Washington's view, urgent.

On Friday, the morning after he had stopped at James McHenry's, Washington set out very early. He stopped at Skerrett's Tavern at the head of the Bird River in Baltimore County for breakfast (Washington liked sliced tongue or cold sliced ham, Indian cakes, honey, and tea) and then went on at once, hoping to beat a threatening spring downpour, to Havre de Grace, a little town on the Susquehannah River, where he meant to catch the ferry across. But the winds that afternoon had become so gusty that Washington decided to put off the crossing, and he took lodgings for the night at an inn at Havre de Grace.

When he crossed the Susquehannah, a fellow Virginian named Francis Corbin caught up with him just on the other side. Corbin, a rich man with great social polish, educated in England, was on his way to Philadelphia on business, and he accepted the general's invitation to ride along in his coach.

The two men proceeded to Philadelphia, then, no doubt engrossed in talk of business. Washington's business interests were extensive. He had risen to his business career in the way quite a few of his compatriots had by marrying up. Born the son of a small planter, he had used his connections (in Washington's case with the neighboring wealthy Fairfax family) to enter a military career; he contracted a prosperous marriage, and then he moved on to large-scale farming and investments in thousands of acres of western lands. When land development schemes or plans for developing canal transportation came to his notice, he was eager to invest. Like so many of his friends and countrymen, he had chronic money troubles. In a few years, when he would make the journey to New York to be sworn in as the first president, he would need to borrow a hundred pounds to finance the trip. But to be overextended was simply to be in harmony with the situation of the new nation—many were taking enormous financial risks, hoping that sheer growth, made orderly by a strong central government, would eventually bail them out.

Washington and Corbin stayed overnight on Saturday at the Sign of the Ship, a tavern run by Patrick O'Flynn, a Delaware militia captain, and had dinner the next day at a hotel belonging to the widow of an English army officer. And then, after dinner, Washington was ambushed by the Cincinnati.

A group of officers who were attending the meeting of the Cincinnati in Philadelphia had ridden out to meet the general. The welcoming party was led by the founder of the Society, General Henry Knox, profane, bighearted, cheerful, three hundred pounds, a former bookseller who had read many books about cannon and so had become Washington's commander of artillery. Knox was accompanied by General James Mitchell Varnum, also corpulent and florid, with a great cockade of white hair, a classics scholar who liked to converse in Latin and who had loved military things from earliest childhood and had been with Washington at Valley Forge. With Knox and Varnum was General Thomas Mifflin, dignified in his bearing, extravagant with his money, Washington's quartermaster general, who had taken a leading part in a conspiracy to unseat General Washington as commander in chief of the Continental Army and turn the conduct of the war over to General Horatio Gates. Astonishingly, Washington had held no grudge; he was remarkably able to look beyond momentary upsets and keep his mind focused on the more important ultimate goal. Washington was even able to restore Mifflin to friendship—and Mifflin was now a delegate from Pennsylvania to the Constitutional Convention, and a fairly dependable supporter of Washington's preferences. The three generals were accompanied by a gaggle of other officers, and they escorted Washington's coach now, all of them splendid on their mounts, swords at their sides, in their old blue-and-buff uniforms, all of them proudly wearing the blue ribbon and gold eagle of the order of the Cincinnati, and the special glory of having ridden with General Washington in the late war.

They were joined by a band of their fellows, the Philadelphia Light Horse Company, at Gray's Ferry—a former Schuylkill River ferry crossing that had been replaced by a shaky wooden pontoon bridge, over which the horses and the general's carriage clattered into Philadelphia. There they were greeted by the chiming of the city's church bells, the firing of cannon, and the applause of a crowd of Philadelphians who lined the way to Mrs. House's boardinghouse.

Madison would have liked to have all of the Virginians stay at Mrs. House's, so that they could work out their convention strategy and be in constant touch with one another. But when Washington pulled up in front of the lodging house, he was presented with a message from Robert Morris urging him to stay just a few doors down Market Street with Morris and his wife, Mary. Washington had already written the Morrises that he could not think of burdening them with what might turn out to be a long stay; now, with their invitation renewed, he accepted at once.

The Morris residence was one of the finest in Philadelphia: a brick house, three stories high, and wide enough to accommodate four windows across the facade of each floor. Just inside the front door was a rectangular entrance hall, grandly outfitted with fluted columns, pilasters, and four arches; a large dining room lay to the right, and a handsome winding staircase, with rails and balusters of West Indian mahogany, rose to the floor above. Perhaps no house in Philadelphia was more sumptuous than this one, with its fine mantelpieces and moldings, its fabrics and furnishings, its cornices and plasterwork and other details of ornamentation. When the British occupied Philadelphia during the war, General Howe had taken it for his own. Now Washington was given a room on the second floor. His bath and quarters for his servants were to be found in the long, narrow backbuilding that adjoined the main structure; and the stables housed his coach horses and riding mount.

Morris was commonly reckoned to be the richest man in America. Born in or near Liverpool, of a mother whose name is unknown, he fetched up in America at the age of thirteen to join his father in the tobacco business. He went to school briefly, dropped out, and got a job with a merchant family, the Willings, whose company was engaged in imports, exports, shipowning, and banking. His rise was stunning. He was a partner by the age of twenty and, soon enough, an outspoken critic of England's policies of taxing the colonies. When war broke out, Congress turned to him as a knowledgeable trader and put him on a committee charged with procuring munitions. As the war went disastrously on, he helped out by arranging loans, juggling and shifting mounds of depreciated currency, bad debts, and undependable promises with the nimble instincts of a great swindler. Always taking a commission for himself on his loans and trades, he nonetheless earned the gratitude of the men responsible for prosecuting the war by his braving the worst days and always finding money. When Congress fled Philadelphia in 1776, Morris stayed on to arrange to get hold of munitions and money. He became known as the Financier of the Revolution, the man single-handedly kept credit flowing to Washington's army, a feat for which he earned Washington's unyielding loyalty.

By the end of the war he was generally despised by the farmers, who charged that his bank drained money from them with its high interest rates and tended to concentrate wealth and political power in the hands of the few. He was also just beginning to engage in speculations in western lands which, by the mid-nineties, would plunge him into bankruptcy.

During the time of Washington's stay with Morris that summer, a business associate came to the door, walked past the liveried servants and the French butler, and interrupted dinner to speak to Morris about an international business matter on which Morris was overextended. (It was, Washington noted in his diary with his habitual reserve, "a little malapropos.") The moment was symptomatic of Morris's financial condition. Within a few years, his whole fortune would collapse. He would flee to his country estate, and hide out there until the sheriff came and got him. He would spend three years, six months, and ten days in debtors' prison, and he would emerge utterly broken in spirit and body.

At the moment, however, Robert Morris represented big money in America, just as Washington represented order. And Washington's acceptance of Morris's invitation to stay at his home reinforced the impression that Washington stood with the men who sought sound money, dependable commerce, steady growth: stability. As William Shippen of Philadelphia wrote, with a touch of raillery, to his son: "much is to be hoped for" from the wisdom and patriotism of those gathering for the convention. "Aristocracy is said to be the Idea of almost all of them—I shall not call it a Miracle if G1 W——n is seen living in Philadelphia as Emperor of America in a few years."

3

THE MAN OF LIBERTY

WASHINGTON TOOK as his first piece of business to pay an official call on Benjamin Franklin, who was then, interalia, the president of the Pennsylvania Executive Council. The general set out just after the had arrived at Morris's to walk the three blocks down Market Street to Franklin's house, but so many people had gathered to shake his hand, to cheer and to gape, that his progress along the street was slow. He crossed Fifth Street, walked down past the Indian Queen Tavern at Fourth Street, and then, between Fourth and Third, he turned in under a little archway, just wide enough for a carriage to pass through, and into Franklin Court.

The passageway and the court were cluttered with loads of dirt and clay and lumber and other evidence of the presence of bricklayers, carpenters, stonecutters, painters, glaziers, lime burners, coppersmiths, carters, and laborers. Franklin, at the age of eighty-one, had decided to build a few new houses on his property along Market Street, for the income from rents, and to add a large addition to his own house—in particular so that he could have a large library and study to work in. "I hardly know," he wrote to his sister, "how to justify building a Library at an age that will so soon oblige me to quit it; but we are apt to forget that we are grown old, and Building is an Amusement." And he was, as he always had been, a shameful materialist.

With its addition, Franklin's house was still quite plain,

45

but it was nothing if not commodious. His wife had died more than ten years before, but his daughter Sarah Bache lived with him, with her three children ("over whom," as one visitor noticed, "she seemed to have no kind of command, but who appeared to be excessively fond of their Grandpa"), and the expanded house had room for them all, and for all of Franklin's own scientific toys and books and his newly acquired specimen, a snake with two heads.

According to one story, the house had actually been built to face on Chestnut Street, just south of Market, but Franklin learned that some legal difficulty might prevent him from having an entrance there and so, without a moment's hesitation, and to save himself the vexation of litigation, he simply flipped the design around and had the house face on this little interior courtyard, which he planted with trees and flowering shrubs, and lined with gravel walks, a front yard tucked peacefully away from the noise of the city, where the doctor himself was often to be found sitting under his favorite mulberry tree.

To enter the house itself was to step into a world propelled by a delight in the new, the odd, the curious, the bizarre, the funny, the wonderful. Franklin had always been the sort of man who could, in the space of a single brief letter, cover such topics as linseed oil, hemp land, swamp drainage, variations in climate, northeast storms, the cause of springs on mountains, seashell rocks, grass seed, taxation, and smuggling. He loved facts. He loved the particular. He was able to talk with knowledge and cheerful interest about mastodon tusks, lead poisoning, chimney construction, the reason canal boats move more slowly in low water than in high water, silk culture, Chinese rhubarb seeds, sunspots, magnetism, a new method for making carriage wheels, the electrocution of animals to be eaten, how to heat a church in Boston, the census in China, the vegetable origins of coal, and the good of keeping a window in the bedroom open at night. Of course, he had experimented with lightning and invented bifocal eyeglasses and a stove and countless other things, and was always intrigued by new inventions. He had seen the first balloon ascension several years before in Paris, and when a skeptic asked him what good a balloon could possibly be, Franklin replied, "What good is a new-born baby?"

As one passed through the house from room to room, curiosities were to be seen on all sides. The entrance hall itself had a fine tall case clock and a set of Windsor chairs ready to be moved out into the garden for outdoor teas, and a Chinese gong to call the children to meals. The parlor behind was outfitted with a card table and its paraphernalia, and on the mantel was a set of little Mandarin figurines whose heads nodded at a touch. All the way upstairs, on the third floor, was what must have been the finest music room in America, where Franklin kept the set of musical glasses that he had had especially blown to his specifications and that he called an armonica, a set of English hand bells, a viola da gamba, and a harpsichord.

The new library was on the second floor, just above the new dining room. Like the dining room, it ran the full depth of the house, and Franklin was inordinately proud of it. It was lined with books from floor to ceiling. Composed of 4,276 volumes, it was perhaps the best private library in America. There were four windows, a fireplace with a marble hearth, a double set of shelves which came out from the end walls and formed four little alcoves. In the center of room, in front of the fireplace, was a special writing table, large enough for Franklin to place his large folios of natural history prints on and open them up for his friends to view. He loved to show off, too, a "glass machine" which exhibited the circulation of blood in the arteries and veins of the human body. "The circulation is exhibited," as one enthralled visitor noted, "by the passing of a red fluid from a reservoir into numerous capillary tubes of glass, ramified in every direction, and then returning in similar tubes to the reservoir, which was done with great velocity, without any power to act visibly on the fluid, and had the appearance of perpetual motion." Another of the marvels in Franklin's study was a long artificial arm and hand that he could used to reach books that were up on the shelves. The chair in which Franklin usually sat was also of his invention; it was a great armchair, with a rocker, and a large fan above, with which he fanned himself, using only the smallest motion of his foot.

He did not get about the house easily this summer, and he had not been getting out much recently. He was bothered by his gout and his kidneystones, which caused him incapacitating pain, and when he did go out he was taken about town in a French-made sedan chair carried by a couple of prisoners from the nearby Walnut Street jail. But he was not given to complaining.

With his plump little figure, his plain, unembroidered brown coat and long, unpowdered gray hair, and his owlish-looking spectacles, he was in splendid contrast to Washington. As one of Franklin's biographers noted, where Washington had schooled himself from his earliest days to be socially correct, Franklin took delight in flouting convention; where Washington was particular and elegant in his dress, Franklin was careless and indifferent; Washington was somber but knew how to be witty, Franklin was affable but knew how to be serious; Washington was most comfortable at home, Franklin enjoyed being in the world; Washington loved women but had sought a wife, Franklin had had a wife but sought mistresses; Washington was a figure of reticence and distinction, Franklin was approachable, a sage wag; Washington was a country man, Franklin was a boulevardier; Washington had a methodical mind, Franklin had a scintillating one. Washington had copied a book of maxims called *The Rules of Civility*, Franklin had written a book of maxims called *Poor Richard's Almanac*. Washington was a gentleman, Franklin was a democrat.

In conversation, Franklin was gentle, humorous, and simple. He seemed always to have some mental powers in reserve, as though he was always more intelligent than the subject at hand quite required. He rarely spoke at length, and when he did speak, an extraordinary serenity and a good-naturedness bubbled up through his words. He tended to converse in little stories, moral tales, or even little songs.

Regarding the topics that preoccupied Washington at the moment, Franklin had his opinions. Washington, for example, still felt somewhat uncomfortable because of his evasion of the meeting of the Society of the Cincinnati in Philadelphia. His most recent troubles over the Cincinnati arose from the fact that the rules of the Society had originally specified that a father might pass membership down to his son. The rule provoked an outcry among Americans who foresaw the establishment of a hereditary organization, a sort of instant aristocracy—

even worse, an aristocracy based in the military, or an elite organization that might one day try to conduct a military coup. The rule was clearly impolitic, and it was soon dropped; but Washington, the honorary president of the Cincinnati, was embarrassed that he had not noticed the rule in the beginning and insisted then that it be stricken out; and he was embarrassed to be president of an organization over which an aura of aristocratic pretension—and even of a possible plot—still hovered.

That anyone should ever have imagined conjuring up a sort of American peerage by way of the Society of the Cincinnati seemed both harmful and comical to Franklin, and he doubtless let Washington know it. As he had written his daughter not long before: "Honour worthily obtained (as for example that of our officers) is in its nature a personal thing and incommunicable to any but those who had some share in obtaining it. Thus among the Chinese, the most ancient and from experience the wisest of nations, honour does not descend but ascends." When someone in China won respect, the credit went to his parents. "This ascending honour is therefore useful to the state, as it encourages parents to give their children a good and virtuous education. But the descending honour, to posterity who could have no share in obtaining it, is not only groundless and absurd but often hurtful to that posterity, since it is apt to make them proud, disdaining to be employed in useful arts and thence falling into poverty and all the meannesses, servility, and wretchedness attending it; which is the present case with much of what is called the noblesse in Europe."

Simple mathematics showed the absurdity of it. "A man's son, for instance, is but half of his family, the other half belonging to the family of his wife. His son, too, marrying into another family, his share in the grandson is but a fourth." Proceeding in this way, "in nine generations, which would not require more than three hundred years (no very great antiquity for a family), our present Chevalier of the Order of Cincinnatus's share in the then existing knight will be but a 512th part." The pretension was not unlike that of those nobles Franklin had met in England who said they were descended from the time of the Norman conquest. Doing his math in reverse, Franklin calculated that such a man would have to have been descended from 1,048,576 persons who had been living at the time of the conquest, which hardly seemed to Franklin much distinction at all.

As for the urgent feeling of Washington that the country was in the midst of dreadful disorder and needed a strong central government, Franklin was skeptical. Pennsylvania, for instance, seemed prosperous enough. "Our husbandmen," as he had written in a recent letter, "who are the bulk of the nation, have had plentiful crops, their produce sells at high prices and for ready, hard money. . . . Our working-people are all employed and get high wages, are well fed and well clad. . . . Buildings in Philadelphia increase rapidly, besides small towns rising in every quarter of the country. The laws govern, justice is well administered, and property is as secure as in any country on the globe. Our wilderness lands are daily filling up with new settlers, and our settlements extend rapidly to the westward. . . . In short, all among us may be happy who have happy dispositions; such being necessary to happiness even in paradise."

Nor did Franklin take too seriously the furor over Daniel Shays' rebellion. As he had written to Jefferson, the insurgents in Massachusetts were speedily quelled, "and I believe a great majority of that people approve the measures of government in reducing them." (Jefferson agreed. He wrote to Abigail Adams in London: "I like a little rebellion now and then. The spirit of resistance to government is so valuable on occasion that I wish it to be always kept alive. It will often be exercised when wrong, but better so than not to be exercised at all." And to her son-in-law, William Smith, Jefferson wrote: "God forbid we should every twenty years be without such a rebellion! What signify a few lives lost in a century or two? The tree of liberty must be refreshed from time to time with the blood of patriots and tyrants. It is its natural manure.")

The anxiety provoked by Shays' Rebellion, the sense of crisis, the call for great measures to make a strong central government, all needed to be taken, in Franklin's view, as in Jefferson's, with a grain of salt—particulary so that they would not be used as a pretext for trimming democratic self-rule.

The concerns that troubled Washington—the postwar in-

flation, the depression, the disruption of trade, the terrible
burdens of both public and private debt, the tendency of the
various states to violate particular treaty obligations toward
the British—all these were, in Franklin's view, merely temporary problems, the usual consequences of the turmoil of war,
and they were already sorting themselves out. There was no
emergency. The country was on its way to prosperity again,
and as prosperity returned, the other difficulties would disappear. Meanwhile, such difficulties should not be used as an excuse for hasty innovation.

These views of Franklin's were widely shared by men who
cherished the old familiar state governments under which they
had so long lived, and did not want, under the presumption of
a crisis, to see them swallowed up in a big new central government. These men spoke eloquently of the virtues of local government (by which they sometimes meant town and village
government, but in the context of this dispute between centrists and localists, they usually meant state government).
Franklin was not himself a leader of this group of localists; he
had indeed always been a champion of union; but he was by
instinct and inclination a man who shared many of their views,
a man who thought in specifics, who loved the unique cultures
of each of the original thirteen colonies, and who loved self-
government. To these men it seemed that a distant central
government was far less able than a government close to home
to understand the problems of everyday life and deal with them
efficiently and quickly—and with direct accountability to the
people most affected. Indeed, many thought that a republic
could not cover too large a territory and remain a republic,
that once a republic tried to take in too much territory it was
destined to develop into a monarchical despotism or disinte-
grate into anarchy. It had been for that reason that Thomas
Jefferson, in debates over whether Virginia should press its
claims to lands in the west, advised his fellow Virginians to
voluntarily limit the size of their state for the sake of preserving republican government.

No doubt, some of the champions of local government
hoped to preserve such unsavory local customs as slavery, or
the local rule of a small group of privileged men. But many of

the defenders of local government argued honestly that the
states presented the best hope of securing liberty. Liberty, in
the eighteenth century, meant not simply liberty from some
intrusive outside power; it meant the active exercise of control
over one's life, the possession of power in one's own hands. It
meant government small enough and close enough to home to
be directly accountable and responsive; it meant self-government, not government handed over to some remote lot of rulers. Strictly understood, the principle of local self-government
meant a share of power more or less equal to everyone else's
share of power, a citizenry more or less equal in wealth and
status, not one dominated by one small group or another; that
is to say, it meant democracy—but this was hardly a view
shared by all the localists, many of whom wanted their local
governments run by the local elite. In any case, having fought
a war to be rid of one distant tyrannical government, these
local-power men where not about to establish another distant,
insensitive government in its place.

Nor did the idea of a central government seem compatible
with sentiment. The states had histories, after all, that went
back two centuries, and each state had its distinctive character and qualities that its citizens were loath to see diminished.
Franklin, back in the 1750s and '60s, when he had been deputy
postmaster general, had traveled up and down the coast on
visits of inspection and seen the wonderful variety of the colonies. Even a brief catalogue of them suggests some of the proud
distinctiveness they cherished.

Massachusetts, settled by Puritans, was populated by mid-
dle-class farmers, tradesmen, and artisans, without extremes
of wealth and poverty. Its economy was stable (save for the
temporary postwar dislocations that led to Shays' Rebellion).
Massachusetts was dedicated from the beginning to providing
free public education. Racially homogeneous, it was a society
in which every man could vote if he joined the church, and
social life revolved around the church and the town government. In sum, it was a society in which nearly everyone could
participate on an equal footing.

Maine, which had begun as the possession of Sir Ferdi-
nando Gorges, who thought he would turn it into a feudal do-
main, was in 1787 a part of Massachusetts. Nonetheless, like

so much of the rest of the country, it was a most independent-minded place: That summer, some of its citizens were holding a convention to consider seceding from Massachusetts.

Vermont, resolutely aloof, had fought in the war but had not been welcome to join the Union. (New York did not want Vermont to come in.) It had a constitution like Pennsylvania's, radically democratic, which provided that any man could vote, without property qualification, and any man could hold office. It sent no delegates to this Philadelphia meeting, and had no intention whatever of abiding by the decisions of the convention.

Rhode Island, founded by three left-wing Puritans who had been thrown out of Massachusetts for their troublemaking, was a state at the mercy of its neighbors. It produced little and consumed little and depended for its sustenance on the scraps of trade that went up and down the coast and across the ocean. Its ports, which were in an unusually exposed position, had been badly damaged by the war, and the state was heavily in debt. So, too, were its farmers back in the interior. To the chagrin, and righteous outrage, of its neighboring states, Rhode Island was printing and distributing paper money as fast as it could—and refusing to send any delegates to Philadelphia to be told to alter their ways.

New Hampshire was seized by nearly a statewide clamor for paper money. Demonstrations and riots had occurred in the central part of the state at the time of Shays' Rebellion, and the towns bordering Vermont were insisting that they ought to secede from their state. Generally, however, the interests of debtors and creditors were so fragmented into small, contradictory aims that New Hampshire was in a swivet of indecision. While the state legislature elected delegates to attend the meeting in Philadelphia, it stoutly refused to appropriate money for the delegates' necessary travel expenses—or, perhaps, really didn't have any.

Connecticut, founded in 1636 by some well-to-do men of Massachusetts, was reorganized in 1662 by royal charter—a charter that the gentlemen of Connecticut felt needed only the most modest alterations to make it suitable to their needs after 1776. There were no riots in Connecticut, no money troubles, almost no agitation for paper money. Its farmers were pros-

perous enough to ride out the postwar problems without undue hardship. After the war, those who had stayed loyal to the
Crown had had no trouble being accepted back into Connecticut society. Few in that state had stayed loyal to the Crown in
any case. Connecticut was pleased with itself, not to say com-
placent.

New York still bore the heritage of its Dutch settlers, the
Van Rensselaers and Schuylers and Van Cortlandts and other
great land-owning families, whose interests tended to coincide
with those of the city's merchants and bankers and lawyers.
This downstate establishment was led by the Dutch, and by
such legal spokesmen as John Jay and Alexander Hamilton.
The usages of aristocracy were well fixed. The Livingston and
Van Rensselaer manors alone had almost a million acres between them. The Philipse family owned another million acres.
Voting rights were restricted by a property qualification so high
that only half the white male population could vote. And there
were more former loyalists to the Crown in New York than in
any other state; they composed possibly as much as half its
population. Then, as now, the farmers upstate fought the
downstaters. Led by George Clinton, the governor during the
entire Confederation period, the upstaters were localists, ready
to secede from the Union. New York would send three delegates to the convention, two Clintonians and Alexander Hamilton, and they would fight one another without hope of compromise.

New Jersey, founded by Sir George Carteret and Lord John
Berkeley in the 1660s, and given extremely liberal political
privileges from the very beginning, including a representative
assembly, dealt from the legacy of pride, and from the humil-
iation of having been dominated by New York on one side and
Pennsylvania on the other. New Jersey had no good ports of
its own and so was forced to send its exports through New
York or Philadelphia, and to pay taxes to both of those bordering states—"a keg tapped at both ends," as Franklin called it.
The New Jerseyans were not eager to let themselves be taken
into a new national government dominated by such large states
as New York and Pennsylvania.

Pennsylvania, the favorite port of entry for emigrants to
the new world, prosperous and vigorous, founded on freedom

of, religion and a basic Quaker belief in the goodness of human nature, was divided between east and west. In the east, along the coast, were the old established families of Quakers and Anglicans, many of them former loyalists. In the west were farmers, radical democrats. The farmers had taken control of the Pennsylvania legislature in 1776, sending a terror of democracy through the ranks of Philadelphia businessmen, and making it more and more difficult for Franklin to defend the democratic constitution he had written for the state at the outbreak of the Revolution.

Maryland, established as a refuge for Catholics, was the only state in which Catholics still played a significant political role. A little state, with a growing port, it could not quite decide whether to be aggressive or self-protective, whether to join a bold new nation or preserve its separate existence. In fact, the political factions had such trouble sorting out their intentions that they could hardly find men willing to go to Philadelphia as delegates. Five of the most obvious leading candidates for the delegation refused to be considered; five others who were elected refused to serve. While Madison and Washington were settling into Philadelphia, and other delegates were setting out on the journey to the city, the Maryland legislature was still trying to find someone willing to go.

Delaware was small and self-protective, a tendency that would become emphatic when its delegation got to town. Its most notable spokesman was John Dickinson, the author of the first draft of the Articles of Confederation, to which he still felt profoundly attached. Tall, slender, modest, pale, his white hair carefully groomed in an out-of-date fashion, Dickinson was an instinctive conservative. he had refused to go along with Britain's new Stamp Act in 1765, and distinguished himself as the author of a number of the American protests against British innovations. Then, when the Americans drew up the Declaration of Independence, he refused to sign. He had never been a man who welcomed change. He would not be now.

Virginia, founded by aristocratic Oxford graduates, the sons of knights and barons, in the early seventeenth century, had been taken over by ambitious men of the middle class whose descendants, by 1787, were aristocratic William and Mary graduates who loved fox hunting, horse racing, rounds of visiting at one another's plantations, and social dancing. The "best" families intermarried, and by the time of the Philadelphia convention, Virginia was run by perhaps no more than a hundred families, who were accustomed, by reason of their zeal, education, good sense, and standing in the community, to occupying nearly all the public posts. There was no unseemly scramble for office in Virginia. Gentlemen stood for election to the House of Burgesses, and freeholders chose from among them. On election day, candidates were present at the polling places; votes were publicly announced; and the candidates thanked their supporters then and there for their votes. The burgesses selected the governors, judges, military leaders, and other public officers from among the leading families, and in this way the government of Virginia remained firmly in the hands of the great property owners, who considered their political careers the performance of public duty.

North Carolina had been settled to a large extent by people pushed out of Virginia, poor whites and former indentured servants who could not survive as small farmers among the Virginia plantations and so carved out small tobacco farms around Albemarle Sound and tried to avoid tax collectors. Some sizable plantations had grown up over the years, but on the whole the North Carolinians remained small farmers, less than half of them rich enough to own slaves.

The South Carolinians were the leading slave owners. On the plantations around Charleston there were about 6,000 adult white males and more than 100,000 slaves. On that foundation the South Carolinians had built a polite society of English-educated "nabobs" and "bashaws," as the northerners called them, who were used to a degree of privilege and comfort that men of Massachusetts and New Hampshire found almost bizarre. South Carolina would send a delegation of four men to Philadelphia, all of them planter-lawyer aristocrats, including Charles Pinckney, a young man of stunning talents and vanity, and John Rutledge, who was, according to the confidential reports of the French minister, Louis Otto, to his government, "the proudest and most imperious man in the United States."

Georgia had been founded as recently as 1733 by General James Oglethorpe, who, as a member of the British Parliament, devoted himself to the plight of the poor. He was especially interested in doing something for those who had fallen into debt and so had been jailed with virtually no hope of ever getting out. With the approval of Parliament, and with funds raised among English philanthropists, Oglethorpe gathered a group of 114 impoverished or otherwise unfortunate people and took them to Georgia, where each settler was given fifty acres of land. Slavery and hard liquor were forbidden. The silk industry was encouraged. More of the poor and unfortunate were encouraged to come and join the first settlers. But the lure of South Carolina was too strong: The most energetic of the Georgians went north, where they could get liquor and slaves. By 1750, Oglethorpe's trustees passed new rules, allowing liquor and slaves, and settlement picked up. By 1752, Georgia had only 1,735 whites and 349 blacks, and by the time of the Philadelphia meeting, the state was still underpopulated, its lands largely uncultivated, and its dependence on slavery increasing lamentably. Like South Carolina, however, Georgia expected to grow, to become a big state, and so it would often side in the convention with the big states that wanted a powerful central government.

Under the circumstances, what was to be done with this historically heterogeneous group of states? The men whose minds were preoccupied with thoughts of liberty, of self-government, of freedom from tyranny, favored recognizing the country for what it was, a collection of distinct, sovereign, and thankfully different polities, each offering a different society. Most of them readily agreed that the Articles were not functioning perfectly; that it was not good to require a unanimous vote to pass an amendment to the Articles, so that a single state could block a necessary reform that twelve others favored; that some means needed to be found to make trade function more smoothly; and that all the states should honor the peace treaty with Britain. But most felt, too, that the United States had not done so badly under the Articles of Confederation: The country had fought a war for its very existence and had won; it had concluded a good peace; it had weathered the postwar depression fairly well; new lands were being settled, population was growing, national income was increasing.

Most of the localists agreed with Franklin, who said: "we discover some errors in our general and particular constitutions; which it is no wonder they should have, the time in which they were formed being considered. But these we shall mend." What was needed was not a whole new government, but only some modest alterations in the old one, and the localists arrived in Philadelphia with that limited aim in mind.

"We have here at present," the doctor wrote to a friend, "what the French call *une assemblee des notables,* a convention composed of some of the principal people from the several States of our confederation. They did me the honor of dining with me last Wednesday." They broached a cask of porter, Franklin said—a cask that his friend had sent him—and the company agreed that it was the "best porter they had ever tasted." And Franklin doubtless regaled the company with his usual tales and songs and snippets of verse, and took them around his house to show them his toys and inventions, including perhaps the mechanism of his bedroom door which he could lock or release by pulling a chain at the head of his bed, and his copper bathtub shaped like a shoe, with a resting place for a book on the "instep."

Some, it is true, among the younger and less experienced men, thought Franklin a garrulous old fool, sentimental and nearly feebleminded, constantly straying from the business at hand to tell some irrelevant anecodote, wandering off on an interminable digression instead of sticking to the point, sitting with his friends under his mulberry tree discussing natural philosophy and his newest musical instrument. But the doctor was still shrewd beyond the younger men's understanding; he knew that the differences they were trying to resolve were enormously complex, and would provoke the most violent emotions, and the doctor's amusing stories and amiable talk helped to soothe away the conflicts that afflicted the assembly of notables and move them, as he hoped, gradually toward a common society.

4

EARLY ARRIVALS

THE SPRING RAINS, the swollen streams, the mired roads, the uncertain ferry service, and the certain sense—from attendance at sessions of Congress over the years—that arriving on schedule for meetings was a waste of time kept the delegates from getting to Philadelphia by the fourteenth of May, the day appointed for the convention to begin. Given the condition of the roads, it was usually easier to sail up and down the American seacoast, or even from London, than to travel by coach from Boston to Philadelphia.

On the fourteenth, none were in Philadelphia except for Madison and Washington, and the Pennsylvania delegates, including Morris and Franklin, who lived there, and one delegate from nearby Delaware—George Read. That evening, however, four more Virginians came to town: Edmund Randolph, of the old Virginia family, governor of Virginia; the jurist John Blair; a doctor, James McClurg; and the scion of another old Virginia family, George Wythe, Virginia's most distinguished and erudite judge, and a professor of law at the College of William and Mary. Madison, still hoping to gather the Virginians in at Mrs. House's, was pleased that Randolph and McClurg had booked rooms there.

Three days later, the last of the Virginia delegates arrived: Colonel George Mason. Accompanied by his son John, he pulled in at the Indian Queen, where, as he wrote home to another son, George, Jr., they were "very well accommodated, & have a good Room to ourselves, & are charged only 25s. Pensylva. Curry. per Day, including our Servants and Horses."

The Indian Queen, as another traveler of the day related, "is kept in an elegant style, and consists of a large pile of buildings, with many spacious halls, and numerous small apartments, appropriated for lodging rooms. As soon as I had inquired of the bar-keeper . . . if I could be furnished with lodgings, a livery servant was ordered immediately to attend me, who received my baggage from the hostler, and conducted me to an apartment assigned by the bar-keeper, which was a rather small but a very handsome chamber, furnished with a rich field bed, bureau, table with drawers, a large looking-glass, neat chairs, and other furniture. Its front was east, and, being in the third story, afforded a fine prospect toward the river and the Jersey shore. The servant that attended me was a young, sprightly, well-built black fellow, neatly dressed—blue coat, sleeves and cape red, and buff waistcoat and breeches, the bosom of his shirt ruffled, and hair powdered. After he had brought up my baggage and properly deposited it in the chamber, he brought two of the latest London magazines and laid on the table. I ordered him to call a barber, and furnish me with a bowl of water for washing, and to have tea on the table by the time I was dressed."

The Indian Queen had sixteen such rooms on the second and third floors, and four large garret rooms above them for servants, stables that accommodated fifty or sixty horses, sheds for carriages, two large kitchens, and a laundry. Downstairs were the public rooms, five large ones furnished with plain and sturdy furniture, cheap engravings (such subjects as the twelve Caesars, the seasons, historical heroes), and maps. In these rooms were to be found both the inn's guests and local men—no women, no blacks except for the servants, no Indians, no laborers, handicraftsmen, artificers, tradesmen, or minors.

The guests sat about in Windsor or rush-bottomed chairs pulled up at large round tables, smoking long-stemmed clay pipes and drinking toddies, flips, lemonade laced with wine, bowls of punch, or Madeira, reading English and American papers and magazines, checking the notices and broadsides tacked up near the bar, exchanging news and gossip in what was still, as it had been for scores of years, the quintessentially natural setting for politics in America.

The wining and dining was in full swing by the time the two Masons arrived. The Philadelphians dispatched invitations for dinner and tea to the celebrated visitors, and Washington at least, ever sociable, plunged in wholeheartedly. He would appear frequently, in the weeks ahead, at the home of Samuel and Elizabeth Powel. The Powels lived in an elegant family enclave in the middle of the city, with four houses set amidst a large formal garden with a "profusion," as Washington noted in his diary, "of lemon, orange, and citron trees, and many aloes and other exotics," which made Mount Vernon seem plain by contrast. Elizabeth was the sister of Thomas Willing, Robert Morris's mentor. Her niece Anne was married to William Bingham, a former British consul and former commercial agent in the West Indies, and the Binghams had a house in the family enclave too, where Washington stopped for tea. The society of the Powels, Binghams, and Morrises—with their teas, and outings in the country, and dinner parties, and occasional forays into the local social events—provided Washington with a diversion from the heavy dose of politics during his stay in Philadelphia. But the principal attraction for him in this society was Elizabeth Powel, who was ten years younger than he was, chatty, slightly neurotic, sometimes deeply melancholy, delighted to talk politics, smart, always fashionably dressed. She loved to tease Washington, and he liked to flirt with her. He enjoyed the company of women always, and especially enjoyed hers.

But he was not only to be found in the little family enclave. He cut a broad swath through Philadelphia society, spreading political goodwill without effort. This mere visible presence of Washington in Philadelphia was doubtless the most important political act occurring anywhere in the country at the time: It gave authority to the convention. And Washington understood that his presence was his most significant act, and he did not go out of his way to do more.

He called for tea at the home of John Penn, the grandson of William Penn. He had dinner at the home of Jared Ingersoll, a Philadelphia attorney who was a delegate to the convention. He attended a charity affair with Mrs. Morris and "some other ladies," where a Mrs. O'Connell read a Dissertation on Eloquence (Washington, diplomatically circumspect even in the privacy of his own diary, described the reading as "tolerable").

He had dinner with Benjamin Chew and the "wedding guests"—
Peggy Chew just having married John Howard, a former officer of Maryland troops who had fought with Washington in
New Jersey—followed happily by tea with just the company
that Washington always savored, "a very large Circle of Ladies." He faced the Society of the Cincinnati over dinner two
days after his arrival; he was both agreeable and distant and
let it be known he could not return.

Colonel Mason, whose tastes ran more along the lines of
Franklin's, was disgusted by the social swirl that so charmed
his Virginia friend and neighbor. "I begin," the plainspoken
country squire wrote George, Jr., barely hours after his arrival
in town, "to grow heartily tired of the etiquetté and nonsense
so fashionable in this city. It would take me some months to
make myself master of them, and that it should require months
to learn what is not worth remembering as many minutes, is
to me so discouraging a circumstance as determines me to give
myself no manner of trouble about them."

While all the others were flitting about town to teas and
dinners, Madison was back at Mrs. House's, engaged in his favorite pastime, preparing his thoughts for the work ahead. The
lateness of the arrival of the delegates was not disagreeable to
the Virginia scholar. It gave him a chance to meet with his
fellow Virginians and prepare a common strategy; for Madison
understood that whichever delegation first presented a working paper to the assembly would set the agenda of the convention. And if Madison was the first to present a working paper
to his own delegation, then he would set the agenda for the
delegation that set the agenda.

"The Virginia Deputies," Mason wrote to George, Jr., "meet
& confer together two or three Hours, every Day; in order to
form a proper Correspondence of Sentiments." It was in these
meetings that the small, unprepossessing Madison set about to
organize the convention.

On the face of it, Madison's task was not an easy one even
for a skilled politician, let alone for a bookish theoretician. And
the delegation that he would try to organize behind his ideas
was not composed of men who were easy to dominate. Colonel
Mason, then aged sixty-two, was himself the principal author

of the constitution of the state of Virginia, the first written constitution of modern times, and of its bill of rights, which set the standard for subsequent bills of rights in America and elsewhere. He would not need the advice of the young Madison. He would have his own ideas about constitutions and how to go about writing them, and he was a local-power man to his bones.

Wythe, aged sixty-one, a signer of the Declaration of Independence, was the first professor of law in America, Thomas Jefferson's mentor in the law, the foremost classical scholar in a state full of classical scholars, and a man of decidedly independent mind. He, too, could be expected to have some things to say about drawing up a set of basic laws of the land, and not feel dependent on the notions of young Madison.

Randolph, who would be thirty-four years old in August, with a quick mind and highly developed political sensitivities, was more Madison's peer. But he was, also, a Randolph, raised in the very midst of politics in Williamsburg, where his father, uncle, and grandfather had all been king's attorneys, and not automatically inclined to defer to the leadership of others. He himself had been Virginia's first attorney general. He was an ambitious young man too, a quality that would cause him to side with the nationalists; yet his sentimental attachments were all with old Virginia, which would lead him to be a localist. In short, he would vacillate.

John Blair was a fine lawyer, educated at Middle Temple in London. In the company he kept in Philadelphia he did not seem astonishing; and in the convention ahead he would never speak and never serve on a committee, but he would cast his vote with the men of order.

James McClurg, a physician without much political experience, was even more clearly than Blair out of his element in this company. He had not been one of the delegates originally selected to attend the convention; when others had declined to serve, McClurg had been chosen as a substitute—and he served, principally, as a reliable vote for the centrists.

Of the five men, then, Madison could count on support from McClurg, from Blair, and also from Wythe, who generally approved of Madison's ideas. But the support from Wythe did not last long. Soon after arriving in Philadelphia, Wythe received word that his wife was dangerously—as it turned out, fatally—ill. And so, after these initial meetings of the delegation, Wythe played almost no part in the Philadelphia proceedings.

By far the most difficult men in the delegation were Randolph and Mason. And Mason, unlike Randolph, vacillated not at all. Mason suffered from gout, stomach trouble, a hatred of political gatherings, and a distrust of strong government. He was prickly and easily irritated, and a powerful, convinced defender of liberty, and of the usages of local government necessary to secure it. He was utterly unimpressed by pretty words or eloquence of any kind, and cared little whether or not he was liked. As a child—so his career of independence began— he had been privately tutored at home, and he had read literary, not political, works: Voltaire, Pope, and Swift were among his favorites. To the extent that such writers were political, they were skeptics and satirists. It may be that all he was interested in doing was protecting his own vast estate—and even more the interests of his children and heirs—but he went about that enterprise by laying all about himself with general principles and lashing his colleagues with enunciations of rights and freedoms.

His plantation was just downriver from Mount Vernon, and he and Washington had been friends since Washington was in his teens, Mason in his twenties. They had surveyed the joint boundaries of their plantations together, hunted together, exchanged plantings, and, in 1759, served together in Virginia's House of Burgesses. That had been the only public office Mason consented to hold prior to the Revolution. His feelings about politics were consummately American: He detested politics and politicians. He was not able to endure the company of the "babblers" in the House of Burgesses even for a year, and quit as soon as he could. As he wrote to Washington, "Mere vexation and disgust threw me into such an ill state of health, that before the Convention rose, I was sometimes near fainting in the House."

He would emerge from his treasured privacy to serve in a crisis—as he did during the Revolution, when he was one of the leading members of the Virginia legislature—but once the crisis was past, he would return at once to his private life. He sought his private life in part out of simple preference, in part because he was constantly beset by the pains of gout, in part because his wife had died in 1773 and left him, as he said, to be both "father and mother" to the four daughters and five sons to whom he was always close. But perhaps in part he believed the principles he avowed, that politicians ought to be returned to private life often in order to see just how it is and what the results of their legislation have been for daily life. He liked a government that was close to home, where politicians were known to their neighbors, where they were elevated to public service if they were men of good character and easy to put out of office if they proved to have poor character or judgment. He was very active in local affairs, serving on all sorts of committees and boards. This trip to Philadelphia was the farthest he had ever been away from home in his entire life.

Together, Randolph and Mason could be expected to combine against any scheme that seemed to propose too strong a central government or, within that central government, too strong an executive. And of course, since Mason had been the author of Virginia's bill of rights, he could be expected to be especially attentive to any threat to those civil rights that were rooted in the Magna Carta and common law. Along with Washington and Madison and Franklin, the old crotchet Mason would be one of the leading characters in Philadelphia.

Madison's job, then, was to bring his disparate fellow Virginians together (including Washington), to come up with a set of propositions specific enough to constitute an outline of a strengthened central government but vague enough to make sure he did not alienate any of his colleagues.

In a letter of April 16, Madison had given Washington a preview (and personal briefing paper) of the plan he would propose. His overall principle was simple: If the central government could not tax, could not ensure that its laws would be obeyed or its treaties honored, could not regulate its trade or its currency, could not repay its debts, could not be certain it had the power to quell internal rebellion or check foreign invasion, then there was no central government. In terms of classical political science, the country lived in a state of anarchy. The individual states could not pretend that they were part of a nation so long as they continued to assert their individual sovereignty. In short, however difficult it might be to bring them to it, the states must give up their sovereignties.

Yet Madison was realistic enough to know that the states would not consent to give up all their powers to a central government. "I have sought," he said, "for some middle ground, which may at once support a due supremacy of the national authority, and not exclude the local authorities wherever they can be subordinately useful."

At the same time, to ensure that the states were clearly subordinate, he would completely erase them from the national government. That is to say, whereas the Articles of Confederation provided that each state send representatives to the central government of the Continental Congress, and that the representatives speak on behalf of their states in Congress, and that each state was entitled to one vote in Congress, Madison simply removed the states from the structure of the central government. He would have the people vote directly for the representatives to the central government instead of their being appointed by the state legislatures, as they were under the Articles; the people and the central government would have a direct relationship without the need of any intervening bodies of the states. And the central government would be supreme.

To be sure, Madison's plan had some difficulties. If the people were to vote directly for representatives, and the representatives represented the people and not the states, then the votes would need to be allocated in proportion to the voters—on the basis of either their numbers or their wealth or the taxes they paid (Madison was not sure which).

On the face of it, allocating votes on the rule of one man–one vote rather than one state–one vote would appear to have no obstacles. Indeed, it would appear to be admirably democratic. But the problem with this change in the principle of voting was that it would give the largest number of representatives to those states that had the largest numbers of people or wealth. The big states would have many representatives, the little states few. The big states would dominate the central government and so dominate the little states.

Given the history of the colonies, the way in which the colonies had developed so that colonists had such strong loyalties to their own states, Madison's plan was destined to arouse violent objection. And Madison knew that the principle of one man–one vote would provoke opposition from the smaller states. They would hardly be eager to have their cherished local governments emasculated and to surrender all political control to a government dominated by a few of their big, arrogant neighboring states. But Madison had no solution to the problem. The smaller states, said Madison, would simply have to give in—for both practical and philosophical reasons. As a practical matter, the larger states would insist on it: They would no longer consent to being pushed around by Rhode Island and a few other small states, which had the power of veto under the Articles of Confederation. They would not give up their powers to a new governmental system unless they were assured of a large influence in it. And as a matter of principle, it was simply not fair that a handful of small states could routinely frustrate the will of a clear majority of the people. Any popular government must, at bottom, be bound by majority rule. Madison did not argue the case further. He pressed ahead with an outline of the sort of government he could build on this base.

Madison would arm this new national government, as he told Washington, "with positive and compleat authority in all cases which require uniformity; such as the regulation of trade, including the right of taxing both exports and imports. . . . Over and above this positive power, a negative in all cases whatsoever on the legislative acts of the states. . . . Without this defensive power, every positive power that can be given on paper will be evaded and defeated."

As for the actual structures to be used to put these principles into effect, Madison proposed a government divided up into executive, bi-cameral legislature, and judiciary. He had no novel inspirations about these structures; he simply took the old, familiar structures of colonial government and recast them in such a way as to transform thirteen separate nations into one.

To see to it that the old Continental Congress did not step in with all its parliamentary rules giving a single state the power to veto any proposed amendment and make a mess of their work, Madison suggested that the Philadelphia conventioneers not refer their recommendations to Congress at all but reach right over the heads of the Congress and obtain ratification directly "from the people." Madison's stratagem was both idealistic and politically ruthless at the same time: The old government would not even have a chance to defend itself. If the people ratified the convention's proposals, then the old government would simply cease to exist, the new one would take its place. And it would establish once and for all the principle that the government was derived from and responsible to the people.

Based on these broad, sweeping notions, Madison had drawn up a set of more specific propositions about the way the new government should be constituted. Some hard choices remained to be made, even among the familiar usages of executive, legislative, and judicial branches. In forming an executive branch, the convention might decide to have the executive come out of the legislature and be answerable to it and removable by it, as was the case in some states. Or, if the executive was to be independent of the legislature, it was possible to reduce the threat of royal pretensions by having a many-headed executive department—as Franklin had successfully advocated for Pennsylvania. And there were many other possibilities. Madison, in his letter to Washington, perhaps out of deference to the man all hoped would lead the new government, and certainly with an eye to the preferences of Randolph and Mason, declared: "I have scarcely ventured as yet to form my own opinion."

As the Virginia delegates looked over these recommendations, Randolph and Mason found nothing to object to. Mason, the most likely critic, perhaps not quite having focused on just how severely Madison meant to cut the power of the states, was pleased enough with the plan to write home cheerfully to George, Jr.: "It is easy to foresee that there will be much Difficulty in organizing a Government upon this great Scale, & at the same time reserving to the State Legislatures a sufficient Portion of Power for promoting & securing the Prosperity & Happiness of their respective Citizens. Yet, with a proper Degree of Coolness, Liberality & Candour (very rare Commodities by the Bye) I doubt not but it may be effected."

Randolph was inclined to go along too, although he did

think, tentatively, that some of the evils in the old system simply needed to be repaired, and that might be accomplished merely by amending the Articles of Confederation.

Madison was not keen on a contest with Randolph. Instead of arguing his point of view, he blandly agreed to a suggestion from Randolph that Madison's own fourteen resolutions, to which the delegation agreed, have a fifteenth added to them—and that the fifteenth be placed first. The fifteenth, which clearly did not belong with the other fourteen, proposed that the Articles of Confederation be "corrected and enlarged" to repair their faults. No one in the convention would be misled by that first proposal for a moment; the delegates would see at once that the following fourteen points called for a whole new scheme of government. But having his proposal there put Randolph's mind at ease, so much so that he agreed—as the governor of Virginia and as the leader of a unanimous Virginia delegation—to present Madison's set of resolutions to the full convention as the Virginia Plan, and so let the meetings begin in an atmosphere of invaluable unanimity.

To help guide the Virginia Plan through the convention, Madison counted on an old friend, James Wilson, a member of the Pennsylvania delegation, who would prove to be without doubt the most thoroughly perplexing man of the entire convention. A Philadelphian who lived just a few blocks from Mrs. House's, Wilson was a tall, stout, ruddy man, aloof and ill at ease, who wore round, thick-lensed glasses and spoke with a distinct Scottish burr.

His house was on Arch Street, near Front, and it was made thoroughly domestic by the presence of six children, and melancholy by the fact that Wilson's wife, Rachel, had died just the year before. Loneliness preyed on him this summer. His study was on the first floor, and in the afternoon, ribbons of sunlight filtered through the venetian blinds there, as he and Madison talked.

Wilson had been born to poor, churchgoing parents in Scotland, and needing to go to work as a boy when his father died, he had soon moved to America and worked his way up through the law. To the wistfully and frequently expressed regret of his mother, he had never looked back. He became famous, and disliked, as an attorney, most particularly for defending Tories in court, and he acquired a facade of haughty aristocratic manners so highly developed as to arouse either hatred or disdain in nearly everyone he met.

He served as attorney to Louis XVI (for some of the Crown's American interests) as well as to Ben Franklin; he was a business partner of Robert Morris's, and he was one of the founders of the Bank of North America. During the war, he once defended a businessman accused of profiteering, an act that so inflamed his fellow Philadelphians that the militia attacked his house, shot out his windows, and smashed down his door before Wilson and his friends were able to repel them. Five men were killed in the encounter. Little wonder that Wilson was detested by the common people of Pennsylvania. When the state legislature voted on a delegation to attend the summer convention, the financier Morris got on the delegation with the least number of votes, Wilson with the second-least number.

His life would never be free of anxiety. His ambitions always outran him. His wish to be rich led him to invest heavily in lands to the west and to go ever more deeply into debt, as, indeed, did Washington and many others. Unlike Washington, Wilson would end his life—although an associate justice of the Supreme Court—fleeing south to avoid his creditors, going from tavern to tavern, hiding from the law, coming to rest finally in a southern tavern, gaunt and listless, his clothes ragged and stained, having suffered a stroke, staring out the window, raving deliriously about arrest, bad debts, bankruptcy, and visions of jails.

A confirmed centrist, this man along with Ben Franklin, and contrary to all that one might have expected, would defend democracy determinedly and eloquently through the whole summer to come. Why he would defend the rights of the people is a puzzle, since the people never liked him, and since their having power would seem to have threatened most of his own interests. Perhaps he wished to use the ruse of majority rule to construct a strong national government in order to subdue the local Pennsylvania government that had given him such trouble. Perhaps he wished only to have a government that could claim to be based on the will of the people but that in practice, by being a distant central government, removed the people as far as possible from direct participation. Perhaps he saw a strong national government as the best way to secure his investments in western land. But no explanation will quite account for the many times, when none of these explanations made sense, Wilson would rise, often making himself appear foolish in the eyes of his colleagues, to speak on behalf of the virtues of democracy. Perhaps at such times he remembered the poor immigrant he had been.

5

THE OPENING SESSION

IT WAS NOT UNTIL May 25, three weeks after Madison came to town, that enough delegates had arrived in Philadelphia to constitute a quorum, and the convention got down to business in Independence Hall—then called the State House. The State House, said Franklin, looked, as one approached it, like a microscope just taken out of its case, or at least the original design for it had looked that way. The building was not in mint condition: The ravages of war, the shortness of money, had kept it from being perfectly maintained. Just recently its wooden steeple (the eyepiece of Franklin's telescope) had become so shaky as to constitute a positive hazard, and it had been carefully removed. What remained was a sturdy, dignified building, with an impressive horizontal spread by virtue of the wings on either side. It had been constructed, in 1732, of good if not lavish materials, with fine, large windows; and it had been embellished with a railed roof walk and elegant carved and gilded clock cases at either end. It bespoke sound government, small and plain but proud, careful with its money but not stingy.

The stroll to the State House was an easy one for the delegates. From Mrs. House's, Madison had only to go a few steps down Market to the corner of Fifth, take a right up to Chestnut (past the piles of lumber set out there for the Philosophical Society's new building), and he was at the front door to the State House. Just at the corner of Chestnut and Fifth was a covered well, with a wooden pump. To the west, up at Sixth Street, a hole had been dug to start work on a new county courthouse. And just in front of the State House, the city commissioner would soon spread fresh gravel over the cobblestones in order to dampen the noise of passing horses and wagons. Standing in front of the State House, one could look all the way back down Chestnut to the river, where the masts of ships could be seen above the wharves. Our the back was the Walnut Street jail, where prisoners thrust their hands through the bars to beg for money and tobacco.

Through the main door at the center of the State House, one entered the great hallway, twenty by forty feet, empty of furniture—but filled, often, with politicians, and with those who had come to have their cases heard in the chambers of the Pennsylvania supreme court, which could be seen through the arches on the right. To the rear, a staircase led up to the second floor, where the Supreme Executive Council (of which Franklin was the president) had its offices. Just at the bottom of the staircase, a door opened out onto a garden, where politicians and suitors of all sorts often went for a breath of fresh air.

To the left was the room where the Pennsylvania legislature met; in short, the State House had accommodations for all three branches—executive, legislative, and judicial—of the state government. The legislature's room was where the Continental Congress had met from 1775 until 1783, where the Declaration of Independence had been signed, and where the members of the Constitutional Convention were now gathering. It was, to most of them, a familiar and comfortable place. The room was large. Just inside the entrance was a wooden railing, with a gate for members, behind which observers could stand when the Congress had had its sessions there. The great windows to both sides, though covered with venetian blinds, let in copious daylight. The ceilings were high. Altogether the room was astonishingly plain, almost bare, certainly simple: a reminder that Philadelphia was a Quaker town.

The speaker's chair was the only piece of furniture of any special distinction. It was a high-backed carved-mahogany armchair with a leather seat. Placed between a pair of Ionic pilasters and framed by a handsomely molded panel topped by a carved frieze of leaves and a cockleshell, the speaker's chair commanded the room with a well-ordered flourish. The wall behind it was painted gray, and when the sunlight struck it early in the morning, it had a faint bluish hue. The speaker's table was covered with green baize. The speaker had no gavel; instead he had a small bell to call the assembly to order. And next to the bell was the most striking object in the room, an exceptionally fine silver inkstand, made some thirty years before by the silversmith Philip Syng. It was the inkstand that had been used in the signing of the Declaration.

Thirteen library tables were set in several rows, more or less semicircularly about the room, facing the speaker's dais, table, and chair. The tables, like the speaker's, were covered with green baize, and set with pewter inkstands, goose quill pens, sand, and writing paper. In time, the tables would come to be littered with papers, journals, reference books, newspapers, brass snuff and tobacco boxes. Windsor chairs were grouped around the tables.

At the moment, the tables for Maryland and New Hampshire and Connecticut were empty. Only one delegate—an earnest young fellow, Rufus King—sat at the Massachusetts table. A lone delegate, William Few, occupied Georgia's table. And the room was made even emptier by the absence of Thomas Jefferson and John Adams, of Patrick Henry and Sam Adams, and of Tom Paine, who set out for France in 1787 to stir up trouble there.

Patrick Henry and Sam Adams were not there because they had chosen not to be. Both were convinced—as were many of their countrymen—that the centrists who had called this meeting would end up constructing such a strong national government as to stifle democracy. He "smelt a rat," said Henry, and he thought that if he and his like-minded fellows stayed away from the Philadelphia convention they would undermine its authority.

Nonetheless, those who had gathered in the hall were an impressive lot: The South Carolina table was already populated by a gathering of nabobs, including John Rutledge, Dictator John as he was called, and two members of the well-known Pinckney family of Charleston. Pennsylvania's delegation was lacking Franklin at this opening session (his gout was giving him severe trouble that morning), but it was distinguished by the presence of Morris and Wilson. North Carolina had fielded Richard Dobbs Spaight, an affable fellow and a staunch defender of democracy, and Hugh Williamson, who tended toward centrism, an old friend of Franklin's who had a famously caustic wit. And the Virginia delegation—with General Washington, and Madison, and Mason, and Randolph, and Wythe—was positively resplendent.

Each state's legislature had elected whatever number of delegates it cared to. The number depended more on proximity to Philadelphia and the ease and expense of travel than it did on anything else. Some states sent only a few delegates; Pennsylvania elected eight. However many delegates it had, each state was accustomed, in affairs of this sort, as under the rules of the Articles of Confederation, to cast just one vote.

Just to the right of center, at the New York table, was another of the most notable delegates to the convention: Alexander Hamilton—his coat open to show cascades of white ruffles at his chest, his long reddish hair swept back like a cockatoo's crest, his five feet seven inches drawn up in a posture of military correctness, his chin elevated just so. He believed that the best form of government was monarchy and that the people were a "great beast."

In some sense, Hamilton could be considered, with Madison, the co-sponsor of the convention. No one had done more than he had to make it come about. No one was more convinced than he that the country was going to be done in by sheer disarray. He had himself called for a constitutional convention as early as 1780. Over his dinner table back in New York, he had badgered and charmed his fellow members of Congress to call a convention. And when the Annapolis convention had finally been arranged, he had worked with Madison to see that it led to this Philadelphia meeting.

An aide to Washington during the war, a colleague of Madison in Congress, Hamilton had been born in the West Indies, the son of a Scottish merchant and a French Huguenot mother—the "bastard brat of a Scotch pedlar," as John Adams once said of him. His father's business "went to wreck," Hamilton said; his mother died when he was eleven; and when he was twelve years old he got a job in a general store and, with the help of his aunts, began to work his way up—to New York, through King's College (now Columbia University), through marriage to the daughter of the wealthy General Philip Schuyler, through a capacity for endless hours of hard work, through his writing: so clear and forceful, it was said, so filled with wit and sarcasm, with bitter invective and elegance and playfulness, as to seem to be "logic on fire."

Having grown to become a connoisseur of elegant clothes and houses and fine wine and fine prints and land, Hamilton believed in the rule of gentlemen, of a strong central government directed by men of wealth and backed, if need be, by a standing army. In his early days he had spoken well of republican government, but by 1787 what he meant by that was a well-buttressed system of senators elected from among the better sort and for life, a president elected for life and armed with powers that the king of England would have envied, a popular house of limited powers and tenure, and the complete crushing of the states. Though Hamilton could not be depended on to like the Virginia Plan, he could be trusted to savage any arguments on behalf of the sovereignty of the states.

And so, the quorum having assembled, the convention commenced at once. The Virginians and Pennsylvanians had arranged beforehand that Franklin, as president of the host state of Pennsylvania, should nominate Washington as presiding officer for the convention. But since Franklin's gout kept him away that morning, his fellow Pennsylvanian Robert Morris, the next senior member of the delegation, and an old friend of the general's, rose to nominate Washington.

The nomination was seconded by John Rutledge, unquestionably one of the slyest politicians in America. From the age of twelve, Rutledge had sat in the gallery—never missing a single session—of the South Carolina Assembly, watching his uncle working on the floor of the legislature, and he knew politics in his bones. In seconding the nomination, Rutledge closed the issue without it having been opened (though debate had hardly been likely in any case, control was a habit with Rutledge), expressing his confidence "that the choice would be unanimous," and observing that "the presence of Genl Washington forbade any observations on the occasion which might otherwise be proper." Thus the leading state of the deep south joined the Virginians and the Pennsylvanians in the first act of the convention.

General Washington was elected unanimously and was accordingly conducted to the chair by Morris and Rutledge. The general thanked the convention for the honor they had conferred on him and then, characteristically (and truthfully), reminded the delegates "of the novelty of the scene of business in which he was to act, lamented his want of better qualifications, and claimed the indulgence of the House towards the involuntary errors which his inexperience might occasion."

Henceforth, Washington would be absolutely silent. He would vote, and his vote would be seen, so that all knew where he stood. And where he stood would carry influence—although, since his vote was only rarely noted in the records, we do not know where he stood on the issues. He would not enter the debates of the convention, either to advocate a position of his own or to comment on another's speech; and so it would seem that he vanished from the convention. But in fact, he was present at every single session of the convention, and his presence was felt daily by the delegates, a presence that argued simply, and indefatigably, for a strong central government.

The delegates were arranged so that the southern states occupied the tables to the left as they faced the speaker; the middle states were in the middle; and the northern states were to the right. At the far left of the semicircle was Georgia's table, then North and South Carolina, Delaware, Virginia, and Maryland. Just right of center was Pennsylvania and New York and New Jersey. Farther right were the tables for Connecticut and Massachusetts, and the empty tables for Rhode Island and New Hampshire. Madison, however, had moved all the way down front and established himself at a table there—so that he could hear all the delegates speak, he said, and keep notes of the debates. In fact, his position down front served, too, to give him the center of the room from which to speak and direct the convention, and to orchestrate his forces throughout the room. He and Rutledge and the Virginia delegation secured the left flank of the room; Wilson managed the Pennsylvania delegation at rear center. Hamilton sat to the right.

The first piece of business in the convention was to read

the credentials of the delegates, a tedious bit of parliamentary ceremony under ordinary circumstances, but this time a significant ritual. In the credentials it gave to its delegates, each state's legislature specified just what it wanted them to do in Philadelphia. Most of the credentials were composed of fine-sounding and vague instructions about improving the efficiency of the government. It was noticed, however, that the credentials of Delaware contained an odd little clause: The delegates from Delaware were prohibited, in any new set of arrangements the convention might make, from departing from the principle of the equality of the states under the Articles of Confederation. At the very outset, then, a warning had been served on the centrists.

After their credentials had been read, the delegates appointed a committee to draw up a set of rules of procedure for the convention. Rules, like credentials, seem a tedious routine of parliamentary procedure, but of course they are crucial: They can be drawn up impartially, or they can be so designed as to tip the balance of power toward one group or another. The rules committee was composed of the judicious Wythe of Virginia, young Charles Pinckney of South Carolina, and Hamilton of New York. And so New York joined Virginia, Pennsylvania, and South Carolina in the opening organizational moves of the convention.

To give the rules committee time to prepare a report, the convention adjourned till the following Monday at ten o'clock. Madison was optimistic, though guardedly so, and he passed the weekend in relative contentment. "A few days now will furnish some data for calculating the probable result of the meeting," he wrote home to his father. "In general the members seem to accord in viewing our situation as peculiarly critical and in being averse to temporising expedients. I wish they may as readily agree when particulars are brought forward."

Washington whiled away the weekend aimlessly. On Friday he had dinner with Morris's partner, Thomas Willing. On Saturday, as he recorded in his diary, he "returned all my visits this forenoon," dined at City Tavern, and spent the evening writing letters. By Sunday he was reduced for entertainment to attending services at "the Romish church," and another evening of letter writing.

By Monday, more delegates had arrived—including Oliver Ellsworth of Connecticut, a famously tenacious (more than one colleague said obstinate) man. Aaron Burr would say of him in later years: "If Ellsworth had happened to spell the name of the deity with two d's, it would have taken the Senate three weeks to expunge the superfluous letter." On occasion, when his days in court had thoroughly exhausted him, Ellsworth would actually gird his loins with a handkerchief so that he could stand up to argue his case. Demanding of himself and others, patrician in manner, particular in his appearance, never to be hurried at his toilet, he was also remarked for his insistent habit of talking to himself, even in the presence of others, and for taking pinches of snuff out of his snuffbox and then, lost in thought, letting them fall to the floor next to his chair, so that he was usually surrounded by a little circular mound of snuff. Ellsworth was the first of the delegates to arrive from Connecticut, a state that, in general, was content with its local government, although Ellsworth could be counted on to be independent-minded in the way he represented that tendency.

Franklin was there, too, on Monday. Suffering from his gout and his stones, he had been carried over the bumpy cobblestones as he would be every day, like a grand duke, in his sedan chair—a little cabin, with a door and windows. He was set down next to the Pennsylvania table, just inside the wooden railing, and his sedan chair was put in a corner behind the railing. He wished, he said, that "I had brought with me from France a balloon sufficiently large to raise me from the ground. In my malady it would have been the most easy carriage for me, being led by a string held by a man walking on the ground." Like Washington, Franklin was not a debater or floor manager. He had rarely made speeches in any sort of assembly in the past; he saved his voice for those afternoons under the mulberry tree at home. But he was certainly a presence.

Wythe of Virginia, who had not yet left, presented the rules. Members were politely reminded of the rules of courtesy, forbidden to whisper, pass notes, read a book or pamphlet, newspaper or manuscript, while another was speaking. They were admonished to address their remarks to the president, to speak no more than twice on a subject unless by special permission, and then only after all other members had had the opportunity to speak if they chose to. Questions presented to the house were to be read through once for information, and then again, a paragraph at a time, for debate and amendment, and then, finally, as a whole again, with whatever amendments had been approved.

The crucial rule, of course, was how the house would vote; and that rule was stated at once, and clearly: Members would vote, as usual, by state, one vote per state. The delegates would poll their own delegations and then, however the majority of the delegation voted, thus would the state cast its one ballot. Seven states would constitute a quorum. Questions would be settled by majority vote.

The rule on voting had not been lightly adopted. In the strategy sessions before the convention, the tough-minded Pennsylvanians, led by Wilson, had told the Virginians that the large states should firmly refuse an equal vote to the small states beginning with the very first day of the convention, to set the ground rules right at once that states had voting strength in proportion to their population or wealth. If the small states were allowed an equal vote, they would simply block any proposal that would come up in the convention that would diminish their powers. And so the convention would be paralyzed from the first day.

Madison and his fellow Virginians demurred: Best not to drive the small states out of the convention before it had begun, they said circumspectly, or to demand of them that they could stay only by giving up their powers and throwing themselves on the mercies of the large states before they had seen what the large states might do; best to let the small states have their equality during the convention and win them over in the course of deliberations so that they would support a new plan with enthusiasm when they returned to their constituents. The argument of the Virginians carried; the small states began the convention on their accustomed footing; and the groundwork was laid for later trouble.

Rufus King of Massachusetts, an ambitious young attorney, aged thirty-two, who had graduated first in his class from Harvard and who had been scrambling his way up through politics ever since, a young man who had at times been thought to be a Tory, at other times a revolutionary, was a master of what would work. While Washington wrote home about farming and Madison corresponded with his father about political philosophy, King wrote friends back home about the minutest details of Massachusetts electoral politics. At the moment, he spotted an imperfect rule. The rules committee had suggested that any member might call at any time for the yeas and nays and have them entered in the minutes; but this, said King, would simply leave the minutes full of contradictions, since the delegates would be changing their minds during the course of the convention. Even more important, though King was discreet enough not to mention it, the practice would leave a record of votes that might get out and prove embarrassing to the delegates. One wanted to be free to say anything at all, and not be held accountable for it. King moved that no record be kept of individual delegates' votes.

Colonel Mason seconded King's motion, and said frankly what King had been too polite to say—that a record of the opinions of members might be broadcast after the convention ended, and even "furnish handles to the adversaries of the Result of the Meeting." The motion carried.

And then the members got into the delicate matter of secrecy. One of their number advised against the "licentious publication" of their proceedings, and that led to another couple of rules: "That no copy be taken of any entry on the journal during the sitting of the House without the leave of the House"; and "That nothing spoken in the House be printed, or otherwise published, or communicated without leave." So precise, and impressive, was this rule, and so punctilious was General Washington, that the general immediately even stopped making in his private diary any entries related to the business of the convention.

Sentries were posted at the door. "It is expected our doors will be shut," Colonel Mason wrote his son, "and communications upon the business of the Convention be forbidden during its sitting. This I think myself a proper precaution to prevent mistakes and misrepresentation until the business shall have been completed, when the whole may have a very different complexion from that in which the several crude and indigested parts might in their first shape appear if submitted to the public eye." There was, of course, an enormous difference between this gentlemen's agreement and later laws of secrecy, by which government officials would be legally subject to punishment if they broadcast some secret—an inconceivable idea to men like Mason.

Jefferson, when he got news in Paris of the convention's rule on secrecy, was outraged that the convention should have adopted even this agreement—not only because it meant he could not discover what was going on, but, as he wrote to Adams in London, because it was an "abominable" precedent to tie up "the tongues of their members. Nothing can justify this example but the innocence of their intentions, & ignorance of the value of public discussions."

Franklin flirted with the rule in his own way, gossiping to visitors under the mulberry tree, provoking his fellow delegates to remind him not to be indiscreet, hushing up at once, and then, soon again, misbehaving. But the rule of secrecy held. Occasionally a delegate would be unable to restrain himself in a letter to a friend, and would let fall the meagerest hint about the work of the convention, but the newspapers knew nothing, at least no details of the debates as they progressed, and editors were reduced to expressions of patriotism and optimism.

In the convention itself, the rule of secrecy had a refreshing effect: The delegates, for the most part, said what they meant. Not always: Some southerners would speak in favor of liberty when they meant they wanted to keep their slaves; some merchants would rail against a suffocating central government when they meant they wanted special privileges from the government. But ordinarily, if a delegate favored aristocracy, he said so—not by way of some elaborate praise of democracy filled with subtle words to indicate another meaning, but by saying he favored aristocracy. If he wanted laws that would protect his own business, investments, or profits, he quite often simply said so.

For all the lateness of arrivals, the irregularity of attendance, the whirl of dinners and teas and outings, and the casual society of tavern life, the seriousness of what they were about to undertake was gradually growing on the delegates. From a little dispute over oyster fisheries, the stakes had distinctly risen to the creation of a new government. The notion of a social contract was a hallowed one in political theory, but in the abstract; here a group of men intended actually to sit down and debate what should constitute it, to vote on accepting it paragraph by paragraph, and to commit this contract to paper. They had gathered, said Madison, "to decide forever the fate of Republican Government"; and the momentousness of the occasion sobered all who took part in it.

George Mason, in a quiet, contemplative moment back in his rooms at the Indian Queen, wrote home to his son: "to view, through the calm, sedate medium of reason the influence which the establishment now proposed may have upon the happiness or misery of millions yet unborn, is an object of such magnitude, as absorbs, and in a manner suspends the operations of the human understanding."

PART II

6

FIRST PRINCIPLES

THE DELEGATES HAVING SETTLED in at their tables, the rules having been established, Washington, as presiding officer, turned gracefully but firmly and gave the floor to Edmund Randolph to present the Virginia Plan.

The handsome young Randolph, speaking in a mellifluous Tidewater voice, the very picture of the old Virginia elite, "expressed his regret," so he said, "that it should fall to him, rather than those, who were of longer standing in life and political experience, to open the great subject of their mission." But, he continued modestly, "as the convention had originated from Virginia, and his colleagues had supposed that some proposition was expected from them, they had imposed this task on him."

He began, as Madison had begun in the meetings of the Virginia delegation, by listing the now familiar crises that the government of the Confederation had not prevented or solved. He spoke of the commercial discord among the states, of Shays' Rebellion in Massachusetts, of the havoc that paper money had created, of the way that some states had violated treaty obligations. If any state could violate treaty obligations, he pointed out, any state could provoke a war with a foreign country, which all the other states would then be obliged to fight. The Congress was unable to defend itself against these or other encroachments on its power by any of the states, or to keep any state from encroaching on the rights of any other state. In this condition of powerlessness, the central government could not be said to be an effective government at all. Indeed, anarchy threatened everywhere; and there were widespread prophecies of America's downfall.

The remedy for the situation he described, said Randolph, was a set of fifteen resolutions that he had in hand, beginning with his own first resolution, which had as their basis "the republican principle," and he now presented those resolutions to the convention, reading out each one in its entirety. Surely this alone was a remarkable act—in a world filled with monarchies, to read out, with the perfect assurance of acceptance, a design for government based on some sort of "republican principle." With all the breeding and high social standing of many of these gentlemen in Philadelphia, it is easy to forget how revolutionary they were.

The first two resolutions called for strengthening the central government enough so that it would be able to defend itself against the evils just mentioned, and for founding the government on a new principle of proportional voting, based on population or wealth, rather than voting by state; the next three resolutions outlined a legislative branch for this new government; two resolutions dealt with the executive branch; one resolution dealt with the judiciary; and the remaining resolutions dealt with the admission of new states, a guarantee of republican government to each state, the amendment process, and the way in which this new constitution was to be ratified.

Because Randolph's resolutions were to be the basis for general debate, because they were a complicated set of interlocking propositions, the delegates were prepared to adjourn for the day and take some time to mull them over. Before they did, however, Charles Pinckney asked for the floor to present his plan for reforming the government. Pinckney was a mere twenty-nine years old, although, to make himself seem even more astounding, he insisted that he was only twenty-four. Vain to the point of exquisiteness, he had a taste for silk and lace; and no matter what he wore, he looked as though he might move in a cloud of pink and powder blue. Many men were vying for recognition in Philadelphia, but perhaps none more feverishly than Charles.

In later years, Pinckney would claim that his plan was the

one the convention adopted. He backed up his claim with a draft of the constitution in his own handwriting that he said was the one he had submitted to the convention, and it had a remarkable resemblance to the finished document. Unfortunately, however, it was written on paper that bore a watermark later than 1787. His reputation was not helped when historians discovered that he had habitually plagiarized the speeches and writings of others and published them as his own. In time, those who knew him best in political circles would take to calling him "Blackguard Charlie."

Just what plan he presented to the convention is not clear, but as nearly as it is possible to piece together from the documents, it would appear that he had some thoughts not for a new constitution but for a revision of the Articles. One of Madison's biographers has suggested that after Pinckney moved in next door to Madison at Mrs. House's—and chatted Madison up in the hall in those days before all the delegates had arrived in town—he swiped some of Madison's ideas and phrases and incorporated them into his plan.

In any case, Blackguard Charlie Pinckney, too, read out his set of resolutions. The delegates listened courteously, and then, without comment, voted to consider Pinckney's plan alongside the Virginia propositions. The session was adjourned then, and the delegates dispersed to their taverns and rooming houses to consider what they had heard.

"They dine without soup," a surprised, and offended, Moreau de Saint-Méry said of the Americans, "at about two o'clock" in the afternoon. "Their dinner consists of broth, with a main dish of an English roast surrounded by potatoes. Following that are boiled green peas, on which they put butter which the heat melts, or a spicy sauce; then baked or fried eggs, boiled or fried fish, salad which may be thinly sliced cabbage seasoned to each man's taste on his own plate, pastries, sweets to which they are excessively partial and which are insufficiently cooked. For dessert, they have a little fruit, some cheese and a pudding. The entire meal is washed down with cider, weak or strong beer, then white wine. The entrée is accompanied by Bordeaux or Madeira, which they keep drinking right through dessert."

The afternoon meal was the main meal of the day. A light

supper sufficed in the evening. And after supper, the tavern-keeper might bring out more beer, cider, wine, or punch to sustain the political talk late into the evening.

The next day, the convention gathered once more in the morning and got down to serious business—a careful first run-through of the Virginia resolutions—taking each resolution at a time, offering initial reactions, asking for explanation or clarification of a clause or a word or an intention. They would spend their first week in this way, meticulously acquainting themselves with the plan conceived by the centrists of Virginia.

To put themselves in the right frame of mind for this preliminary review, the delegates reorganized themselves into a Committee of the Whole. This parliamentary device would allow the members to debate and vote and debate and change their vote and not be formally bound by any actions they took until they could see the shape of the whole plan for which they were voting. It is an admirable device, fostering exceptional openness of speech and mind. As the convention proceeded, the delegates would move in and out of this committee repeatedly to report its own actions to itself; and, ultimately, no vote could be counted final until the very last day of the convention.

To preside over the Committee of the Whole, the delegates appointed Nathaniel Gorham, who had just arrived from Massachusetts. A robust man, forty-nine years old, Gorham had just finished a term as president of Congress, and so his selection to preside in committee paid formal obeisance to the Confederation. Gorham, a man of modest birth and little education, sent off at the age of fifteen to an apprenticeship as a mechanic, had managed to become a moderately well-to-do merchant. His selection as chairman placed in that highly visible presiding officer's chair a self-made man, a man whose very presence argued, if not for democracy, at least against aristocracy.

Randolph's first resolution came before the house: "Resolved that the articles of Confederation ought to be so corrected & enlarged as to accomplish the objects proposed by their institution; namely, common defense, security of liberty, and general welfare"—and so the issue was posed at once for debate whether the Articles were to be amended or a wholly new plan proposed.

Gouverneur Morris of the Pennsylvania delegation rose to speak. No relative of Robert Morris, Gouverneur was a young-ish man of high style and casual impudence, who enjoyed his own arrogance enormously. He was a notorious womanizer. A rich, landed aristocrat, a man of order with a near-Hamilton-ian contempt for the people, he favored a high-toned central government. He had a wooden leg, which was the subject of constant gossip and which he loved to use, pacing up and down the room, to punctuate his sentences with a thump. Some said he had had to jump from a second-floor window to escape the husband of a woman with whom he was having an affair. John Jay wrote to him from Madrid: "I have learned that a certain married woman after much use of your legs had occasioned your losing one." (In truth, he lost the leg in a carriage acci-dent on Dock Street in Philadelphia, but he did not discourage the more colorful rumors.) Of all the men at the convention, Gouverneur, with his jaunty brilliance, was perhaps the only one who could outshine Hamilton in sheer hauteur.

Gouverneur was not the sort to indulge Randolph in the vague language of the first Virginia resolution—or a sort of woolly-headed attachment to the Articles—and he swept it aside with a casual declaration that this first resolution was unnec-essary, since "subsequent resolutions would not agree with it." And he urged that the resolution be dropped so that the con-vention could get right on with considering three propositions:

"1. that a Union of the States merely Federal will not ac-complish the objects proposed by the articles of Confederation, namely common defence, security of liberty, & genl. welfare.

"2. that no treaty or treaties among the whole or part of the States, as individual sovereignties, would be sufficient.

"3. that a *national* Government ought to be established consisting of a *supreme* Legislative, Executive & Judiciary."

Given Gouverneur's peremptory demand, Randolph duti-fully moved to consider these propositions; Gouverneur sec-onded the motion. The issue was joined. A slight tremor of unease passed through the convention.

Young Charles Pinckney ventured to speak up first, in a

quiet, understated way. Did Mr. Randolph mean "to abolish the State Governments?"

Randolph, young as he was, had been well schooled by his Virginia mentors, and he was not to be drawn so easily into taking a clear position on a controversial issue so early in the convention. He answered by not answering, saying that he meant by his general propositions only "to introduce" the outlines of his system.

The South Carolinians were put at once into an uncomfortable position. They wanted to champion Madison's notion of a strong central government dominated by the large states (which would include South Carolina). Such a government might be good for international trade, for the export of rice and tobacco and indigo, and so for the present and future of South Carolinians' fortunes. But as southerners and plantation owners, they wanted, too, to protect the state governments that protected their slave-based society. And so, while they were careful not to oppose the Virginians, they were careful, too, not to accept the Virginians' ideas too quickly.

General Charles Cotesworth Pinckney, the smooth, pink cousin of young Charles, a serene and courtly forty-one-year-old southern gentleman and as suave a politician as Charleston ever produced, took the floor and quietly "expressed a doubt" too (picking up the threat first suggested by the credentials of the delegation from Delaware) whether the delegates were actually empowered to discuss a system of government based on principles different from those of the Articles of Confederation. A strict construction of the credentials of the delegates would not allow the convention to do anything but remain with the Confederation. The South Carolinians thus fired their early warning shots: They might give strength to this new government, but only if a new government was formed so as not to threaten their society.

Doubts and hesitations were expressed now on other sides of the house. Elbridge Gerry, a dapper, birdlike, stuttering merchant from Marblehead, had just arrived in Philadelphia the day before, and he was struck at once by this talk of a powerful new central government. Gerry was a man passionately devoted to local rule—quick, as it was said, to "sniff tyranny in every tainted breeze," an old friend of radical Sam

Adams, a man committed to liberty, to equal rights for all and special privileges for none, an independent-minded New Englander who could not bear the thought of a meddlesome government. On the other hand, he was also a businessman, who depended on the special privileges that government, whether local or central, could grant, a man who could see the possible advantage in a strong central government dominated by such large states as his own Massachusetts.

Caught thus in the classic dilemma of the businessman, suspended between his love of liberty and his love of profits, unable, as the honest man he was, to reconcile his conflicting interests, Gerry flailed desperately. Where Edmund Randolph vacillated in a well-mannered way, Gerry pitched from side to side, frantic with worry. At the moment, however, he contented himself with joining the South Carolinians to express "the same doubt."

Indeed, he said, picking up the theme voiced by the delegations from Delaware and South Carolina, it was not at all clear whether this convention had the power to propose a wholly new government. If it did, stuttered Gerry, then "we have the right to annihilate the confederation"—that is to say, to overthrow the existing government entirely, to conduct a coup d'état.

Gouverneur Morris—not an easily frightened man—did not bother to reply to the anxious charge that he was conducting a coup; he wasted no effort in trying to reassure Gerry or the others. Rather, he condescended in his inimitable way to explain "the distinction between a *federal* and *national, supreme* Govt.; the former being a mere compact resting on the good faith of the parties; the latter having a compleat and *compulsive* operation. In all communities, concluded Morris, "there must be one supreme power, and one only." It was as simple as that. Warnings that the delegates were conducting a coup d'état did not move him.

Roger Sherman had just taken his seat with the Connecticut delegation—and, the moment he arrived, he displaced all the other delegates as the voice of New England. Sherman, a venerable sixty-six years old, was a peculiar-looking man, and whenever he entered a room his contemporaries tended to take out their pens to draw caricatures. A farm boy, self-taught, dressed in plain and ill-fitting clothes, with large hands and blunt fingers, thick muscular wrists sticking out of his coat sleeves, he had worked his way up from shoemaker to shopkeeper to almanac publisher. Unlike Franklin, he was inclined to fill his almanacs not with shrewd wit and casual wisdom so much as with a bit of moral verse or a homily ("He that would be happy, must be Virtuous" and "Plain down right Honesty, is the Beauty and Elegancy of Life").

He was the very quintessence of a New Englander—a Puritan, nurtured in the town meetings of New England, a man who believed in self-reliance, in small-town government taking care of its own business. Had John Adams or Sam Adams or John Hancock been present in the convention, they would have been the voices of that New England political culture. But since John Adams was in London, and Sam Adams was sulking in Boston, and John Hancock, having shown himself sympathetic to the farmers, had just been elected governor of Massachusetts, Roger Sherman spoke for New England—though always in only a few words.

The Confederation, Sherman said cautiously, stepping into the midst of this great controversy, "had not given sufficient power to Congress." Additional powers were necessary, particularly the power to raise money, a power that would come to involve many other powers. It was not an easy matter to sort out just how to do this, but he was not disposed "to make too great inroads on the existing system."

The convention paused to consider these early declarations of positions. It was not clear at once how the sides were lining up in this debate. A bit more feeling out seemed called for. A motion was offered that called—ambiguously—for "a more effective government."

But the Virginians were not prepared to have their initiative blunted on this very first resolution. Before the advocates of local power had quite organized their ideas or their forces— in fact, before all the defenders of local government had even arrived at the convention—the Virginians wanted to press the issue to a vote. The Virginians and Pennsylvanians marshaled their forces, called for a vote, and put a stop to this vague motion calling for mere reform of the Articles.

Then Pierce Butler, another nabob from South Carolina, stood up and proposed the wording on which the Madisonians

were eager to vote; Butler moved that a "national" government be established, with a "supreme" legislature, executive,
and judiciary.

Again the Madisonians marshaled their forces. Franklin's
friend Williamson brought his fellow North Carolinians into
the Madisonian camp, and the South Carolinians went along
for the time being with their big-state aspirations, keeping their
reservations to themselves. Massachussetts was brought tentatively into the large-state fold. Gerry's colleagues, Gorham
and Rufus King favored a strong central government. And so
the motion passed with six votes in favor, Connecticut opposed, New York divided. Thus, the principle of a supreme national government, the basis of the whole Madisonian plan,
was set in place at once—albeit very precariously.

With high spirits, the Madisonians moved immediately to
their second resolution: "that the rights of suffrage in the National Legislature ought to be proportioned to the quotas of
contribution, or to the number of free inhabitants, as the one
or the other rule may seem best in different cases." This was
the resolution that would establish the principle of one man—
one vote, and that would also necessarily give the advantage
to the big states in the new arrangement.

Now, however, some of the other delegates were quicker
to object. This phrase "free inhabitants," for example, was a
nasty pair of words. Were the southerners not to be allowed to
count their slaves in determining their voting strength? Here
was an issue—slavery—that might split South Carolina off from
Virginia and Pennsylvania at once. Madison asked for the floor
immediately. He suggested that the words "or to the number
of free inhabitants" be struck out of the resolution. They might
occasion debates over slavery—an issue he would rather postpone so that it not get entangled with the issues of whether
voting was to be proportional on any basis.

Ever practical Rufus King took the floor. He saw some other
nits to pick in the business of proportional voting. If voting
was not to be based on population, then it would be based on
wealth, or taxation. But if voting was based on taxes, and if
taxes varied from year to year as the productivity of the states
varied, the apportioning of votes could become hopelessly cha-
otic.

Unable to agree at once whether to base proportional voting on population or wealth, the convention came to a momentary standstill. Then Hamilton threw aside all considerations for the sensibilities of the southerners and moved flatly that "the rights of suffrage in the national Legislature ought to be proportioned to the number of free inhabitants."

Hamilton's motion was seconded—and then, just as the Madisonians seemed on the verge of another victory, a countermotion was put before the house to postpone Hamilton's motion, and at once the motion was checked. The convention came to a pause. The presence of the slave-owning states was felt.

Randolph had another formulation to offer: that "the rights of suffrage in the national Legislature ought to be proportioned"—Randolph did not say according to what. That was nice. Perhaps the southerners could count their slaves to increase their representation and perhaps not. His resolution was adopted. Another amendment was put forward: that the rights of suffrage ought to be proportioned, "and not according to the present system"—and this wording passed too. It seemed the convention was easing toward agreement.

Madison tried to work his way back, then, by degrees, toward his preferred phrasing, which would establish the principle of majority rule. He moved that the convention agree: "the equality of suffrage established by the articles"—that is, the principle of the equality of the states—"ought not to prevail in the national Legislature" but "an equitable ratio of representation" ought to be substituted.

Then George Read, of the little state of Delaware, called a halt to this whole pussyfooting debate. Read, a slight man, very punctilious in his dress, was in favor of a strong central government—he made that clear. But he wanted to make certain that the small states were not swallowed up in a central government. The clause related to voting ought to be postponed, said Read. He reminded the convention of the credentials of the Delaware delegation, which prevented them "from assenting to any change of the rule of suffrage." (Read should know what the credentials said; he had written them.) If "such a change should be fixed on," said Read, then the delegates from Delaware would have "to retire from the Convention." The dissolution of the Union could begin at once.

Read's little ultimatum sobered the delegates considerably, although, for all its effect, it could not subdue the ebullient Gouverneur Morris, who found nothing more delightful than a dare. Of course, said Morris, the "valuable assistance" of the delegates from Delaware "could not be lost without real concern," and that they might thus give the world proof of discord so early in the convention was a matter of real regret; nonetheless, the change in voting procedure that was proposed was "so fundamental" that "it could not be dispensed with," whatever the cost. As far as Morris was concerned, Delaware could walk out.

Madison quickly interposed to soothe his colleagues' feelings and hold the Union together. Whatever logic there may have been, he said, for equality of suffrage among the states when the Union was really a treaty among sovereign states, that logic must cease to operate once a single, sovereign, national government was put in place. Nonetheless, out of consideration for the sentiments of the delegate from Delaware, he suggested that the members might vote in Committee of the Whole simply to take a sense of the sentiment of the members on this point, but that their official report (to themselves) in the convention itself might record the matter as having been postponed.

This was a sweet piece of parliamentary maneuvering, but Read was not taken in for a moment—and several other members rose up to take exception. The Madisonians must not try to slip by this objection from the local-power men with any parliamentary sleight of hand.

Then the Madisonians replied in their turn and tersely: No proper construction of the credentials could permit the members from Delaware to withdraw from the convention. They had been appointed to the convention and must serve. Threats to withdraw were unacceptable.

The smallest hint of frayed tempers showed through the courteously spoken exchanges. An urge to adjourn overtook the delegates. But before they could adjourn they had to deal somehow with all the motions on the floor; thus, to give themselves respite, they voted to accept Read's motion to postpone the inflammatory issue of suffrage to a later day.

So it was that just three days into their summer of debate,

as the delegates dispersed to their taverns and rooming houses, they left the convention hall with an awakening sense of the intricacy and depth of the differences they must resolve if they were to live together in the same country.

7

THE QUESTION OF DEMOCRACY

ON THURSDAY, MAY 31, the delegates put aside for the time being their differences about central and local authority and began a week-long review of Virginia resolutions 3 through 15, which spelled out the broad structure of the proposed national government, should such a government finally be accepted. One day was devoted to the legislature, four grueling days to the executive, and only a brief few hours to the judiciary. The week seemed to be taken up with the mere mechanics of things—of branches and duties and procedures—and it was. But like the discussion of the shape of the table before a peace conference, this talk necessarily became involved at once with whom this structure was to serve: who was given power, and who was not.

Just how democratic the new government was to be was certainly at the center of these questions. All the delegates assumed they were discussing the framing of a republic, a representative government. They used both the word "republic" and the word "democracy" to speak of the government they were framing, but to the extent that they meant something different by their choice of words, it was a difference of emphasis, not of kind. In theory, the most democratic form of government they might imagine was a form of egalitarian local self-government. But not all the localists were egalitarians, and some of the centrists (most notably Wilson) favored direct popular voting. The question of democracy, in other words, cut across all lines of the debate.

The issue was present from the opening phrases of resolution 3, the first of four resolutions about the legislature, and democracy did not fare well right from the beginning. Resolution 3 looked innocuous enough—"that the national legislature ought to consist of two branches"—and in fact it was agreed to at once, without debate. All voted in favor of it—except Pennsylvania, which clung to its old ideal of the one-house legislature (probably only in deference to Franklin; Wilson, Robert and Gouverneur Morris, and the others didn't like the unicameral legislature). The two-house legislature was based on the British model, and it was adopted not only without question but also without anyone quite having articulated what the second house was meant to be and do.

The second house was meant, of course, as all second houses are meant, to provide a check, to see to it that all the "passions" of the majority do not carry the government away. The defenders of the two-house legislature would argue that in this way the government would be able to check momentary urges, to allow a cooling-off period for mature reflection. The opponents of a two-house legislature felt, on the other hand, that there were other ways to allow for a cooling-off period if that was what was wanted—a piece of legislation could simply be set aside for a cooling-off period once it was passed, be publicly debated, and then be passed again—that the two-house legislature would act permanently to frustrate the will of the people and to protect the privileged, and that the defeat of the one-house legislature was a defeat for democracy. Nonetheless, there was an easy majority to be mustered in favor of the bicameral legislature. No doubt the fresh memory of Shays' Rebellion sustained the delegates in their natural inclinations.

The delegates moved on to consider resolution 4—"that the members of the first branch of the National Legislature ought to be elected by the people of the several States." This was the first time the proposed constitution mentioned the people.

Roger Sherman, the farmer's son, the former shoemaker, objected at once. Despite his background, Sherman was no egalitarian. He believed in a government by the elite. The people, said Sherman, "should have as little to do as may be about the Government. They want information and are constantly liable to be misled." He said no more; it was a brief enough speech, and firm enough too: So much for the warm feeling toward democracy, and for the thought that the localists were necessarily democrats.

Elbridge Gerry agreed. "The evils we experience," stuttered Gerry, "flow from the excess of democracy. The people do not want virtue; but are the dupes of pretended patriots." He did not bother to mention Shays by name—he didn't need to—but he spoke of the "baneful measures" and "false reports" that had been circulating even more recently in Massachusetts, and the activities of "designing men," and he said that he had himself been "too republican" in the past; he was still republican, he said, but he had been taught "by experience the danger of the levelling spirit."

Given such forthright arguments against democracy, delegates such as Hamilton and Gouverneur Morris, who would have taken even more elitist positions, could afford to sit back quietly. And anyone who had anything good to say about the people might be expected to be suitably chastened, even silenced, by these pronouncements of the current fixed opinion. Who would dare to rise and reply to such fashionably scathing denunciations of the people?

The man who did rise at least was that patrician country gentleman who so loved the comforts of a privileged home, whose family had settled in America 130 years before, a man with five thousand acres of land to protect, the owner of several hundred slaves, an indubitable member of the elite, George Mason of Virginia.

The first house of the legislature, the crusty old gentleman instructed his colleagues, "was to be the grand depository of the democratic principle of the Government." It was to be America's House of Commons. What did the delegates have in mind when they advocated not having the people vote for its members? The first house "ought to know and sympathize with every part of the community." It ought to be taken not only from different parts of the entire republic but from different parts of the states, from different communities, so as to bring into it all the "different interests and views" one found in the country as a whole.

To be sure, the people were not infallible, but neither was any individual or group; and the government could not sensibly cut itself off from the common knowledge and accumulated wisdom that resided in the people as a whole. An individual's vote was like a vote on a jury: It was not supposed that any one man possessed the whole truth of human affairs. It was only supposed that a proposition that could get past the various intelligences and prejudices and knowledge of daily life of twelve people of different backgrounds and native endowments had a better chance of being a true proposition than any other. The same principle applied to the democratic franchise.

Perhaps the Americans had, Mason acknowledged, "been too democratic" in the recent past; but he was afraid that "we should run incautiously into the opposite extreme. We ought to attend to the rights of every class of people." Indeed, he had himself "often wondered at the indifference of the superior classes of society to this dictate of humanity & policy." Did they never think, "however affluent their circumstances or elevated their situations" were at the moment, that the course of time would certainly "distribute their posterity throughout the lowest classes of Society"? Under the circumstances, said the man who so loved his family, who had been raising his nine children single-handedly for more than a dozen years, "every selfish motive . . . every family attachment, ought to recommend such a system of policy as would provide no less carefully for the rights and happiness of the lowest than of the highest order of Citizens."

Madison then summed up the argument in favor of popular election of the first house. First of all, and simply, he thought "the popular election of one branch of the national Legislature . . . essential to every plan of free Government." Like Wilson, he thought that principle was so well established as to require no elaborate defense.

Second, said Madison, in some of the states, members of the legislature were already removed from the people, having been elected by a body of electors. (This was done intentionally as a "refining" process: With each step of the electoral process, the people were removed one more step from the government, and the government was placed increasingly in the hands of the professionals so that they could run it for themselves, and ensure that no popular firebrand was too easily elected; but even professionals recognized that this device could be taken too far.) Now, if the first branch of the national legislature was placed at still another remove from the people by being elected by the state legislatures, then the national legislature would be twice removed from the people. If, in addition—though none of this had yet been decided—the second house of the national legislature was elected by the first, and if the executive was elected by the second house, and if the executive then appointed officers to carry out the laws of the nation, "the people would be lost sight of altogether; and the necessary sympathy between them and their rulers and officers, too little felt." Perhaps, said Madison, the second branch and the executive could be elected by indirect means, but the first branch must be elected directly by the people.

The question was called to a vote: whether the first branch of the legislature should be elected by the people; and the motion carried. With this vote the issue of the legitimacy of the new government was settled once and for all. A monarchy may derive its legitimacy from God; but the American government would derive its legitimacy from the people. There was, and could be, no other source of legitimacy; and no ruler could set it aside when it suited his convenience or ambitions.

Resolution 5 read "that the second (or senatorial) branch of the National Legislature ought to be chosen by the first branch out of persons nominated by the State Legislatures."

A question came at once from Pierce Butler, the son of an Irish baronet, who had come to America to seek his fortune and had found a Charleston heiress, married her, and settled down into a comfortable life of South Carolina politics and planting. Perhaps the popular house could be checked by an avowedly upper-class senate? Butler wondered what more detailed thoughts Randolph had about the legislature. For instance, he asked, how many members did he mean the senate to have?

Randolph replied—as circumspectly to Butler as he had to Pinckney, but leaving a bit more room for Butler to infer some favorable meaning—that he had not thought it proper to provide details when he originally offered his plan, but that if his personal opinion was being sought, he thought the senate ought to have rather fewer members than the first house, that the senate ought to be "so small as to be exempt from the passionate proceedings to which numerous assemblies are liable." If the task of the delegates here was to "provide a cure for the evils under which the United States labored," then, "in tracing these evils to their origin," Randolph said, "every man had found it in the turbulence and follies of democracy: that some check therefore was to be sought for against this tendency of our governments: and that a good senate seemed most likely to answer the purpose." The senate, in short, ought to be the house of the elite.

Madison's ally James Wilson was acknowledged by the chair, and he promptly set himself apart from those two other allies Randolph and Pinckney and their notions of the follies of democracy. Both branches of the national legislature, said the Scotsman, sending a shock through the whole convention, "ought to be chosen by the people," by direct democratic election.

The idea could not have been more surprising. No one had been clamoring for a democratically elected upper house. There was no precedent for the idea, and Wilson's colleagues could not have been more amazed. Evidently no one knew what to reply to Wilson. And no one did reply.

Instead Sherman mentioned briefly how he would like to see the senate elected. In fact, he spoke so briefly that few of the delegates notice the importance of the remark he made: He would favor, he said, an election of one member by each state legislature. In this way, each state would have equal representation in the senate, just as each state under the Articles currently had equal representation in the Continental Congress.

Sherman's suggestion had a novel appeal: It would recognize the sovereignty of the states in one branch of the legislature, and soothe the fears of the localists so that they might surrender the equality of the states in the other branch. And it would leave the centrists unchallenged in their preference for majority rule in the house. But no one picked up on Sherman's idea. The problem that it solved was not under discussion at the moment. The delegates were preoccupied with questions of class and property, not with the erstwhile business of big and small states. Sherman did not press his idea. He made his suggestion and then lapsed back into silence.

The resolution about the senate was brought to a vote, and it lost in a welter of unresolved thoughts. The whole notion of the senate, of just what purpose it really ought to serve beyond the one of checking "popular passion," remained hazy in the extreme.

Resolution 6 contained several provisions. Some were easy: On the question whether both branches should be able to initiate legislation, and on the question whether all the powers of the existing congress ought to be transferred to this new legislature, the convention agreed without debate.

On the next provision, however—to give the new legislature "legislative power in all cases to which the state legislatures were individually incompetent"—the ever present centrist-localist issue flared again, and both Pinckney and Rutledge sprang up to object to the "vagueness of the term incompetent." Their colleague Butler joined them, asking again for Randolph to clarify his thoughts.

At last Randolph answered the South Carolinians uniquivocally; he had no intention, he said, of giving "indefinite powers to the national legislature." He was, said this scion of an old Virginia family, "entirely opposed to such an inroad on the State jurisdictions," and he did not think "any considerations whatever" could ever change his determination. His opinion was fixed on this point.

Madison decided to reassure the South Carolinians without being quite as unequivocal (or, frankly, as honest) as Randolph—for in fact, as it would later come out, Madison favored giving the national legislature an absolute veto over state laws.

He had come into the convention, Madison said circumspectly, with "a strong bias in favor of an enumeration and definition of the powers" to be exercised by the national legislature—in order to avoid just this problem of leaving the legislature with broad undefined powers that caused South Carolina such anxiety. But he had also come with "doubts" about the practicability of drawing up a list, for fear that the delegates would leave out something that would later be found to be crucial—or include something better left out. As he had listened to the debate, "his doubts had become stronger." What his opinion might eventually be "he could not yet tell." But for the time being he favored a general delegation of powers.

Madison's words could not have been entirely reassuring to the South Carolinians—they must have noticed that he had left all possible options open. And they were not quick to surrender their trust to him. For their part for the time being they subsided, and joined the other states in voting for this delegation of authority to the federal legislature. (Connecticut alone held back: The skeptical Sherman voted no, causing Connecticut's vote to be split between himself and Ellsworth, who sometimes saw some virtue to the centrist argument and always cast his vote according to his own lights. The managers of the convention—Madison and his allies—must have cast an anxious eye at the two Connecticut delegates, and hoped that the remaining, tie-breaking member of the delegation would arrive soon, and side with Ellsworth against Sherman.)

Several other clauses in resolution 6 dealt with the relationship between state and national legislatures: whether the national legislature could veto any state law that contravened the articles of union, or any state law that contravened a treaty with a foreign nation; and these clauses passed with ease. The last clause of resolution 6, however, made the delegates hesitate. This clause gave the national legislature the power "to call forth the force of the union against any member of the union failing to fulfil its duty under the articles thereof"—in short, it gave the Union the right to punish, with military force, any state or group of states that dissented from the Union as a whole.

Elbridge Gerry found it a ferocious clause—although he did not disagree with it on that account. Rather, he suggested, with the deviousness one heard a Marblehead merchant was capable of, that the clause "ought to be expressed so as the people might not understand it," and hence not be alarmed by it.

But the idea that one might write the constitution in such a way as to give the politicians some secret knowledge or understanding that was not shared with the people could not have been more contrary to eighteenth-century American belief.

Nearly all the delegates took it as an article of faith that any good system of government had to be completely clear and open to the understanding of the people, and Gerry's suggestion seemed to take the other delegates by surprise. They turned it down at once, on account of its "artifice."

The more Madison thought about the use of force, he told his colleagues, the more he doubted its "practicability." The use of force against a state would not be seen as an enforcement of the law, or a punishment for its breach; rather, it would be seen "as a declaration of war," and it would probably be seen "by the party attacked as a dissolution of all previous compacts." He hoped, he said, "that such a system would be framed as might render this recourse unnecessary."

Had a state the right to dissolve its bonds with the Union? Men of the eighteenth century were inclined to think that political contracts could be unmade as freely as they were made. Certainly, if the thirteen states were sovereign governments, they had the right to enter and leave a union with other sovereign states at will. But if the new government eliminated the states as sovereign governments, and if the whole American people ratified a new constitution, could the states undo what the people had done? This was not, perhaps, given the sensitivities of both the small and the southern states, the most politic time to go deeply into the question—to declare, for example, that the Union would have the right to coerce the southern states, by war if necessary, to abide by the will of the majority once the majority had approved the new system of government. The scholarly Madison, showing that he had some political instincts too, moved that consideration of the clause be postponed—and it was.

With this specter of dissolution, or even civil war, hanging over the proceedings, the delegates adjourned, having completed their review of Virginia's resolutions for the legislature. Some of them no doubt were feeling a degree of anxiety, but Dr. Franklin, for one, was delighted. The interests of the centrists had led the convention as a whole into a train of thought from which, happily, there seemed no turning back: If one was to have a national government at all, only one device could bring it into being—the principle of majority rule. Furthermore, the government would have to be based on the popularly elected house of representatives. To Franklin's mind, at least a basis of democracy was inescapable. As he told his old friend Benjamin Rush, he thought that the convention "will soon finish their business, as there are no prejudices to oppose, nor errors to refute." As was so often the case, Franklin was outlandishly optimistic.

But if any single message emerged from these first exploratory debates, it was this: When the convention sat down to consider the structure of the government, the first thing considered was the legislative branch. Some delegates wanted to give it more power, to increase the power of the central government. Others, because they favored a weak central government, wanted to restrain it. Some wanted it more democratic, some less. But very few of the delegates wished to move the legislature from its central position in the American government. The legislature, for better or worse the depository of the will and collective wisdom of the people, and not the executive, was to be the foundation of the government, the place in which its main business was done, the location of its principle authority and power. Not until many years later, when the president was seen as the only official elected by all the people, could he presume—and it was an act of presumption that would have staggered the men of Philadelphia—to best represent the whole people.

8

THE EXECUTIVE

ON THE MORNING OF JUNE 1, resolution 7 came to the floor—
"that a national executive be instituted, to be chosen by the
national Legislature for the term of ——— years, to be ineligible thereafter, to possess the executive powers of Congress
&c." No sooner was the word "executive" mentioned than
Charles Pinckney, still trying to make an impression, rose to
express the common fear of all: He recognized that any government needed a "vigorous" executive; but he feared that the
delegates might end in creating "a Monarchy of the worst kind,
to wit an elective one." With that the debate on the executive
branch was opened—a debate that went on for three days, as
the delegates tried to protect themselves against what they saw
as a profound and everlasting danger.

To be sure, Hamilton and some others thought a monarch
would be a fine thing; quite a few delegates believed that at
least a very strong executive was needed to administer as large
and diverse a country as America; and others talked of the unruliness of a large and diverse country when they meant the
unruliness of the people. But most of the delegates feared the
tendency of an executive to draw power to himself until he
had all the prerogatives of a king; and the most dangerous start
on this road to creating an uncrowned king was to grant the
executive, as Charles Pinckney said, the powers "of peace &
war." If the executive has the ultimate powers of the state in
his hands, he can use those powers to draw others to himself

until he holds nearly all power in his hands. If the executive was to be given the executive powers of the old Congress, as resolution 7 specified, such powers would include those of peace and war. It was an indisputable point, and young Pinckney must have been pleased with himself to have been the first to make it.

But before Pinckney could propose an amendment to limit the executive's powers, Wilson wanted to clarify just who and what this executive was to be. It might be that delegates would like to have an executive composed not of a single man but of several men, or of a committee, with its various members responsible for different aspects of policy, and that that arrangement would in itself provide a check of sorts against the danger of elective monarchy. Wilson himself preferred "a single person" as the national executive, and he moved that the resolution be amended to specify a single executive.

The room lapsed into silence. Gorham, as chairman, asked if the delegates wished to vote on this motion. The delegates were embarrassed. Washington's presence was felt in the room. A subject had been broached that required the utmost tact. Surely, if the executive was a single person, Washington would be that person; to question whether or not one could trust a single person was to appear to question whether or not Washington could be trusted. No one knew quite how to get around this momentary stumbling block.

It has been said that the framers of the Constitution shaped the office of chief executive around Washington, that they were deeply influenced by the sort of man he was, and would not have designed the office as they did had he not been there to fill it. But the delegates to the convention were not so lacking in imagination; they were easily able to see past Washington to the future. Washington might fill the office first, but obviously not forever.

Washington's presence at the convention was rather an obstacle of the moment: The delegates must talk about the executive office frankly, even if some of their fears about a bad executive did not apply at all to Washington.

Dr. Franklin rescued the delegates from their impediment. His age, and his friendship with Washington, entitled him to speak. It was a point of great importance, said Franklin, and he wished that "the gentlemen would deliver their sentiments" without inhibition.

Franklin's remark smoked out John Rutledge, who had escorted Washington to the chair on the opening day and then all but vanished into his usual studious inconspicuousness. Rutledge was famous for never taking an open position on the losing side of a case, either as a lawyer in court or as a politician in the South Carolina legislature. And so when he did speak, people listened. Now, in that well-bred Charleston accent that always blended the sound of the south with that of an English education, Rutledge allowed that he favored vesting the executive power in a single person. A single person would feel the greatest responsibility (and could be most clearly held responsible), though, of course, Rutledge would be against giving him the powers of war and peace.

Roger Sherman, rudely contradicted Rutledge. The executive, he said, was a mere instrument of the legislature, nothing more. The executive should be appointed by the legislature, accountable to the legislature, charged by the legislature to carry out their commands. And the number of the executive should not be fixed; rather, the legislature should appoint as many executives as it wished, and change the number at will, for the legislature was "the depository of the supreme will of the Society," and the executive simply a servant or servants for carrying that will into effect.

Had another man made Sherman's speech, it might have been an argument in favor of a most democratic device—to have an executive be something even less than a prime minister in a parliamentary system, to place all power in the legislature and have the executive be the legislature's mere instrument. Coming from Sherman, however, it was nothing of the sort; it was his old argument in favor of the continued existence of the Articles of Confederation—a union of sovereign states, with a mere administrator for chief executive—and the other delegates dismissed it as not being to the immediate point.

An executive, declared Wilson briskly, explaining why a single executive was best, needed to have the powers of "vigor and dispatch"—and even of "secrecy"—to conduct the nation's business. Wilson hardly meant, with this, that presidents should be able, among other things, to wage secret wars—to put the lives and fortunes of the people at risk without their consent, or even their knowledge. He would have been horrified to see what later presidents would claim was necessary to do in secret. Wilson would not give the powers of the British monarch to his executive; indeed, he would not even give the executive the powers of war and peace. The only powers he contemplated giving the executive were those of executing the laws and appointing officers—not much more, in fact, than the powers Sherman would give the executive—but he thought the executive must be a single person.

Edmund Randolph was upset. No matter what powers were or were not delegated to the executive, Randolph opposed a single executive. A single executive, said the young man conclusively, was "the foetus of monarchy." Too much of what he was hearing seemed to resemble the British system of government, with its House of Commons, House of Lords, and king. He did not mean to censure the British model, he said, "but the fixt genius of the people of America required a different form of Government." He did not see why the requisites of vigor, dispatch, and responsibility could not be found in three men as easily as in one. He thought the executive ought to be independent of the legislature; in that event, by consisting of more than one man, it would best guard against its tendency toward monarchy.

Too many possibilities, without many clear preferences, intruded on the delegates. Like the question of democracy, the question of the executive did not divide the house neatly along the same old centrist/localist lines. Rather, it introduced a new layer of complexity, which cut across those first divisions and set the delegates searching for some constellation of beliefs on which they could finally unite.

Unable to decide just what to do about the number of the executive, they postponed the issue briefly and went back to the question of executive powers. For all their indecision about some questions, the delegates were definitely and unanimously clear on one: The executive should not have the power of war and peace. The issue was one of enormous moment, for their own time and for the future—but it required hardly any debate, so eloquent and settled were the lessons of history. None of the delegates wanted an executive who could take them to war on his own judgment or that of himself and a few hand-picked advisers. None wanted him to be able to plan an aggressive action in secret and then claim that a sudden emergency compelled him to act. None wanted him to define ever increasing areas that needed defending and so have the country constantly responding to attacks on its "interests." None wanted an executive who would use the excuse of sudden or continuing crisis to gather more and more powers to himself, to draw political power away from states and communities to the central government, and, within the central government, away from the legislature and the judiciary to the office of the executive. In sum, none wanted him to use the warmaking power, the assumed ultimate responsibility for the nation's security, as a ruse to transform his office into that of an elective monarch, with all the inevitable consequences which would finally reduce citizens to mere petitioners whose needs and wisdom would be commonly sacrificed in the name of national defense, and whose criticisms would bring charges of disloyalty against them. The vote against giving the executive the powers of war and peace was informed by centuries of experience, and it could not have been more emphatic.

As for the other duties of the executive, the delegates were able to agree at once, at least in the most general terms, that the executive should have the rather modest powers "to carry into effect the national laws" and to appoint officers. In the view of most of the delegates, then, although the executive was not to be quite the cipher Sherman had in mind, he was to be a public servant of very humble constitutional standing. He might be George Washington; but he was not to imagine that he was George III.

Then the delegates moved on to consider how the executive was to be chosen, and James Wilson astounded his colleagues by saying he was "almost unwilling to declare the mode which he wished to take place, being apprehensive that it might appear chimerical. He would say however at least that in theory he was for an election by the people." To say that the other delegates were stunned would be an understatement. They were entirely dumbfounded.

Wilson tried at once to explain himself. He wished, he said, "to derive not only both branches of the Legislature from the people, without the intervention of the State Legislatures, but the Executive also." In this way, Wilson thought, the two branches would be "as independent as possible of each other, as well as of the States." Once again Wilson's suggestion would favor both democracy and the national government. The government would have its own built-in checks and balances, which would, at one and the same time, endow it with independent authority and prevent it from devolving into tyranny. The mechanics of the government—and the fact that it was based on popular suffrage—would keep it from falling into the hands of one interested group or another. This was the classic eighteenth-century notion of a rational mechanism with inherent checks and balances, like the Newtonian model of the universe: distinterested, impartial, harmonious, perfectly constructed, impossible to corrupt or discommode once it was put in operation.

No doubt Wilson was too sanguine about how sheer structure would keep a government pure and just. But that was not all that was working against him; what was more important was that there were those who positively wanted to give undue influence to special interests. John Rutledge, for one, immediately suggested an election of the executive by the second branch of the legislature only—that is, by the senate.

Rutledge's notion was certainly aristocratical. However, Rutledge had another purpose in suggesting it. South Carolina's continuing dilemma was to find a way to back this new national government dominated by the large states, and, at the same time, protect its society from the new national government it joined in making. South Carolina did not seek a position of outright domination. It only required a means of self-defense, a way of keeping others from imposing upon South Carolina.

Of course, Sherman's erstwhile proposal—that the house have proportional representation and the senate have one vote per state—offered a possible solution to South Carolina's problem. The senate, if endowed with one vote per state, gave the south that means of self-defense—a solid several votes that could always block an issue that required a two-thirds majority, and would go far toward holding off a simple plurality. And now

Rutledge recalled it and probed it further: What if the executive was elected by the senate—by the body that gave each state one vote? That would offer further protection to the southerners. And that would begin to construct a national government with which the south could feel quite comfortable.

It seemed, indeed, that Sherman's old proposal—having gone originally unnoticed—had begun to attract the interest of a number of delegates, as it was increasingly seen to solve a problem that troubled them. It was, for the Madisonians, an insidious influence. If Rutledge, for instance, should embrace Sherman's idea, then South Carolina would be pried loose from Madison's group and moved toward an alliance with the small states and the localists. Nothing in the record indicates that either Madison or Wilson yet realized the threat coming from Sherman's proposal. While the proposal attracted more and more delegates, Wilson went right on with the thought that was on his mind and made a detailed suggestion for popular election of the executive.

If, as the response of the delegates seemed to indicate, direct popular election was too radical an idea, Wilson had another thought. He suggested that the states be divided into electoral districts, that the people vote for special electors, who would in turn vote for the executive. In this way, the radical notion of direct election would be avoided, but the election would still not depend on the state legislatures, and it would, at least ultimately, be derived from the people.

But Wilson had lost the interest of the other delegates. No one quite saw the point in a popular election; they saw even less point in these electors; the electors served to make election of the executive indirect, but they were an obvious ruse, and not sufficiently useful in any other way, and Wilson's suggestion was voted down. Yet there in the record was the beginning of an idea for an electoral college, and it would be resurrected when it was needed to serve more exquisite and pressing needs.

The delegates, unhappy with Wilson's proposals, unmindful of Rutledge's suggestion, settled for accepting the wording in Randolph's original resolution, that the executive would be chosen by the national legislature—a proposal, in effect, for a parliamentary system—and there they left it for the time being.

And so, having settled on a way of electing their executive, the delegates turned to consider how they could get rid of him (or them) if he (or they) didn't work out.

John Dickinson moved that the executive be removable merely on the request of a majority of the legislatures of the individual states. Sherman allowed that the national legislature ought to be able to remove the executive at its pleasure, even without a request from the state legislatures. Hugh Williamson of North Carolina proposed that the executive be "removeable on impeachment & conviction of malpractice or neglect of duty." And Williamson's motion was seconded and passed at once.

The impeachment clause as first passed was not destined to stay in the constitution in just that form, but its casual inclusion at the moment was revealing: It showed that even those delegates who hoped for a strong executive thought he should be removable from office on the easiest of grounds. The chief executive was not to be a monarch who ruled by divine right, not a pope or a duke or any other sort of person elevated above his fellow citizens, but a public servant who would do his job or be fired.

Dr. Franklin had a thought, or perhaps it ought more properly to be called a pet peeve. He was bothered by one of the provisions in the resolution on the executive, a provision that called for paying the executive a salary. He was not feeling well enough to stand for any length of time to address the delegates, and so he had painstakingly written out a speech at home. He handed it now to James Wilson, who rose to read it on Franklin's behalf, while the old doctor sat back and listened.

In general, said Franklin, he found the Virginia Plan a good one, and he wished it well. Yet he was bound to say that he differed on the idea of giving the executive any compensation for his labors. "Sir, there are two passions which have a powerful influence on the affairs of men. These are ambition and avarice, the love of power, and the love of money. Separately each of these has great force in prompting men to action; but when united in view of the same object, they have in many minds the most violent effects. Place before the eyes of such men a post of *honor* that shall at the same time be a place of *profit*, and they will move heaven and earth to obtain it."

Evidently Franklin was about to suggest that the chief executive should not be paid any salary at all, and one can well imagine the other delegates trying not to wince at the old man's thought. Politicians would want salaries, as all the delegates knew, to defray their expenses if nothing else; and furthermore, if no salaries were to be paid, then only saints or rich men could afford to serve as chief executive. Franklin's proposal was palpably silly.

And yet the doctor had a point, and he knew it: Rapacious men should not be allowed to dominate the government. At the very least, they should not be rewarded for doing so. Perhaps Franklin did not have the device to keep such men out of government, but he knew his principles were correct. He knew, too, that rapacious men had been kept from executive office before, and that they could be again. The techniques might have to change, even change constantly, but the principle did not change; and framers of law should not give up seeking ways to enforce the principle just because human beings were so devilishly inventive.

What kind of men "will strive for this profitable pre-eminence, through all the bustle of cabal, the heat of contention, the infinite mutual abuse of parties, tearing to pieces the best of characters? It will not be the wise and moderate, the lovers of peace and good order, the men fittest for the trust. It will be the bold and the violent, the men of strong passions and indefatigable activity in their selfish pursuits. These will thrust themselves into your Government and be your rulers."

In time, a permanent class of strivers after power and privilege would be established. Generally, said the doctor, the ruling power prevails, "the revenues of princes constantly increasing, and we see that they are never satisfied, but always in want of more."

It will be said, said Franklin, "that we don't propose to establish Kings. I know it. But there is a natural inclination in mankind to Kingly Government. . . . I am apprehensive therefore, perhaps too apprehensive, that the Government of these States, may in future times end in a Monarchy." Whether the convention would establish an executive committee or a single executive would not matter if the government itself was made a source of both power and profit. In that case, the convention would have sowed the seeds of "contention, faction & tumult," which could only end in the establishment of a king, whatever he might be called.

To suggest that an executive serve without salary might seem a utopian idea, but history provided instances of such actions. One instance was that "of a respectable Society who have made the experiment, and practiced it with success more than a hundred years. I mean the Quakers." Another instance, nearer to home, was that of the general who commanded the American forces for eight years without pay, "a Patriot whom I will not now offend by any other praise."

Silence fell on the convention; perhaps the delegates were overcome with longing for the world of public service that Franklin conjured up; perhaps they were trying to think of some way that Franklin's ideas could be put into practice. Perhaps they were only thinking whether or not they would care to serve without salaries in the new government. Whatever the case, they did not think for long. Hamilton rose to second Franklin's motion, "with the view," he said, "of bringing so respectable a proposition before the Committee." But there was no debate; the proposition was postponed; it had been seconded just to move it along and off the agenda. The proposal was treated, Madison noted, "with great respect, but rather for the author of it, than from any apparent conviction of its expediency or practicability."

John Dickinson, the tall, distinguished, old-fashioned gentleman from Delaware, the man who had served as chairman of the committee that had written the Articles of Confederation, had not said much yet through all this debate. Of an older generation—though not as old as Franklin—he, too, was concerned about the power that some of the ambitious young men of the convention were so eager to place in the hands of the national government and, in particular, in the hands of the executive, who would, no doubt, be afflicted by many of the flaws of character that Franklin had just mentioned. Dickinson's preferred defense against such dangers was to retain the Articles of Confederation—and the dispersion of political power into many local governments that the Articles provided—and now he took Franklin's concerns and wove them into an argument on behalf of the Articles.

Such an executive as some of the delegates had in mind, Dickinson said, "was not consistent with a republic." A "firm executive," he said, could only exist "in a limited monarchy." Of course, there was much to recommend a monarchy; certainly monarchy provided a stable government. A limited monarchy, he thought, was one of the best governments in the world. "It was not *certain* that the same blessings were derivable from any other form. It was certain that equal blessings had never yet been derived from any of the republican form." Yet a limited monarchy was out of the question. One could not simply conjure a House of Lords into existence on the American continent to provide the necessary limitations on a king.

But America, fortunately, already possessed, by accident, a source of restraint against too forceful and corrupt a central government and its executive: "the accidental lucky division of this country into distinct States." If this happy accident was not abolished, it might provide just the restraint against monarchy for which the delegates longed.

He hoped that each state would retain "an equal voice at least in one branch of the National Legislature," and that the other branch would be based on proportional representation. To this structure, he thought, all the delegations could be brought to agree. It gave recognition to the principle of majority rule in the house, and a means of self-defense to the small states in the senate.

And so Dickinson joined Sherman, and possibly Rutledge, in what began to assume the form of a faction opposed to the Virginia Plan—in which, it almost seemed after Dickinson had finished his speech, Dr. Franklin belonged too.

But Dickinson's remarks were not taken up by the convention. Instead the delegates returned obsessively to the debate on whether the executive should be single or plural, and by now Edmund Randolph, who had become entirely preoccupied with his fears about the "foetus of monarchy," opposed a single executive with a fixed passion. He felt he would not do justice to the country that had sent him to this convention if he were "silently to suffer" the establishment of a single executive. "He felt an opposition to it which he believed he should continue to feel as long as he lived."

The people were averse, he said, "to the very semblance of Monarchy." A single executive was unnecessary, "a plurality being equally competent." His mind was made up. While the other members of the convention continued to search for ways to accommodate their ideas and interests, Randolph had taken a stand.

Wilson did not trouble to hide his scorn. It seemed that Mr. Randolph objected not so much to the measure itself, said Wilson, as to its presumed unpopularity (courting popular approval, as one might imagine, was not high on Wilson's list of priorities). Wilson could see no evidence of the antipathy of the people. Indeed, he thought it did not exist. "All know," said Wilson curtly, almost contemptuously, "that a single magistrate is not a King." In fact, all the thirteen states, though they agreed in almost nothing else in their constitutions, "agree in placing a single magistrate at the head of the government. The idea of three heads has taken place in none. The degree of power is indeed different; but there are no co-ordinate heads . . . Among three members, [I foresee] nothing but uncontrolled, continued, & violent animosities." Three executives might never agree on any policy; reason alone showed that such an arrangement could not depend on a simple vote of two against one to come to a decision. In courts of law, there were ever only two sides to a question; but in the legislative and executive branches, there were often very many sides to a question. Each of the three members of the executive branch might therefore espouse a separate point of view, and no two might be able to agree at all.

Wilson's argument was strong, no doubt about it. It even changed Sherman's mind, as he acknowledged at once. But then Sherman bent the argument around to slightly different grounds. Even if a single executive was best, he said, nonetheless, "it should also be remarked that in all the States there was a Council of advice, without which the first magistrate could not act." A council, Sherman said, that could effectively veto the chief executive's decisions might go far toward allaying reservations about the monarchical aspect of the executive office.

Hugh Williamson asked Wilson if he meant the executive to have a council.

No, replied Wilson emphatically, he meant to have no council, "which oftener serves to cover than prevent malpractices."

Niceties had dropped away from the debate; exchanges had become brief and direct, and Wilson at least spoke with apparent confidence that his logic swept all before it. The question of a single executive was called to a vote at once, and passed in the affirmative, seven to three.

The Wilson tone of voice was not, however, very politic. The convention was, after all, still in its early phase—not the time to make uncompromising enemies. And some of the local-power men, and others who were fearful of the power that might be exercised by a central government and a strong executive, began to bridle at the way the centrists were dismissing them.

The next, and last, provision of the clause on the executive dealt with the question whether the executive ought to have some veto over legislative acts. Wilson sprang to the offensive at once, saying that he thought the executive ought to have an "absolute veto" which the legislature could not afterward overturn. "Without such a Self Defence the Legislature can at any moment sink [the executive] into non-existence." To make the notion more palatable, Wilson suggested that the executive and judiciary together might exercise this absolute veto.

Hamilton did not hesitate for a moment to back Wilson; he, too, favored an absolute veto. There was nothing to fear from it, he said offhandedly; the king of Great Britain had not exercised his veto since the Revolution, and the veto power would not be much used in America either.

Dr. Franklin was surprised at this cavalier attitude. He was sorry, he said, to differ from his colleague, "for whom he had a very great respect," but his memory went back a long way; he had some experience of this veto power under the government of Pennsylvania back before the days of the Revolution. "The negative of the Governor was constantly made use of to extort money. No good law whatever could be passed without a private bargain with him . . . till at last it became the regular practice to have orders in his favor on the Treasury presented along with the bills to be signed, so that he might actually receive the former before he should sign the latter." Franklin feared that if an absolute veto was given the executive, more and more power would be demanded until the executive had at last brought the legislature "into a compleat subjection."

Sherman, too, was offended by the proposition of an absolute veto. He was against "enabling any one man to stop the will of the whole. No one man could be found so far above all the rest in wisdom."

Madison offered a compromise. Let some proper proportion of the legislature be designated as able to overrule the veto of the executive, and that would serve the same purpose as an absolute veto. "It would rarely if ever happen that the Executive constituted as ours is proposed to be would have firmness enough to resist the Legislature, unless backed by a certain part of the body itself."

"We are, Mr. Chairman," said old Colonel Mason, "going very far in this business. We are not indeed constituting a British Government, but a more dangerous monarchy, an elective one. . . . Do gentlemen mean to pave the way to hereditary Monarchy? Do they flatter themselves that the people will ever consent to such an innovation? If they do I venture to tell them, they are mistaken. The people never will consent. . . . Notwithstanding the oppressions & injustice experienced among us from democracy; the genius of the people is in favor of it, and the genius of the people must be consulted." It had been a hatred of the oppressions of monarchy, Mason reminded the convention, that "had carried the people through the late Revolution." They would not now willingly embrace what they had fought a war to be rid of.

"Will it not be enough," asked Mason, "to enable the Executive to suspend offensive laws" for a set period of time, "till they shall by coolly revised, and the objections to them overruled by a greater majority than was required in the first instance."

"The first man put at the helm," Franklin joined in, in obvious reference to General Washington, "will be a good one." None need fear what he would do; but "nobody knows what sort may come afterwards. The Executive will be always increasing here, as elsewhere, till it ends in a monarchy." The stoutest defenses ought to be erected to delay that moment, and when the moment arrived, to give others the means to defend themselves against the monarch.

On the question of an absolute veto, the vote was ten against, none in favor. On the question whether the executive ought to have a veto, which the legislature could then override by a two-thirds majority vote, the convention accepted the proposition at once.

Thus, the initial review of the executive branch in the Virginia Plan was ended. And surely this initial consideration of the executive branch was remarkable in one respect above all others: The system that was preliminarily adopted was a parliamentary system; it called for an executive elected by Congress, as is the prime minister in a parliamentary system, removable merely for malpractice, and with very circumscribed powers, most particularly in his powers to take the country to war. When it came to establishing an executive for their new government, the delegates were extraordinarily cautious—and even so, many feared that even such a weak chief executive as they had established might be, or become, too monarchical.

9

THE KEYSTONE OF THE CONSTITUTION

TUESDAY, JUNE 5, was given over to a review of the last half-dozen resolutions of the Virginia Plan—that a national judiciary be established, that provision be made for admitting new states to the Union, that each state be guaranteed a republican government, that the Continental Congress be continued until a new government was established, that a method of amending the constitution be established, that the officers of the various states be bound by oath to support the Union, that the constitution be ratified by special conventions of the people. It was a relaxed, almost carefree day compared to the occasional moments of tension of the past several days, as though these final resolutions were almost taken for granted compared to what had gone before. When the delegates considered resolution 9, dealing with the establishment of the judiciary, Dr. Franklin turned positively expansive. The delegates could not decide whether judges ought to be appointed by the legislature or the executive, and Franklin said he wished they would consider other modes as well. And then he launched into one of his meandering stories—this one about the way judges were appointed in Scotland. There, he said, "the nomination proceeded from the Lawyers, who always selected the ablest of the profession in order to get rid of him, and share his practice among themselves." He hoped the delegates might think of some equally clever device to make it in the interest of those who chose the judges "to make the best choice."

Nothing occasioned so little debate in the course of the convention as the role of the judiciary. The principles of common law going right back to the Magna Carta, of the rights to such usages as trial by jury, which had been incorporated into the constitutions of the states, and the actual practices of the judges and courts as they had evolved in the colonies were fairly widely accepted by the members of the convention. All that needed discussion was the exact way the judiciary was to be incorporated into a new national government.

Two serious differences did arise. The first involved the means of judicial appointment. Some delegates favored having the executive appoint judges; others thought that would give the executive another array of monarchical powers; some delegates favored appointment by the legislature; still others thought the legislature too numerous and not well qualified to choose judges. Madison suggested, halfheartedly, to get around the legislature's poor qualifications to appoint judges, appointment by the senate alone. In this early stage of review, the matter was postponed.

The second, and more serious, difference over the judiciary involved the question whether the national government, in addition to establishing the Supreme Court, was to establish inferior courts, dispersed throughout the country, with final jurisdiction in certain cases—a provision that would enable the federal judiciary to reach directly into the states to adjudicate cases.

Rutledge objected instantly, naturally enough, arguing that the state courts "might and ought to be left in all cases" to render an initial decision. Litigants would have the right of appeal to a federal court if they chose, and that was sufficient to ensure "uniformity of judgments."

But Madison was not happy to leave certain cases to state courts, with the only remedy a time-consuming and costly appeal. "A Government without a proper Executive & Judiciary," said Madison, "would be the mere trunk of a body without arms or legs to act or move." If the constitution was not to provide for inferior courts, then at least it ought to provide that Congress could, at its initiative, provide them.

Butler of South Carolina objected to this notion. ("The people will not bear such innovations. The States will revolt at such encroachments." Even if such a system was best, it should not be adopted; the people would not accept it. "We must follow the example of Solon who gave the Athenians not the best government he could devise, but the best they would receive.") Nonetheless, Madison won his point; his idea was accepted as a presentable compromise.

As for the rest of the Virginia Plan, the convention rattled through the remaining resolutions quickly: resolution 10, which provided for the admission of new states to be carved out of the western territories, was approved; resolution 11, which guaranteed these new states republican governments, was postponed; resolution 12, which provided for the continuance of government under the Articles until a new constitution should emerge from the convention, was passed as a matter of course.

Resolution 13, providing for an amendment procedure for the new constitution, which could be put in effect without the assent of the national legislature, caught young Pinckney's attention.

He doubted, said Pinckney, "the propriety or necessity" of a mode of amendment. "The novelty and difficulty of the experiment," replied Gerry, who always anticipated trouble, would necessitate "periodical revision." Also, he said astutely, the knowledge that the constitution could be revised would tend to win supporters to it. Resolution 13 was approved.

Resolution 14, requiring an oath from state officers to support the national government, was postponed (those local-power men holding back again).

When the last resolution came up for consideration, however, the delegates roused themselves out of their hot-weather torpor. Resolution 15 called for ratification of the new constitution by the people. It was another of those devices to reach over the heads of the state legislatures, and Roger Sherman was quick to react. Popular ratification was "unnecessary," said Sherman; the Articles of Confederation provided a mechanism for changes with the assent of Congress and the approval of the state legislatures, and no new device was necessary.

On the contrary, Madison said, ratification by the people was essential. If the states ratified the new constitution, then in the future, if there was ever a conflict between the states and the central government, it would seem that the states had the ultimate authority, that they could repudiate what they had originally agreed to—that if the states created the federal government, they would have the power to dismantle it or withdraw from it. The new government must be ratified by "the supreme authority" of the people themselves. Then the states (or the central government, for that matter) could not set aside what the people had made.

But sensitivities about the centrist/localist split had been too sharply exacerbated. The delegates were not of a mood to accept Madison's argument. Rather, the vote on resolution 15 was postponed.

Thus, by June 5, the full Virginia Plan had been presented to the convention, and on the whole, the Madisonians had done a good job. All fifteen resolutions of the plan had been laid before the delegates, explained, reviewed clause by clause, their implications spelled out, and their intent understood by all. Even in this most introductory phase, some important issues had been argued out, some crucial provisions evidently accepted. Doubtless the Madisonians would have been pleased if at this point the delegates had simply voted to accept the whole plan and go home.

But clearly, not all the delegates were entirely pleased with the plan. Some wanted to go right back to the beginning and raise some basic questions of principle that they had postponed only to give the Madisonians a chance to present their ideas.

Young Charles Pinckney, for instance, from that slippery key state of South Carolina, was not convinced of the rightness of the very first provision of the Virginia Plan, which called for the lower branch of the legislature to be elected by the people. The people, said Pinckney in his best highborn manner, might well prove to be "less fit judges" than the state legislatures for such elections. Furthermore, said Pinckney, gently threatening, if the state legislatures were excluded from this role in the national government, they "would be less likely to promote the adoption of the new government." He was then supported by his colleague Rutledge. The South Carolinians seemed to be sliding back again toward the local-power faction.

Wilson carried the counterargument. He hoped for a vigorous government, he said. And a vigorous government had to flow from "the legitimate source of all authority," the people. The government needed to possess not only the force of the people but also "the *mind* or *sense* of the people at large. The Legislature ought to be the most exact transcript of the whole Society. Representation is made necessary only because it is impossible for the people to act collectively."

Roger Sherman tried to state what he took to be Wilson's intentions in terms stark enough to discredit them. (Sherman's "air," John Adams once said of him, "is the reverse of grace; there cannot be a more striking contrast to beautiful action than the motion of his hands. . . . when he moves a hand in anything like action, Hogarth's genius could not have invented a motion more opposite to grace." But, said Adams, "he has a clear head.") If, said Sherman, it was the intention of the convention to abolish the state governments, then the convention should say so frankly, without hedging; and in that case, "the elections ought to be by the people." If, however, state governments were to be continued, and the delegates honestly pursued that end, the elections to the national government ought to be made by the state governments.

As for those who favored abolishing the state governments, Sherman thought they were carried away with their fancies about the national government and the need for some new, strong government. The objects of the Union, after all, were "few." The Union ought to provide defense against foreign danger, defense against internal disputes, treaties with foreign nations, regulation of foreign commerce, and taxation on that foreign commerce. "These and perhaps a few lesser objects alone rendered a Confederation of the States necessary." All other matters were best left in the hands of the states.

Liberty was most secure, self-government best guaranteed, and efficiency and responsiveness most certain, if most powers were left to the states. This had always been the case, and would always be so. The people had no wish for a large central government and saw no necessity for it. "The people," Sherman said, "are more happy in small than large states." Of course, some states were too small and therefore "too subject to faction." BUt others were too large—so large as to be ungovernable. And in any case, whether large or small, local governments were to be preferred to a central government. Thus, he was for giving the central government certain powers, but only the most essential powers, and for having those powers very strictly circumscribed.

Colonel Mason, who had long been most comfortable with local government, nonetheless disagreed with Sherman now. Under the new government that was proposed, said Mason, it was the people who would be represented, not the states; therefore, reason would seem to dictate that it was the people who ought to choose the representatives. The whole principle of representation, said this trustee of the town of Alexandria, this vestryman of Truro parish, required that representatives "should sympathize with their constituents, should think as they think, & feel as they feel; and that for these purposes should even be residents among them." Much had been said against democratic elections in this convention; indeed, he admitted much might be said against them. But "no government was free from imperfections and evils . . . improper elections in many instances were inseparable from Republican Governments. But compare those with the advantages of this Form in favor of the rights of the people, in favor of human nature."

Still, Pinckney and Rutledge and Sherman were not moved. And in the end Madison was forced to enter the debate, and to give, finally, the rationale for his system, the argument on which his whole structure depended.

The election by the people of at least one branch of the legislature, said Madison, was "a clear principle of free government," and he did not labor the point by adducing any arguments in its favor. The delegates all knew them perfectly well. Furthermore, he differed from Sherman in thinking that the objects Sherman had mentioned were the only ones required of a national government. Life would be simple and carefree indeed if that were all a national government needed to do. But a national government needed also, said Madison, to provide "for the security of private rights and the steady dispensation of Justice." Interferences with those needs were the evils that had "perhaps more than anything else" produced the very convention they were attending. Perhaps the delegates had forgotten about those disputes over fishing rights and commerce and trade arrangements with foreigners and problems with currency that they had all talked about at the beginning of the convention.

But then Madison went beyond these practical matters to the very heart of his argument. "Was it to be supposed that republican liberty could long exist under the abuses of it practiced in some of the States?" Mr. Sherman had admitted that small states were particularly subject to faction and oppression. "It was to be inferred then that wherever these prevailed the state was too small." To be sure, faction and oppression existed in some of the larger states too—but not as much as in the smaller states. Thus, said Madison, the delegates were "admonished to enlarge the sphere as far as the nature of government would admit. This was the only defense against the inconveniences of democracy consistent with the democratic form of government." Madison was inclined to agree with the thought that Sherman had introduced but had failed to take to its inevitable conclusion.

All civilized societies, observed Madison, were divided into different groups or factions, which vied for domination of the whole: "rich and poor, debtors and creditors, the landed, the manufacturing, the commercial interests, the inhabitants of this district, or that district, the followers of this political leader or that political leader, the disciples of this religious sect or that religious sect." Wherever one of these groups was in the majority, it threatened to smother the rights of others. What was there to restrain them?

In Greece and Rome, "the rich and poor, the creditors and debtors, as well as the patricians and plebeians alternately oppressed each other with equal unmercifulness." And in America itself, said Madison, throwing aside all caution over the sensibilities of his fellow southerners, "we have seen the mere distinction of color made in the most enlightened period of time, a ground of the most oppressive dominion ever exercised by man over man."

How, then, was a tyrannical faction to be opposed? "The only remedy," said Madison, taking up a suggestion of one of his favorite philosophers of the Scottish Enlightenment, David Hume, "is to enlarge the sphere, & thereby divide the community into so great a number of interests & parties that in the first place a majority will not be likely at the same moment to have a common interest separate from that of the whole or of the minority; and in the second place, that in case they should have such an interest, they may not be apt to unite in the pursuit of it"—that is, to add more factions to the polity, to make it harder for any one to dominate, or to make it impossible for such a faction to dominate without compromising with others in such a way as to mitigate its ambitions and prejudices.

Madison's system was not foolproof; it could not work at all times or in all instances. It left room for the permanent oppression of some factions—certainly for the oppression of blacks and of women for many more decades. Those who were, in one way or another, left outside the polity were clearly defenseless. Even some minorities brought into the system could be permanently oppressed if a concordance of other minorities joined in that oppression. (Madison's theories, Hamilton jotted in his journal, contained a good deal of truth; although, said the New Yorker, "they do not conclude so strongly as he supposes.")

Yet Madison's system had an extraordinary principle built into it to repair its own limitations: The answer to the problems of democracy was more democracy, to extend the franchise ever more broadly, to bring in more and more constituencies, for the sake of liberty and justice not just for them but for all. The more who were brought in on equal footing, the more secure were those already inside. In principle—though Madison did not carry his argument so far—the system could be enlarged not only geographically but also in such a way as to bring in other races, classes, sexes, and factions, the poor and the outcast, both those who were already in the country and foreigners who wished to enter; and with the welcoming of each one the system would be strengthened for all. Any attempt to limit the franchise deprived the whole polity of knowledge and experience, of particular intelligence and of balance—and weakened the system for all.

This, then, the principle of the extended republic, was the centerpiece of Madison's constitution, the point on which all else rose or fell, around which all else was constructed to make that principle vital. It was the principle that would be at the heart of the debate for the rest of the summer, indeed for the rest of the life of the republic.

PART III

10

THE OPPOSITION IN PLACE

ALL THE WHILE the Virginia Plan was being presented and explained, defended and rationalized, new delegates were arriving on the convention floor—from New York, from Connecticut, from Delaware and New Jersey—until, by June 6, the hall was nearly full. Altogether, sixty-one delegates had been elected by their states to attend the convention, although more than a dozen were absent most of the time, six did not bother to come at all, and only about thirty of them were in attendance more or less full time. But in any case, as the Madisonians looked around the room, they found themselves now no longer so much among friends.

Over in the New York delegation, John Lansing, a man of Dutch descent and ponderous dignity, had taken his seat as a representative of those New Yorkers who believed in the virtues of local government. Before Lansing arrived, New York had been represented by Hamilton, a centrist, and Robert Yates, a localist. On vote after vote, the two New Yorkers had brought one another to a standstill. Now Lansing arrived with the tie-breaking vote, and immediately rendered Hamilton's vote useless.

In the Connecticut delegation, which had also been often divided, with Sherman going one way and Ellsworth the other, William Samuel Johnson arrived—and the delegation tipped to Sherman's localist point of view. Johnson, who would play a significant part in the debates, was a cautious man, always carefully picking his way through an argument in search of the middle ground. He was, in fact, so exasperatingly painstaking in this way that his father had once said to him impatiently, "even caution, one of the best things in the world, may be carried too far." When Johnson embarked on a political career in that corner of Connecticut, near to New York, where several religious factions kept everyone in constant turmoil, and where conservative loyalty to the Crown was firmly established, he became a master of avoiding tangled passions, a man widely known for his noncommittal fellow feeling.

When the Revolution broke out, Johnson—who only a few years before had been seeking an office under the Crown and promising "to serve his Majesty faithfully"—simply retired from public life, and his lack of commitment to the revolutionary cause had made him suspect in much the same way that John Dickinson's caution had made him suspect. Now, with the fashion running against democratic tendencies, Johnson found himself happily back in style.

Johnson favored keeping the Articles of Confederation and preserving the power of the states, and he must have been inspired at least in part by the time he had spent in England before the Revolution. He had come to believe then that the English were mistaken in their administration of the colonies simply because they were so remote from America. "I heard a respectable counsellor at law ask . . . gravely in the Hall [Westminster] whether Philadelphia was in the East or West Indies and said he had a Notion it was upon the coast of Sumatra." Such observations as that made Johnson tend to believe that small governments were best, and that Madison's plan for a large, remote central government was a mistake that he had seen before.

Along with Dickinson and Read of Delaware and, occasionally, the erratic Elbridge Gerry of Massachusetts, and aided sometimes by the independent-minded Colonel Mason of Virginia, Johnson joined what was forming into a solid faction of localists surrounding Roger Sherman.

Some of Sherman's strongest and most consistent allies came from New Jersey: David Brearly, William Livingston, and William Paterson. Brearly was such a quick, outspoken patriot early in his life that he had been arrested for treason in the very first moments of the Revolution and had to be freed by a mob of his fellow citizens. Now aged forty-two, he had learned discretion, but his instincts were still those of an independent-minded man, a man who did not like distant governments telling him what to do.

William Livingston, aged sixty-three, was a well-born lawyer, a petulant and impatient character, who had loved, in his early days, to pass as a radical aristocrat, to make sweeping denunciations of the stuffy, established order, and to write satirical verse and witty broadsides. In 1752, he had founded a weekly publication "to oppose superstition, bigotry, priestcraft, tyranny, servitude, public mismanagement and dishonesty in office" and to champion "the inestimable value of liberty." He still liked to be disruptive around those who had too much love of order.

William Paterson, who would emerge with Sherman and Dickinson as one of the most important leaders of the local-power faction, was the son of a storekeeper. He had gone to Princeton and started on a career of social climbing there that he had never stopped. He adopted an aristocratic view of society, saying, among other things, that inferiors (such as storekeepers, one supposes) ought to be treated "with Generosity and humanity, but by no means with Familiarity, on one hand, or Insolence on the other." He filled his private notebooks with useful reminders to himself: "As simplicity of language constitutes the best style so simplicity of behavior constitutes good breeding. The true gentleman is easy, without affectation, grand, without haughtiness, cheerful, without levity, and humble, without meanness." He catalogued the maxims of manner and style in music, dance, and dress, and he always had a certain stiffness of manner that he could not quite smooth out. His affection for local government seemed to come in some measure from a wish to reestablish—and to join—the simpler, more austere aristocratic society that he imagined had existed a generation or more before, to become a gentleman of the older generation.

In the Delaware delegation, in addition to Dickinson and Read, Sherman had another more or less dependable ally in Gunning Bedford. Bedford was a huge, colorful fellow—big enough to make two or three Madisons—"a bold and nervous speaker," as one of his fellow conventioneers jotted in his diary, with "a very commanding and striking manner . . . warm and impetuous in his temper . . . and very corpulent." He was old-fashioned to his bones; he did not need, like Paterson, to try for the effect. Out of natural habit, he would never adopt trousers but would wear short breeches with knee buckles to the end of his life. He would be noticed in the convention for his "intensity of feeling and frankness of utterance"—that is to say, his hot temper and tactlessness.

In the North Carolina delegation, Hugh Williamson and Richard Dobbs Spaight and William R. Davie, all of whom tended toward nationalism, were joined by Alexander Martin, a man who loved poetry and hated both the English and the sort of government at a distance that the English had imposed on America.

In the Maryland delegation, a man bearing the elegant name Daniel of St. Thomas Jenifer, a sociable, good-humored, sixty-three-year-old bachelor of aristocratic background and no apparent serious political persuasion, voted frequently with the emerging opposition. Although he was a friend of Washington's, and something of a nationalist, he could often be mobilized to vote with the old-fashioned, tradition-loving aristocrats among the localists.

With the addition of these men to the convention, then, the Madisonians were suddenly opposed by New York and Connecticut, Delaware and Maryland (though not quite certainly), New Jersey and, often, North Carolina—that is, by a possible six votes—which composed the Shermanites, or as they might equally well be called, the Dickinsonians or, now that the New Jerseyites were present in full force, the Patersonians. The Madisonians, on the other hand, could count on only five votes: Virginia, Pennsylvania, Massachusetts, South Carolina, and Georgia. (The delegates from New Hampshire had still not arrived—and would not until July 23.) Massachusetts, with the anxious Elbridge Gerry, was not always a certain vote; and the two southern states had to be treated with extreme care to keep them in the fold. From time to time, depending on whether Williamson's or Martin's point of view dominated, North Carolina could be lured into the Madisonian camp. But all in all, the Madisonians were on the defensive.

Just what Madison's opponents had in common—the social climber Paterson, the overconfident Bedford, the exceedingly cautious Johnson, the gentleman farmer Dickinson, the
aristocrat Jenifer, the former shoemaker Sherman—is difficult
to sort out, just as it is difficult to sort out exactly what all the
individual Madisonians had in common.

If a delegate had looked about the room in Philadelphia
with a completely objective eye, he would have been very hard
put to see much difference at all in the two factions that were
taking shape in the hall, aside from their outspoken declarations in favor of central or local government. He would see a
room filled with males, all of a class of white property owners
of some sort, all of them bound by the social and intellectual
conventions of their time, all more conservative than the fire-
brand democrats of the Revolution had been a dozen years before. On the other hand, he would see, too, a group of men
who, for all their establishmentarian manner, their property
ownership, their social conservatism, and their newfound caution, had in fact overthrown a government by force.

Of the delegates elected to attend the Philadelphia meeting, nearly all (excepting those few, like William Samuel Johnson, who had tended to be more cautious) had put their lives
at risk by joining the Revolution; and so all vividly understood
the implications of political judgments, and were not likely to
hold political positions out of inattentiveness, or a careless
hoping for the best, or a lazy habit of making nice-sounding
phrases. They were all thoroughly practiced in political realism. Eight had committed treason by signing the Declaration
of Independence; and five others would have if they had not
already left for the battlefield. Thirty did some sort of military
service during the war. A dozen had been with Washington at
Trenton, Monmouth, or Yorktown. Another dozen had supported the guerrilla general in the wartime Congress or been
his fishing companions on the Potomac.

They were, on the whole, a young group. The average age
of the delegates was forty-two. Madison, at thirty-six, was older
than eleven other delegates—including Gouverneur Morris
(thirty-four), Edmund Randolph (thirty-three), Rufus King
(thirty-two), Hamilton (thirty), Pinckney (twenty-nine years and

seven months), Spaight (twenty-nine years and two months), and Jonathan Dayton of New Jersey, who, at twenty-six, was the youngest delegate. Franklin was the oldest at eighty-one, with Sherman a distant second (at age sixty-six), Daniel of St. Thomas Jenifer and Livingston next (both sixty-three), then Mason (sixty-two), Wythe (sixty-one), Washington (fifty-five), Blair (fifty-five), Dickinson (fifty-four), Read (fifty-three), and Robert Morris (fifty-three).

In a day when a college education was rare, twenty-six delegates were college educated, in curricula that often owed much to the Scottish Enlightenment. They knew their David Hume, and John Locke, and Montesquieu. They were sophisticated about political theory and about history. Hamilton and Gouverneur Morris had gone to King's College; Elbridge Gerry and Rufus King had gone to Harvard; the Virginians Blair, Randolph, and McClurg had gone to William and Mary; Johnson and Livingston had gone to Yale; and fully nine delegates had gone to Princeton, including Madison, his opponent Paterson, and Paterson's allies Luther Martin, Alexander Martin, and Gunning Bedford. Some had studied law at the Inns of Court in London. (Eight of them had been born in the British Isles. Many were the sons of immigrants from Britain. The flavor, and accents, of Britain were much in evidence.) They knew, from their readings of history as well as their experience of it, the significance and long-term consequences of such abstractions as liberty and justice or the lack of them. None of these words were, to them, merely popular expressions to be mouthed without a real understanding of their implications.

Every single one of the delegates in both factions had at one time or another been on the public payroll. They were professional politicians, not amateur political theorists. Forty-two had been in the Continental Congress. More than forty were at the moment in their state governments in some capacity, ten of them as judges, thirty as legislators, and several as governors. As many as twenty of the delegates had had some part in writing the constitutions of their own states. They were thoroughly schooled in the issues they had gathered to debate. They understood arguments when they heard them; they were neither naive nor cynical.

They were accustomed to living amidst enemies. A man

Madison's age, for instance, had grown up among Tories who wanted to restrict his religious and political freedom; had taken part in a war that was civil as well as revolutionary; and now continued to live among men who had been Tories, who had wished him dead, who still wished that the new government would collapse or (some of them) that a counterrevolution could sabotage the new nation. It was to these Tories that men like Madison wanted to give freedom of speech, freedom of assembly, freedom of the press, and the right to bear arms that were fully as powerful as any arms the government itself could give its soldiers. These were not timid men.

At least sixteen of the delegates could be classed as aristocrats, including Washington, George Mason, Gouverneur Morris, Daniel of St. Thomas Jenifer, Randolph, the Pinckneys, Rutledge, William Samuel Johnson, and William Livingston. Another eight or ten were of unquestioned "first families," and a great many others, such as Hamilton and James Wilson and Robert Morris and even Washington, had shown a talent for marrying up and establishing themselves as members of the upper class.

Ten were unquestionably rich, including Washington (despite his cash-flow problems), his neighbor Mason, Robert Morris, Gerry of Massachusetts, Dickinson, and Daniel of St. Thomas Jenifer. Almost as many were intently trying to become rich, or had been rich, including all the delegates from South Carolina, James Wilson, and Nathaniel Gorham. About the same number again could be classed as well-to-do, including Franklin, Gouverneur Morris, William Samuel Johnson, Livingston of New Jersey, Edmund Randolph, young Richard Dobbs Spaight and his colleague from North Carolina Alexander Martin, Washington's friend McHenry from Maryland, and Dr. McClurg from Virginia. The emerging factions of centrists and localists could not be neatly divided along lines of wealth or class.

Perhaps sixteen could be classed as comfortable, including Rufus King, Ellsworth of Connecticut, Alexander Hamilton, George Read, Gunning Bedford, and Wythe and Blair of Virginia. A half-dozen could be said to have been men of modest means, including Madison and his opponents Paterson, Brearly, and Luther Martin. And a few could be called men of very modest means, most notably Roger Sherman.

It is a measure of the economic chaos of the times that in the future, ten of the delegates would experience excruciatingly difficult financial times or fall into bankruptcy. It is a measure, too, of the tendency so many of these men had toward taking risks.

It has been said that the Madisonians tended to be wealthier than their opponents, and that the Shermanites tended to represent the small farmers and frontiersmen, although that seems not to be true. A number of Sherman's men were clustered around the bottom of the economic ladder, but their allies were distributed among all classes.

It has been said, too, that the Madisonians tended to own a large amount of personal property, to hold securities of various sorts, to derive their wealth from large plantations and slaves, while the Shermanites tended to have their wealth in smaller farms, but this notion, too, disintegrates on close examination. Twenty of the delegates to the convention got their wealth from the cultivation of land; ten had investments in city real estate; twelve had speculative investments in the undeveloped lands of the west. But the two factions cannot be sorted out according to such investments.

Sixteen of the delegates owned productive slaves (as distinguished, that is, from domestic servants). The slave owners included Washington, all of the South Carolinians, Daniel of St. Thomas Jenifer, George Mason, Edmund Randolph, Blair, Spaight, and Alexander Martin. And domestic slaves could be found in the households of Madison, Wilson, Wythe, Robert Morris, Dickinson, Read, Johnson, Livingston, and Luther Martin. Once again, slave owners are to be found among both Madisonians and Shermanites.

Both Madisonians and Shermanites seem relatively evenly distributed among planters and farmers—the planters and big farmers included Washington, Mason, Jenifer, Lansing of New York, the Pinckneys, Spaight, and several others—and among the lawyers too, who included Rufus King, Ellsworth, Hamilton, Paterson, Gouverneur Morris, Wilson, Read, Dickinson, and Alexander Martin.

Among the merchants, who were, perhaps, disproportionately Madisonian, were Gorham and Robert Morris—but also the anti-Madisonian Gerry. Among those whose principal profession was the holding of state office were Yates of New York, Livingston, Brearly, Bedford, Luther Martin, Blair, Wythe, Randolph, and Rutledge. There were a couple of small farmers, a couple of physicians, a retired lawyer, Sherman, who did a bit of everything, and Franklin, who, in this as in everything, was in a class by himself.

All of these men had gathered with the conviction that some sort of improvements needed to be made. The Shermanites disagreed with the Madisonians often and fundamentally about what that "improved" government would be; but all agreed that the central government must be more effective than the current one provided by the Articles of Confederation.

In sum, there were not two well-formed and easily identified parties to be found at this convention. The politics of 1787, like the country, were unformed, and composed of scores of shifting alliances. There were at least two dozen factions represented at the convention: There were representatives of large landowning interests, of commercial interests, of shipowners, of slave owners, of speculators in land, of speculators in government debt, of those opposed to slavery and those in favor of it, and all these shifting allegiances did not easily form themselves up into two opposing sides.

Nonetheless, in the most general sense, and with exceptions at every turn and every moment, it can be said that the Madisonians seemed to attract a slightly younger group of men than the Shermanites, men more given to risk, more oriented toward the future, perhaps more cosmopolitan. If they owned slaves, they tended to be large slave owners, or, on the other hand, urban lawyers with a few domestic servants, men whose business interests turned them out toward the larger world. They tended to live in port cities—or up along rivers that put them in direct touch with commerce and even international trade. They tended to be merchants and men of a speculative bent, men who were not instinctively averse to bigness or growth. They tended to think nationally, continentally. The Madisonians seemed often to be forward-looking, to embody something of the nineteenth century.

The Shermanites, on the other hand, tended to be con-

servative, cautious, even nostalgic for an older order. Some were
small farmers, some country gentlemen with large farms, some
alumni of New England town meetings; all tended to prefer a
rural, small-scale order of things. Many of them felt a simple
attachment to their states, which still bore the distinctive
characters that had marked them as Pilgrim or Catholic or
Huguenot or Dutch settlements, characters that seemed worth
preserving for their own sakes, and for the sake of offering
Americans a free choice among a multiplicity of societies.
Shermanites put a high value on local self-government. They
were suspicious of a juggernaut of a powerful nation serving
the interests of large commercial interests. Some were intent
on standing apart on their farms or in their town councils
against combinations of such economic interests. Some had
more selfish reasons—a wish to see that the large states did
not squeeze them out of their share of profitable land specu-
lation in the large western territories, or an intention to see
that their ownership of slaves was not threatened. Most seemed
anxious about being swept up in something larger and more
powerful than they could control—whatever ends they had in
mind. And whatever their motivations, while the Madisonians
spoke most often of their fears of disorder, the Shermanites
spoke repeatedly of their fears of tyranny. While the Madisonians spoke most consistently for order, for the uniformity of
law and equity, the Shermanites spoke fiercely for liberty, for
a direct share in the government. The more remote their government was from them, they felt sure, the less it would ap-
proximate self-government. All of these passions and convictions would endure in American politics, but they would not
always form themselves in the same two clusters of conviction
and interest—or be easy to find, always, monopolized by one
party or another.

It has been said that the Shermanites represented in some
sense not just the noncommercial interests, not just the men
of the country, the frontiersmen and the small farmers, but, in
a more general sense, the "outsiders" of American society, those
who simply wanted the government to get off their backs. The
truth is that the real outsiders were not represented at the convention at all.

Those who were opposed altogether to the federal government, those on the fringes of settlement who mainly wanted the government to leave them completely alone and free, found the Shermanites often speaking their language. In truth, they did not have any group at the convention pledged to represent their views. They might have had; but to the extent that they had a chance to participate, they refused to lend their names to the enterprise. As it was, they had to hope that others would somehow take care of their interests—always a risky proposition in politics.

11

THE LOCALISTS ATTACK

THE SHERMANITES WERE NOT foolish enough to try to attack the Madisonians on all fronts at once. Instead they singled out a few choice issues on which to express their disagreement, to pick away at the Madisonians, and to see whom they could split off to their side. John Dickinson carefully introduced the first of these trial issues.

It might be essential, Dickinson conceded, to draw one of the legislative branches from the people; but it was equally essential, he said, that the other branch be chosen by the state legislatures. He had always been in favor of a strong national government, Dickinson informed the Madisonians, but the states needed to be left with "a considerable agency in the System"; and if the state legislators could choose the senate—something resembling the House of Lords would be best, Dickinson thought—endowed with a "becoming freedom," that might serve the purpose well. The senate would not run the country; it would only see to it that no unnecessary encroachments were made on the states.

Doubtless many motivations persuaded Dickinson to take just the position he did—his innate comfort with the way things were, his social and economic interest in the status quo in general—but one motivation was altogether specific. He owned vast tracts of land in both Delaware and Pennsylvania, and so he could easily see reason to protect both large and small states. "Let the Property of the larger states be secured," he jotted in his notes for his speech. "Let the Property and Liberty of the lesser be also secured. Let Neither dictate to the other."

The preservation of the states in some role was indispensable, said Dickinson. "It will produce that collision between the different authorities which should be wished for in order to check each other." If all the thirteen state governments were formed into one single government, he said, nothing would have been achieved but to "unite 13 small streams into one great current pursuing the same course without any opposition whatever." For these reasons, he favored a senate chosen by the state legislatures, and resembling the House of Lords, made up of men whose influence came from "family weight."

Wilson, the lowborn Scotsman who had come to America with no lingering affection for the House of Lords, retorted at once: "The British Government cannot be our model. We have no materials for a similar one. Our manners, our laws, the abolition of entails and primogeniture, the whole genius of the people, are opposed to it."

And yet, as the debate progressed, it soon became apparent to Wilson and Madison that their allies were conspicuously silent. Even worse, Elbridge Gerry joined the Shermanites. Charles Pinckney of the crucial state of South Carolina joined the Shermanites. And finally, Virginia's own country gentleman George Mason, never much of a continentalist, found himself more at home with the Shermanites on this point: "It is impossible for one power to pervade the extreme parts of the U.S. so as to carry equal justice to them. The State Legislatures also ought to have some means of defending themselves against encroachments of the National Government. In every other department we have studiously endeavored to provide for its self-defence. Shall we leave the States alone unprovided with the means of this purpose?"

Prudence dictated a tactical withdrawal on the part of the Madisonians. Wilson and Madison dropped out of the debate and let the Shermanites have the point—and the vote to have the senate elected by the state legislatures—for the time being.

But now, having given power to the states, Charles Pinckney turned around, to the delight of Madison, and tried to balance that power by giving the national legislature absolute veto over state laws. (This veto power was—shrewdly—already balanced by virtue of the fact that the senate was elected by the states.)

Madison came to Pinckney's support at once. This veto was, to Madison, the most crucial provision of the whole plan. Experience, said Madison, had "evinced a constant tendency in the States to encroach on the federal authority . . . A negative was the mildest expedient that could be devised for preventing these mischiefs . . . Should no such precaution be engrafted, the only remedy would lie in an appeal to coercion"—that is to say, the threat of civil war.

But here was talk suddenly of absolute, undefined power—which certainly seemed to undo what the states' rights men were fighting for—and Elbridge Gerry did not like it. Where, the merchant of Marblehead wondered, would the national power stop? Would the nation be empowered to dictate to every citizen of every state just how businessmen must do business?

He "could not see the extent of such a power," Gerry fretted, and he was against "every power that was not necessary." He thought that if states got out of line, a "remonstrance" would be sufficient. If it was not, then force ought to be used. But an all-purpose veto was out of the question. "The National Legislature with such a power may enslave the States. Such an idea as this will never be acceded to." At the very least, the cases in which the veto could be exercised should be defined.

No one, Wilson replied in exasperation, could define all the cases in which the veto could be exercised. The delegates could hardly imagine all the issues that might arise over the course of decades or centuries. Obviously, discretion would have to be left either on one side or the other. And Wilson thought it might more safely be lodged on the side of the national government (especially if the senate was to be, in any case, a creature of the state legislatures).

However novel an idea this veto seemed to the delegates, said Wilson, "the principle of it when viewed with a close and steady eye is right. There is no instance in which the laws say that the individuals should be bound in one case, and at liberty to judge whether he will obey or disobey in another." What was true of individuals was also true of states.

By the time Wilson had finished speaking, John Dickinson, astonishingly enough, had changed his mind, and he abruptly deserted the localists on this point. It was impossible, said Dickinson, picking his way meticulously through the issue, "to draw a line between the cases proper and improper for the exercise of the negative . . . We must either subject the states to the danger of being injured by the power of the National Government or the latter to the danger of being injured by that of the States." Dickinson accepted the idea that there could be only one sovereign government, and that that had to be the central government. Dickinson's desertion on such a key point was a blow to the local-power men.

But Gunning Bedford took up the cudgels then and carried the fight on. His colleagues wondered, he said, "where would be the danger to the States from this power." Well, let them look to "the smallness of his own state which may be injured at pleasure without redress." The delegates proposed to strip the states of their right to equal representation. Bedford had done some calculating. If the federal government was to be based on proportional representation, then his state of Delaware would possess one ninetieth of the power of the central government, while Pennsylvania and Virginia would share one-third of the whole power of the government.

"It seems as if Pennsylvania and Virginia by the conduct of their deputies wished to provide a system in which they would have an enormous and monstrous influence." Sheer selfish interest was running wild.

Once again, despite Dickinson's change of position, sentiment was shifting against the Madisonians, and before the vote was called, Madison made another effort to save the national veto. The difficulties that had been mentioned, said Madison, were worthy of attention. Just how the central government would deal with state legislation that needed urgent attention was a concern. But it was not an insoluble problem. Perhaps, to simplify matters, just the senate could be given the veto power. (That was an artful suggestion on Madison's part and quite a concession: The Shermanites might be mollified if the veto power was given to a senate chosen by the states. Then, later on, Madison could try to get the senate elected differently.)

But the men of the small states were unmoved. The Madisonian proposal for an absolute federal veto of state laws was brought to a vote and failed. It was rejected decisively, seven to three, with one state divided.

William Paterson, no doubt feeling buoyed by this show of weakness among the Madisonians, proposed to have the delegates go all the way back to the very beginning and reconsider the whole basis of the Madisonian plan: the principle of proportional representation as the basis for choosing the national legislature.

The Congress of the Confederation had established this convention, said Paterson, and each delegation was bound by the credentials it brought to the convention and by the *original intention* of those legislators who had framed those credentials. The delegates had been empowered to suggest amendments to the Articles of Confederation and nothing else. They ought to keep within those limits or they would surely be charged by their constituents, said Paterson ominously, "with usurpation." Here was no attack on the details of the Virginia Plan; here was a full-fledged attack on its very foundation.

The delegates had not been charged to make a large, centralized nation, said Paterson; they had been charged to repair the confederacy. Now, a "confederacy" supposes exactly "sovereignty in the members composing it & sovereignty supposes equality." The principle of the equality of the states could not be thrown out. The small states "would never agree to it."

The idea, said Paterson contemptuously, that "a great individual State, contributing much, should have more votes than a small one contributing little" had no more logic to it than the argument that 'a rich individual citizen should have more votes than in indigent one."

It had once been proposed that America should be represented in the British Parliament and then bound by its laws. Would that have been a good idea? America "could not have been entitled to more than one-third of the number of Representatives which would fall to the share of Great Britain. Would American rights & interests have been safe under an authority thus constituted?" The Madisonians clearly wanted to smother local government and liberty altogether under their massive central government.

For his own part, said Paterson, he was much attached to

the Confederation. All that was wanted were some amendments "to mark the orbits of the States with due precision, and provide for the use of coercion," and leave well enough alone.

Mr. Wilson and Mr. Madison had suggested that the large states might confederate on their own and leave the small states out. Paterson was not frightened by such a prospect. "Let them unite if they please," Paterson concluded grandly, "but let them remember that they have no authority to compel the others to unite. New Jersey will never confederate on the plan before the Committee. She would be swallowed up." Paterson "had rather submit to a monarch"—nay, "to a despot, than to such a fate."

Here was rhetoric that had not been heard before in these debates. Echoes of 1776 were resounding now in the hall, and it may be safe to assume that prides were touched and pulses quickened. The Madisonians roused themselves.

It was, said Wilson, because "all authority" was derived from the people that "equal numbers of people ought to have an equal number of representatives, and different numbers of people different numbers of representatives." What could be more clear? "This principle had been improperly violated in the Confederation, owing to the urgent circumstances of the time." And if persons were the measure of suffrage, not property, then "are not the citizens of Pennsylvania equal to those of New Jersey? Does it require 150 of the former to balance 50 of the latter?" Was Paterson arguing against the principle of majority rule?

"If the small states will not confederate on this plan," well, then, so much the worse for them. Pennsylvania," said Wilson, and he presumed some other states, "would not confederate on any other."

And then Dr. Franklin asked for the floor. The time had come, he thought, to calm some nerves. He was not feeling strong enough himself to deliver a speech, but he had written something out, and be begged the delegates' indulgence in having James Wilson read it out for him.

"It has given me great pleasure," Wilson read in Franklin's name, "to observe that till this point, the proportion of representation, came before us, our debates were carried on with great coolness of temper. If anything of a contrary kind has on this occasion appeared, I hope it will not be repeated; for we are sent here to *consult* not to *contend*, with each other; and declarations of a fixed opinion, and of determined resolution, never to change it, neither enlighten nor convince us."

He had thought himself, said Franklin, that it hardly mattered whether members of Congress would vote by state or individually, since they would be inclined in either case to think of the common good. But in the course of debate, he had come to change his mind. He thought now that the representatives ought to bear some relationship to the numbers represented, and that "the decisions should be by the majority of members, not by the majority of States. This is objected to from an apprehension that the greater States would then swallow up the smaller. I do not at present clearly see what advantage the greater States could propose to themselves by swallowing the smaller."

Franklin, too had done a little arithmetic. It appeared to him that in the present mode of state equality, it was in the power of six or seven of the smaller states to outvote and swallow up the greater. The minority was empowered to overawe the majority, "contrary to the common practice of Assemblies in all countries and Ages." He could not conceive that some gentlemen wished to use the argument in favor of local government as a ruse to destroy the principle of majority rule.

The convention was properly stalled now. The Shermanites, having launched their attack, had lost momentum. But the Madisonians were not able to finish them off, either. The time had come to stop talking principles and to resort to some pure, hard political dealmaking. And at that moment, Wilson and Charles Pinckney, who had evidently been conferring with one another off the convention floor—perhaps at the Indian Queen, more likely in the quiet of Wilson's home—combined together in a striking new move that abruptly turned the convention on its head. They proposed that representation be based "in proportion to the whole number of white & other free Citizens & inhabitants of every age, sex & condition including those bound to servitude for a term of years and three-fifths of all other persons [i.e., slaves] not comprehended in the foregoing description, except Indians not paying taxes, in each State"—the three-fifths rule being a formulation that Congress had adopted in 1783 in a revenue amendment, and so a familiar compromise formula for counting slaves.

All at once the southern states were to be granted a disproportionate share of power based on the number of slaves they held. All at once the south was given the big share of power they had sought in the new government to protect themselves. All at once they no longer needed a Shermanesque senate to protect them from a tyranny of the majority. And all at once the balance of the convention swung back around again in favor of the Madisonians. Crucial votes deserted the Shermanites. The three-fifths rule drew the south solidly into the Madisonian camp. The Wilson-Pinckney phrase was accepted as the basis for suffrage in the lower house.

Roger Sherman, instantly alarmed, and hoping to keep this combination from sweeping the localists aside, proposed again that each state have one vote in the senate. Everything, said Sherman, "depended on this," Sherman's proposal, however, no longer came from strength. Rather, he was pleading. The centrists should not use sheer voting power now to ride roughshod over the interests of the localists, he argued; if they did, the localists would be left ever resentful.

But the Madisonians, having a suddenly strengthened grip now on a new, unholy majority, voted down Sherman's proposal without a moment's debate, six to five. And then Wilson and Hamilton followed through with a motion that the senate be elected according to the same proportional rule as the house, and this time they slammed it through by six to five. The Madisonians had Virginia, Pennsylvania, Massachusetts—and North Carolina, South Carolina, and Georgia. The majority voting bloc was now freshly constituted of the three large states and the deep south; and for the first time, it seemed steadfast.

The worst fears of the localists were enacted before their very eyes. With a quick succession of votes, the Madisonians went on to jam a score of votes through the convention: a specification of terms of office, veto powers, rights of suffrage, the establishment of inferior federal courts, the admission of new states. As the Madisonian avalanche swept through the hall, Elbridge Gerry objected querulously: New Englanders, he said, would never consent to some of these Madisonian provisions. Nonsense, said Madison; no one knew what the people wanted: "we ought to consider what is right and necessary." And so the right and necessary Madisonian provisions were voted one after another into a new constitution.

Phrasing was brought up, reconsidered, rewritten, subjected to vote, until, on June 13, the Virginia Plan—debated, revised, and voted on clause by clause—was complete. It called for a "national" government consisting of legislative, executive, and judiciary branches. It called for a house elected by the people, its members to serve three years. It called for a senate to be chosen by the state legislatures, with different numbers of senators for each state, depending on population, to serve terms of seven years. It specified that both branches could originate bills. It specified that the national legislature could pass laws in all cases in which the state legislatures were not competent, and that the national legislature had no absolute veto but could veto those state laws that contravened the articles of union or any foreign treaties. It specified that the rights of suffrage for both house and senate were to be proportioned according to the complex formulation of free whites and three-fifths of all slaves.

For the executive branch it was specified that the executive was to be a single person, chosen by the national legislature for a term of seven years, with power to execute the laws and to veto any law that was not afterward passed again by two-thirds of both house and senate; was to be ineligible for reelection, and impeachable for malpractice or neglect of duty.

For the judiciary it was specified that a supreme tribunal be established, with judges appointed by the senate, to hold office on good behavior. It was specified, too, that the legislature had the power to establish inferior courts, and that the national judiciary would have jurisdiction over all cases with respect to the national revenue, impeachments of any national officers, and "questions which involve the national peace & harmony."

All that remained was for the convention to accept the plan as a whole.

The Shermanites were stunned and utterly silenced. At last,

an embittered William Paterson spoke. Several of the delegations, he said crisply, had another plan, which they wished to present to the convention before a final vote was taken on the proposals presented by the Virginians.

12

THE LOCALISTS ATTACK AGAIN

PERHAPS SOMETHING should be said about the weather. Beginning on June 11, the day on which Wilson and Pinckney put together their alliance on the three-fifths formula, the usual summer heat wave hit Philadelphia, and the delegates were plunged at once into a sweltering, humid torment that went on and on, relentlessly, with only an occasional break, for the remainder of the summer.

These Philadelphia summers were famous with travelers, who found the climate torturous—and they were excruciating especially for the New Englanders, who naturally wore their customary wool suits throughout the summer. Nor did it help that the delegates kept the windows closed. If, as sometimes happened when the room became too impossibly stifling, the windows were thrown open, the flies came in, the notorious Philadelphia flies that lit on faces and hands, biting, and turning everything black with the filth they left behind.

Such days were enough to make one long for night—until, back at the inns and boardinghouses, the decision had to be made again: whether to leave the windows open or closed. There were no screens. And flies and mosquitoes bred in the moist garbage in the back streets below one's window. Not even the finest houses in the most salubrious neighborhoods escaped this plague. Just a hundred feet from the stately home of Bishop White, the garbage was piled so high that a stable owner complained he could not get his carts in and out. A hundred feet

farther on was an open sewer, which, in addition to other efflu-
via, carried the infernal odors of the refuse of tanning from
Howell's tanyards.

The mosquitoes that sprang out of these breeding grounds
and those of the nearby swamps were supplemented by those
imported by the ships from the West Indies and Central and
South America. Not surprisingly, Philadelphia was visited often
in the summer by whooping cough, malaria, smallpox, and
yellow fever. At least one man, driven to real desperation by
these insects, brought a hornets' nest into his house and hung
it in place of a chandelier from the parlor ceiling, to let the
hornets feast on the mosquitoes and flies.

Under the circumstances, even the most equable of tem-
pers began to flare after the midday sun had heated the State
House up to the full fierceness of a Philadelphia summer day.
Under the circumstances, too, it cannot be surprising if, by
June 15, when the priggish and pretentious William Paterson
came to present his alternate proposal to replace the Virginia
Plan, a certain civility was on the wane.

Paterson's proposal, commonly called the New Jersey Plan,
was in fact a joint product of the delegation of New Jersey,
New York, Connecticut, and Delaware. It provided, as could
have been expected, not for a new plan of government but rather
for the Articles of Confederation to be "revised, corrected &
enlarged" in such a way as to strengthen the central government while preserving the sovereignty of the states.

As Paterson presented his plan, Wilson made notes of the
differences between the Virginia and the New Jersey plans, and
considering who made them, they are remarkably dispassion-
ate and objective.

Propositions

From Virginia
1. A Legislature consisting of two
   or three branches
2. On the original Authority of
   the People
3. Representation of Citizens
   according to Numbers and
   Importance [i.e., wealth]

From New Jersey
1. A single Legislature
2. On the derivative Authority of
   the Legislatures of the States
3. Representation of States
   without Regard to Numbers
   and Importance

4. A single Executive Magistrate	4. More than one Executive Magistrate
5. A Majority empowered to act	5. A small Minority able to control [because each state has one vote]
6. The national Legislature to legislate in all Cases to which the State Legislatures are incompetent, or in which the Harmony or the Union may be interrupted.	6. The United States in Congress vested with additional Powers only in a few inadequate Instances.
7. To negative Laws contrary to the Union or Treaties	7. To call forth the Powers of the confederated States in order to compel Obedience
8. Executive removeable on Impeachment and Conviction	8. —by Congress on Application by a Majority of the Executives of the States
9. The Executive to have a qualified Negative	9. —to have none
10. Provision made for inferior national Tribunals	10. —None
11. The Jurisdiction of the national Tribunal to extend to Cases of national Revenue	11. —Only by Appeal in the dernier Resort
12. —to Questions that may involve the national Peace	12. —Only limited and appellate Jurisdiction
13. The national Government to be ratified under the authority of the People by Delegates expressly appointed for that Purpose	13. The Alterations in the Confederation must be confirmed by the "Legislatures of every State"

In sum, then, the New Jersey Plan drew together the objections that the local-power men had been making thus far in the debates. The New Jersey Plan had been hurriedly worked out, and it was not as finely crafted as Madison's plan—debate could refine it—but it provided a rallying point for all of Madison's opponents who felt they were being pushed too far, too fast, into a big, consolidated government. Doubtless, Madison could not have been heartened as he saw this cohesive opposition taking shape, especially when old John Dickinson, the master of prudence, caught his attention long enough to say: "You see the consequence of pushing things too far."

As soon as Paterson had finished presenting his plan, the New Yorker John Lansing rose to express his support. "He has

a hisitation[sic] in his speech," wrote William Pierce of
Georgia in his journal (Pierce was a modest man who made no
mark on the convention, but who watched the others closely and
made incisive little character sketches of them), "that will prevent him from being an Orator of any eminence;—his legal
knowledge I am told is not extensive, nor his education a good
one"—altogether not the ally one would pray to have on one's
side.

The convention, said Lansing succinctly, according to the
original intention of the state legislatures, did not have the
authority even to discuss the Virginia Plan. New York would
never have sent delegates to the convention if it was supposed
that they would participate in a scheme to destroy the Confederation. To augment the power of the Congress would be to
improve a good, and acceptable, system, and to expect approval of the work of the convention.

Paterson followed immediately after Lansing; and perhaps
the New Jerseyan was not any more the man than Lansing
was to lead the opposition to Madison. It was not simply a
matter of class: The delegates did not hesitate to give respect
to Sherman and Gorham and the many other self-made men
at the convention; but Paterson, the storekeeper's son who would
be an aristocrat, a man who used his law practice as little more
than an agency for bill collecting, discredited himself with his
tendency to assume a high moral tone.

How, asked Paterson at once, did the delegates presume to
throw away the Confederation? All thirteen states had agreed
to enter the Confederation. A few delegates in Philadelphia could
not simply tear up that compact. "What is unanimously done,
must be unanimously undone."

Had the delegates even tried to repair the old system before flying to a completely new and untried idea? Did they seek
a new system because the people clamored for it? "Do the people at large complain of Congress? No: what they wish is that
Congress may have more power."

Maybe this New Jersey Plan would not be a thoroughgo-
ing enough solution to the country's problems. Still: "at least
a trial ought to be made" before they flew to some radical solution. What was the rush? In such important affairs, surely it
was best to proceed by degrees, to let a system grow naturally

rather than to impose on the country some notion that sprang from theory more than experience.

If the weather had been more agreeable, if it had been earlier in the course of the convention, if the Madisonians had been less sure of the voting power they had put together, these proposals of Paterson might have been treated with more respect. But by this time the Madisonians were in no temper even to hear what their opponents had to say.

Wilson, his chin no doubt raised to its usual haughty altitude, replied to Paterson in almost disdainful terms. "with regard to the *power of the Convention,*" said Wilson, making Paterson's concern seem almost the product of a lack of manly confidence, "he conceived himself authorized to *conclude nothing*, but to be at liberty to *propose anything.* . . .

"With *regard to the sentiments of the people,* he conceived it difficult to know precisely what they were . . . He could not persuade himself that the State Governments & sovereignties were so much the idols of the people, nor a National Government so obnoxious to them, as some supposed. Why should a National Government be unpopular? Has it less dignity? Will each Citizen enjoy under it less liberty or protection? will a Citizen of *Delaware* be degraded by becoming a Citizen of the *United States?*"

The Shermanites, in their affection for small political bodies and the sanctity of state governments, should not forget that men are venal—that this venality is the rule, not the exception—and that the smallest political bodies in Great Britain, for instance, were "notoriously the most corrupt"; smaller political bodies were always easier to corrupt than larger ones, to turn to serve the special interests or prejudices of the few. (The abolitionists and civil rights advocates of later years would certainly find this a sympathetic argument.) To advocate local rule was to advocate leaving the citizenry prey to cabals of plotting commercial interests, or oligarchs, or even fraternities of army officers who wanted to bend local government to their selfish interests with nothing to check them. Such men might gather under the rubric of liberty, but they meant to have untrammeled liberty for the few, the rich, and the powerful, not liberty for all. Whatever security of rights was enjoyed in Britain was owed entirely to the purity of Britain's judges. The political liberty of Britain was entirely "at the mercy of its rulers" to preserve at their whim, or from their own sense of enlightenment, but not because they were bound by law—hardly a perfect, or even minimally safe, state of affairs.

The Shermanites seemed to think, too, that nothing was to be feared from legislative government, and yet, "despotism comes on mankind in different shapes." History gave many examples of tyranny by the legislature. The only way to prevent the danger of legislative tyranny was to divide the legislature so that it will restrain itself. "In a single house, there is no check, but the inadequate one, of the virtue & good sense of those who compose it."

Beyond this, however, Wilson argued no more. He had covered this ground before; and if the Shermanites would not be persuaded, they would simply have to be outvoted.

Then, to everyone's astonishment, Alexander Hamilton, who had played something less than the spectacular part one might have expected of him in the debates so far, spoke. He spoke, indeed, extravagantly—for six hours. And he outlined an entirely new plan, all of his own devising, presented to the convention without his having prepared the delegates for its reception, without his having lined up support for it in advance. Sick of the debate he had heard to date, appalled at the lack of daring of the plans that had been presented, chafing at the way Lansing and Yates had reduced him to powerlessness within his own delegation, Hamilton, the elitist par excellence, presented a splendid, high-flying plan for monarchy, or at least a well-entrenched oligarchy that made Madison's plan for a central government look very tepid indeed.

Hamilton did not stint when it came to making speeches. He had always had an astonishing capacity for work, and when he prepared a piece for writing or speaking, he put every effort into it. He would customarily work over the draft of a text by candlelight through the night, until dawn. Or he would sometimes sit down and mull over a problem hour after hour until he felt he had it right. Then he would go to bed, no matter what time it was, rise after a short rest, take a cup of strong coffee, sit down to his desk, and write his thoughts out, for six or eight hours, straight through, whether it was day or night.

He spoke with famous eloquence. Although he never liked to speak to the people at large, preferring always to address his remarks confidentially to the elite, his abilities as a speaker were so great that in later years, Congress would not allow him to make his reports in person for fear that his oratorical powers would too greatly influence their judgment—or so, at least, they said of the learned, and arrogant, speaker.

This particular speech was vintage Hamilton, full of well-turned phrases, sharp thrusts at his opponents, and impeccable furnishings of history and philosophy. He managed, in the course of his observations on the tendency of local governments to subvert the central government, to work in a nice study of the Greek republics as well as Charlemagne's empire and the Swiss cantons, and, later on, to give well-crafted little moral lessons from the histories of Sparta, Athens, Thebes, Rome, Carthage, Venice, and the Hanseatic League, to drop offhand references to Aristotle, Cicero, and Montesquieu, and to make it appear, in fine, that an *elected* monarch was really no different in principle than an elected executive. "If this Executive Magistrate [that he proposed] would be a monarch for life," why then, so what? The executive proposed by the Virginians "would be a monarch for seven years." Both would be elected.

What was the great controversy between the Virginians and the Shermanites? To Hamilton's way of thinking, the Virginia Plan was not such a departure from the Articles of Confederation. What was it really, he asked, but "pork still, with a little change of the sauce"?

For his part, said Hamilton, "he had no scruple in declaring, supported as he was by the opinions of so many of the wise & good, that the British Government was the best in the world: and that he doubted much whether any thing short of it would do in America."

In every community, said Hamilton, "there will be a division of it into the few & the many." Some might want to protect the many; he wanted to be certain that the few were not left unprotected. Now, the British House of Lords, Hamilton thought, "is a most noble institution. Having nothing to hope for by a change, and a sufficient interest by means of their property in being faithful to the National interest, they form a permanent barrier against every pernicious innovation."

No senate, however, that was elected for only a temporary term of office, whether for three years or seven years or whatever the term, would provide the sort of check against popular passions that the House of Lords did. The senate, therefore, should be elected for life, or at least during good behavior.

As for the executive, "the English model was the only good one on this subject. The Hereditary interest of the King was so interwoven with that of the Nation, and his personal emoluments so great, that he was placed above the danger of being

Indeed, one of the weakest aspects of a republic, said Hamilton, was its liability to "foreign influence & corruption"—its liability to have its legislators and governors bought by foreign nations and delivered into the hands of enemies. "Men of little character, acquiring great power become easily the tools of intermeddling neighbors." This was a very real danger, the result of having so many hostile or ambitious foreign nations actually established on the soil of the American continent, so many foreign intriguers trying to get around or undermine the uncertain new country, so many thousands of former supporters of the Crown still unpersuaded that the new government could or should survive, any one of them perhaps with the ability to turn a state or two or three against the central government. Any man, with his right to bear arms, possessed the ability to take to the streets to start a counter-revolutionary war in a matter of only a few brief minutes—a danger far more real and immediate than the panicky fear of foreign spies or "subversives" would be in the future.

In later years, Americans would look back on the early days of the republic as though to a pastoral time of simple problems and pathetically small dangers—and consider its usages inappropriate to a modern era full of terrorists and subversives. Yet the real and immediate dangers to the republic of 1787 make the fears of those subsequent years seem the exaggerated phantoms of a timid people.

One can hardly imagine how fearful a modern government might be if every citizen had a rifle in his home—indeed, if every citizen were entitled, as he was in eighteenth-century America, to have the most powerful weapon of his age in his hands to use not for petty crime or sport but to turn against his own government if that government seemed unjust or tyrannical. One can hardly imagine what a check such an armed citizenry was on its own government—how thoroughly was the government at the mercy of the people.

"Let the executive," then, said Hamilton, establishing a strong bulwark against the passions of the people, "also be for life." An executive for life would be "a safer depositary of power" than a string of men elected for only seven years.

"But is this a Republican Government it will be asked? Yes," answered Hamilton carelessly, "if all the Magistrates are appointed and vacancies are filled, by the people, or a process of election originating with the people."

Let the executive have an absolute veto on all legislation. Let the senate have the sole power for declaring war. Let the judges, too, serve for life. Let the state governors be appointed by the central government, and let those governors have absolute vetoes on state laws. And let the assembly be elected by the people for terms of three years. (It was revealing that Hamilton overlooked giving the popular body any powers.) In this way the government would be stable and vigorous, it would protect the few from the many, and it would be safe from foreign subversion.

No one commented on Hamilton's plan, although there was a comment on Hamilton's *speech*. In one of the only two instances in which Johnson of Connecticut wrote anything at all about the convention in his memorandum book, an entry was sandwiched between two recordings of the weather, and it consisted of a single word: "Hamilton." If there have been a good many Hamiltonians in later years, there were few in Philadelphia in the summer of 1787.

Madison, trying to bring the delegates back to the point (that is to say, to his plan), set about in his piping voice to attempt now, in one summary statement, to demolish the opposition.

He made no effort to charm or cajole Paterson. Rather, he simply attacked straight ahead. It had been said by Mr. Paterson, said Madison, that the Confederation, having been formed by unanimous consent, must be dissolved by unanimous consent. Madison plunged at once all the way back to the "theocratic origin" of the "fundamental compact by which individuals compose one Society" and argued that a breach of the compact by one part of the society absolved the other from its obligations to that society. (Madison and Paterson had not been at Princeton during the same years; Gunning Bedford, who had been a college classmate of Madison's, could have told Paterson not to begin such a debate.)

Such violations—numerous and notorious violations—had already occurred. Where had they occurred? "Among the most notorious was an Act of New Jersey herself; by which she *expressly refused* to comply with a constitutional requisition [tax] of Congress."

"He did not," said Madison, "wish to draw any rigid inferences from these observations"—that is to say, he would not directly say New Jersey had been dishonorable, and that New Jersey itself had acted so as to dissolve the very Confederation that Mr. Paterson now defended.

Proceeding, then, to the substance of Mr. Paterson's plan, Madison saw several mortal flaws in it. It would not prevent the several states from violating foreign treaties, which could, as a result, plunge the whole country into war with a foreign power. It would not prevent encroachments on the federal authority by the state; for example, the federal government could not keep the states from entering into treaties, or wars, with the Indians against the country's interest, or making agreements or other pacts with one another that would cause economic and political conflicts between states.

Did Mr. Paterson not believe such omissions in his plan significant? Madison pelted him with historical examples of other confederacies in which "the tendency of the particular members to usurp" the authority of the central government had brought "confusion and ruin on the whole."

Nothing could keep a state from issuing paper money under Mr. Paterson's plan. In certain circumstances, the issuance of paper money could be seen as an act of aggression. How? "The states relatively to one another" were in the position of being either debtors or creditors. If the debtor states issued paper money, the creditor states suffered—and could do nothing to protect themselves against such acts. In hundreds of other ways, too, by handling ultimate power over to the states, individual states could be hostile and destructive toward their neighbors, passing laws that would shift economic and social burdens across state lines, producing conflicts that could not be resolved without a central authority. Unless the central government could veto the acts of state legislatures, no state was safe from the active or passive aggression of another. Competition among the states (over trade, commerce, the settling of western lands, fishing rights, and scores of other issues) was inevitable. Either informal agreements or formal treaties between states would result. Competition would increase. The best prospect was constant tension, impositions, injustices perpetrated by the strongest states against the weakest. A possible prospect was war.

Nor did the New Jersey Plan protect the Union against the "influence of foreign powers over its members" that Mr. Hamilton had mentioned—putting the entire Union at peril by inviting a foreign power to infiltrate the weakest state, or to join one state against another—or even against one faction of the rich or the merchants, the military or the farmers, in their conflicts with other states or factions. In the past, such intrigues had caused enormous havoc to nations. He cited "the intrigues practiced among the Amphictyonic Confederates first by the Kings of Persia, and afterwards fatally by Philip of Macedon. [Madison's little notebook held him in good stead here.] Among the Achaeans, first by Macedon and afterwards no less fatally by Rome. Among the Swiss by Austria, France and the lesser neighboring powers; among the members of the Germanic [body] by France, England, Spain, and Russia—and in the Belgic Republic by all the great neighboring powers." Mr. Paterson's plan, by not giving to the central government the right to veto the acts of individual states, "left the door open for the like pernicious machinations among ourselves."

What, in any event, did the little states imagine they had to gain from Mr. Paterson's plan? In a confederacy of the sort Mr. Paterson recommended, in which each sovereign state was free to obey the common will or not—or in which coercion would be applied against those who did not obey the common will—the large states or the large interests dominating them would be free to do what they wished and to resist any coercion; and the small states or the small interests would be the ones that would have to bow to coercion or to endure the injustices created by the legislatures of their neighboring states. In such a confederacy, the weak were always the hopeless victims of the big powers and the big interests. The Amphictyonic Confederacy, said Madison, showed that such arrangements were "the cobweb which could entangle the weak, but would be the sport of the strong."

Consider the situation, Madison said, in which an adherence to the New Jersey Plan would simply cause the convention to dissolve without arriving at any solution. What would happen then? "Either the states must remain individually independent and sovereign; or two or more Confederacies must be formed among them of a size and power resembling the emerging, and constantly warring, nation-states of Europe. In the first event would the small States be more secure against the ambition and power of their larger neighbors than they would be under a general Government pervading with equal energy every part of the Empire, and having an equal interest in protecting every part against every other part?"

Or, in the second instance, where two or more confederacies were formed, "can the smaller expect that their larger neighbors would confederate with them on the principle of the present confederacy, which gives to each member an equal suffrage; or that they would exact less severe concessions from the smaller states than are proposed in the scheme of Mr. Randolph?"

Madison must by now have had the most attentive following of his audience. "The great difficulty lies in the affair of Representation; and if this could be adjusted, all others would be surmountable." Now, the delegates from New Jersey had acknowledged that it was not *just* to give Virginia, which had sixteen times the population of Delaware, "an equal vote only." But at the same time, they said it would not be *safe* for Delaware to allow Virginia sixteen times as many votes.

Thus, it seemed, the issue resolved itself as a matter of safety for the small states. But did they suppose that they were, in fact, safer under a plan for the equalization of the states, "in which case they would necessarily form a junction with their neighbors"? If forming an alliance with their neighbors was to be the source of safety, why could they not form such an alliance under the Virginia Plan—only be free to form and dissolve it at will within the free give-and-take of a national legislature, instead of, as under Mr. Paterson's plan, being bound to it for eternity?

And let them consider, too, said Madison, how they will like this principle of the equality of the states when the western territories begin to come into the Union as new states—each one of them entitled to an equal vote, until a score of new states outnumber the thirteen original states, until the new west, with all its radical, coonskin-wearing frontier democrats, routinely dominates the old east, and has its will in everything. If, on the other hand, the new states voted according to their "proportions of inhabitants, all would be right and safe. Let them have an equal vote, and a more objectionable minority than ever might give law to the whole."

It was a masterly speech. The vote, called for at once, proved it. By seven to three, with Maryland divided, the convention voted its preference for the Virginia Plan. New York, New Jersey, and Delaware voted against it; but all the others voted in favor, including Connecticut.

The New Jersey Plan was crushed, and crushed decisively. The Articles of Confederation were dead, whatever a strict construction of the delegates' credentials might say, whatever had been the original intention of the legislatures that appointed the delegates; and the New Jersey Plan could not revive them.

Yet even so, such an overwhelming defeat did not cause Paterson and his allies to accept the Virginia Plan. On the contrary, it simply maddened them. Right or wrong, they clung to their passion for local control, and they turned now—as Madison had turned on them—and tried to enfeeble the plan they could not destroy.

13

THE LOCALISTS ATTACK YET AGAIN

LANSING, THE STOLID upstate New Yorker whose only interest was obstruction, led the assault. The convention, declared Lansing, no matter how it had just voted, must in the end adhere to the Confederation in some form. A strict construction of the credentials of the delegates left them no choice in the matter. And in any case, the people would not conceivably approve a plan in which the federal government assumed such enormous power.

Abstract political theory might recommend the Madisonian view of a supreme national government, but "will a gentleman from Georgia be a Judge of the expediency of a law which is to operate in New Hampshire?" For the federal government to have a veto over state legislation would be even more injurious than the administration of Great Britain had been in the past.

Colonel Mason, back in the camp of his fellow Virginians on the recent course of debate, disagreed flatly and at once. He thought that Lansing's objection about the power of the convention was groundless. In a great crisis, said the man who had stepped into the center of many crises, public men were right to rise to the occasion.

Nor did Mason think there would be public hostility to the Virginia Plan. On the contrary, exactly the opposite would be the case: it was the New Jersey Plan, with its idea of expanding the powers of the Continental Congress, that the public would dislike. "Is it to be thought that the people of America, so watchful over their interests, so jealous of their liberties, will give up their all, will surrender both the sword and the purse, to the same body, and that too not chosen immediately by themselves? They never will. They never ought."

Much had been said, Mason continued, about the "mind of the people of America" in this debate; and perhaps it was unsettled about some things; but it was definitely settled in its attachment to republican government and in an attachment to more than one branch in the legislature. The state constitutions "accord so generally in both these circumstances that they seem almost to have been preconcerted. This must either have been a miracle, or have resulted from the genius of the people." Certainly, then, the people would approve the Virginia Plan in its broad outline.

Nonetheless, said the ever independent Mason, in a pointed remark to Madison, he could "never agree to abolish the State Governments or render them absolutely insignificant. They were as necessary as the General Government, and he would be equally careful to preserve them." Logic might be on Madison's side. Yet there was a passion for liberty, for self-rule, in America, and it must be accepted.

Roger Sherman, awkward and plainspeaking, tried to articulate the deepest sentiments of the localists. In later years, and with other men, the argument for states' rights would be used as a ruse to protect slavery or the unequal treatment of blacks, or even to weaken the central government altogether in order to allow private interests to have their unimpeded way. But such was not the case with Mason and Sherman, whose love for local government came from an honest passion for liberty. If the centrists were so insistent on proportional representation in the house, said Sherman, that was well and good; he would agree to a two-branch legislature. But he must insist, as a quid pro quo, that each state have an equal voice in the senate. The rights of the lesser states, he said, must be preserved: "Each state like each individual had its peculiar habits, usages, and manners, which constituted its happiness. It would not therefore give to others a power over this happiness, any more than an individual would do, when he could avoid it." Only the senate could provide an effective means of self-defense.

The Union was, and ought to be, composed of thirteen distinct states, each one offering a distinct way of life to its citizens; it should not be a single nation imposing a single vision of society on all. A central government might best ensure order and even uniform standards of justice by way of uniform laws. But local governments were best able to see to it that individuals actually participated in their own government; controlled their own affairs; had the direct experience of governing themselves and so knew best from their own experience how to govern and what they could reasonably expect and demand from their representatives; and had the power, because their government was so close to them, to insist that the government do their bidding. Local government actually bred better citizens than did a central government which sent down its rules from on high to a distant, uninvolved, and even apathetic population. In sum, local governments were indisputably the best guardians of the genius of self-government; and the localists would not ever give up such a treasure.

If Madison could not or would not see the force of this argument because of his abiding fear that any concession to local power might expand to tear apart the Union, no matter; other delegates agreed with Sherman's view, and they struggled to find a way to incorporate something of Sherman's notions into the Virginia Plan.

General Pinckney tried to slip through a seeming compromise resolution. The house of representatives, said the general, instead of being elected by the people, might be elected "in such manner as the legislature of each state should direct." That would bring some recognition of the states into the Madisonian scheme.

Hamilton leapt on Pinckney. Pinckney's idea was "intended manifestly to transfer the election from the people to the state legislatures, which would essentially vitiate the [Virginia] plan. It would increase that state influence which could not be too watchfully guarded against."

Rutledge came to Pinckney's defense. Still the ally of Virginia, but still also the protector of South Carolina's society, Rutledge moved like quicksilver from one side of the issue to the other. At the moment, he was interested in seeing to it that representatives were not chosen in such a way as to threaten the South Carolina oligarchy. He could not see much difference, he said with studied blandness, between "a mediate and immediate election by the people." In either case, the people were the ultimate electors.

The difference, declared Wilson acerbically, between a mediate and an immediate election was obvious and immense; in this particular case, the difference was especially worthy of notice, since "the legislatures are actuated not merely by the sentiment of the people, but have an official sentiment opposed to that of the General Government and perhaps to that of the people themselves." The people must vote directly for their representatives, or else the people are not certainly represented.

Then Ellsworth, that practiced Connecticut country lawyer, who had been sitting back, taking snuff, and talking to himself, came up with a canny suggestion. Like Sherman, Ellsworth had no trouble expressing a thought in a few words. His business letters were always brief and to the point, as were his letters home. Once, when he had been away from home for a long stretch and had not written his wife for longer than usual, he sent her a letter which could seem either very taciturn or very passionate, but was, in either case, very short: "One week and then— Oliver Ellsworth." At the moment, Ellsworth contented himself with the crisp suggestion that the federal legislators be paid by the states rather than out of the national treasury.

Once again Hamilton jumped in: "Those who pay are the masters of those who are paid." To have the states pay the members of Congress would simply provide another device to undermine the national government: Only a member who represented the views of the state legislature would receive compensation. With such a provision, the states could effectively disband the national legislature.

Defeated on their efforts to change the house, the localists merely returned their attention to the senate. But before anyone else had had a chance to speak, Charles Pinckney was recognized by the chair and proceeded to deliver a long, intricate justification for Sherman's proposal on the senate—a justification so sinuous in its reasoning as to be breathtaking.

First of all, said Pinckney, one must start by observing that the people of the United States "are perhaps the most singular of any we are acquainted with. Among them," said the young Charleston nabob, all decked out in his regalia of silk and lace, "there are fewer distinctions of fortune and less of rank than among the inhabitants of any other nation."

(To some extent, one must admit, what Pinckney said was true: America was not burdened by a handful of nobility who owned whole principalities, whose families had ruled for centuries, and who naturally took their places in the House of Lords in Britain or in other privileged positions in the courts of Europe. From this observation, however, Pinckney was led to an extravagant conclusion: that America was an egalitarian society.)

"Every freeman," said the slave owner, "has a right to the same protection and security; and," said the plantation owner, "a very moderate share of property entitles them to the possession of all the honors and privileges the public can bestow."

Pinckney went on to envision an even more democratic future: The immense tracts of open land in the west would ensure that there would always be "few poor, and few dependent— Every member of the Society almost will enjoy an equal power of arriving at the supreme offices and consequently of directing the strength and sentiments of the whole Community. None will be excluded by birth, and few by fortune, from voting for proper persons to fill the offices of Government."

The people of the United States, said Pinckney, could be divided into three classes: professional men, commercial men, and the landed interest. (The poor, the female, and the black, among others, did not thrive in Pinckney's imagination—as, indeed, they did not in the imaginations of most of his colleagues.) Although they are each different from the other, altogether they have but one interest. "The dependence of each on the other is mutual. The merchant depends on the planter. Both must in private as well as public affairs be connected with the professional men . . . Hence it is clear . . . that after all there is one, but one great and equal body of citizens composing the inhabitants of this Country among whom there are no distinctions of rank, and very few or none of fortune."

For this reason, said Pinckney, there were not two great classes to check one another, such as Britain had for its House

of Commons and House of Lords. Thus, America would have
to look elsewhere for some naturally balancing forces. And
where were they to be found? The states, declared Pinckney
triumphantly, were the elements to provide balance, if only
they were given the proper means for doing so—namely, the
senate. Let the states be represented in the senate, and the states
would provide that essential mechanism for checking and balancing the other branches of the government.

In Madison's view, this debate on the senate had become
entirely cut off from any sense of political reality. And he rose
at last to clarify what he thought was the right way to regard
the senate.

The first function to be served by the upper house, said
the political theorist succinctly, was obviously "to protect the
people against their rulers." All the institutions of government
must be so formed as to protect the people against their rulers:
This understanding that the members of government were
themselves the greatest threat to liberty and justice must never
be forgotten. The politicians themselves were the primary force
in society to be defended against, because they had the power
no other element in society had: the power to make the rules
by which they and all others lived—to grant and withhold
privileges, to create and destroy fortunes, to define the outlaw
and the traitor. No other person or faction or group had so
much power. And even American politicians, as these patriots
were among the first to know, had the capacity for great wrong,
and even for tyranny.

Second, the senate must protect the people "against the
transient impressions into which they themselves might be led."
Sudden passions were always liable to overcome calm reflection. The members of the convention must remember that those
who would be charged in the future with the protection of "the
public happiness might betray their trust. An obvious precaution against this danger would be to divide the trust between
different bodies of men, who might watch and check each
other."

Finally, however, it must be acknowledged that "in all civilized Countries the people fall into different classes having a

real or supposed difference of interests. There will be creditors and debtors, farmers, merchants, and manufacturers. There will be particularly the distinction of rich and poor."

It was true, said Madison, "as had been observed (by Mr. Pinckney) we had not among us those hereditary distinctions of rank which were a great source of the contests in the ancient governments as well as the modern States of Europe . . . We cannot, however, be regarded even at this time as one homogeneous mass . . . In framing a system which we wish to last for ages, we should not lose sight of the changes which ages will produce. An increase of population will of necessity increase the proportion of those who will labor under all the hardships of life, and secretly sigh for a more equal distribution of its blessings. These may in time outnumber those who are placed above the feelings of indigence. According to the equal laws of suffrage, the power will slide into the hands of the former."

What will keep these numerous poor from simply voting all the wealth into their hands? The senate. That was the need for it in the scheme of government. This wish to recognize the states should not lead the delegates to protect some frivolous interest at the expense of a real one. The natural war waged in all societies forever was that of rich against poor. If the rights and livelihoods of the many were to be protected in the house, then the rights and livelihoods of the few must be protected in the senate. The senate would be the bulwark against the tyranny of the majority over the minority, against the many, against the poor. If the senate was elected by the house, as the original Virginia Plan had provided, then the senators might naturally tend to be men of greater national standing. Being put at one remove from the people in the way they were elected, they would be less subject to popular sentiment.

In its design, then, the Madisonian system was placed at war with itself; The rights of the minority were protected in the senate, the rights of the majority in the house; the rich in the senate were set against the poor in the house—or they would have been, had the poor been represented in the house. What Madison designed, really, was for the rich to have the senate, and the middle class to have the house. The poor would have to hope, as always, that a government pledged to justice did not mean to risk the foundation of justice by restricting it to the few.

Still, at least some of the advocates of local power were not content with this notion of giving the senate to the rich and leaving the old local governments to their own devices to protect themselves. As the days wore on into late June, and the heat drew their tempers into a finer and finer fragility, the local-power men became increasingly strident. "The hot season in Philadelphia," wrote Moreau de Saint-Méry, "is so debilitating that it deprives people of all energy and makes the slightest movement painful . . . As Talleyrand said, 'At each inhaling of air, one worries about the next one.' " And the "innumerable flies" were a constant torture, constantly lighting on one's face, "stinging everywhere . . . many among them are a sort of blisterfly, and once they have attacked you, you can have no peace until they are killed. If one writes, the paper is spotted with flyspecks. If a woman is dressed in white her dress is in like manner spoiled . . . The upholstery and bell-pulls are sticky. At table and above all at dessert they light upon and befoul all food, all drinks. They taste everything they see . . . [some] persons use saucers filled with vitriol; all the flies which pass its poisoned atmosphere perish, but in a state of eroticism which forces them, before they die, to taste the irritations of love's delights. In large stores the dead flies must be swept up at least four times a day."

In this atmosphere, Luther Martin of Maryland, a wild, slovenly, heavy-drinking fellow, chose to speak or, rather, to harangue the delegates for a full day and a half, speaking on the side of the local-power men—to their intense chagrin.

Martin was a man who had hated Tories; as attorney general of Maryland, in 1778, he had prosecuted them with a vengeance. This talk he heard in the Constitutional Convention, of establishing a senate to protect the rich, did not set well with him. (His motives for taking exception to the idea were not entirely pure. He had some land-speculating friends back home, who did not want their real estate ventures threatened by a new central authority.)

Martin was a smart man—he had graduated first in his

class at Princeton—but not a smooth or socially comfortable one. He was often in debt, had been arrested on five different warrants of attachment, and said toward the end of his life, "I am not even yet, I was not [in the past], nor have I ever been an economist of anything but time." He was a steady and faithful churchgoer—although, as one preacher confessed of his follower, he made "notorious sacrifices at the shrine of Bacchus," and he was always in arrears for pew rent. Yet, as Aaron Burr once said of him, "his heart is overflowing with the milk of benevolence."

He was, at least sometimes, a terrific trial attorney. There were many stories about how Martin would stagger late into a courtroom, wearing the clothes he had slept in, having evidently been too drunk for days to have prepared his case. He would introduce himself, swallow a pint tumbler of brandy (they called him "Brandy-Bottle"), and then begin to talk, in broken sentences, sometimes mispronouncing his words—and yet astounding his listeners with his command of the law and of the facts. Usually, to the growing astonishment of the opposing attorney, he pressed his case to a successful conclusion. And so, when he rose to speak in their behalf, the local-power men must have been anxious—and at the same time hopeful that this would be one of Martin's good days.

Because he had arrived late, and missed much of the early debate, Martin had no idea what had already been covered—and thus he launched into an argument in his usual ramshackle manner on many topics that had already been thoroughly exhausted. He did have the unfortunate tendency, when he got hold of something, never to let it go. As William Pinckney (who was often on the losing side in cases against Martin) once complained, Martin would often quote "authorities without number to support what nobody denies."

Martin declared that "the convention had no right to form a new government," that a correct construction of their credentials did not permit them to set off on new, unprecedented experiments, lacking foundation in the Articles, without consulting the intention of the states the delegates represented. He said that an equal vote for each state was essential to the federal idea. To prove it, he commenced to quote swatches of John Locke's theory that before individuals have entered into a social contract with one another they are still in a "state of nature" and so are equally free and independent. Similarly, he said, the states were in a state of nature, free and independent, and could not be compelled to surrender their sovereignty by some ruse of appealing to the people over their heads. He proceeded from theory to history, presenting the American past not as a story of constant experiment and change within the context of general political principles but rather as a bond that could not be undone. The small states, he said, would never allow a negative to be exercised over all their laws; no state that had ratified the original Articles had objected to the equality of votes; complaints had not been lodged against this equality of votes but rather against the Confederation's lack of power, and so forth.

When Martin had finally finished, on the second day, his colleagues sat, as one of them said later, overcome by "fatigue and disgust." The delegates were no longer captivated by talk of the sanctity of past arrangements. The mood of the convention had passed Martin by. And in any case, although Martin had been at his most passionate in his presentation, he was not at his most persuasive.

The speech drew no more votes to the side of the small states. Rather, by annoying the delegates with its hectoring in the very midst of the summer heat wave, it helped drive the convention further into two hardened camps, and Madison, who should have had the wit to reply with some gracious words to clinch the advantage Martin had given him, instead turned on Martin in exasperation.

The idea of the states having equal votes, said Madison, was demonstrably wrong. The Shermanites were confusing the principle of treaties (in which each sovereign state agreed to abide by certain rules) and the principle of a compact, "by which an authority was created paramount to the parties," able to make laws for all. If France and England were to enter a treaty for the regulation of commerce with, say, the Prince of Monaco and four or five other small countries, the large states would not hesitate to treat the small ones as equals. But if a council were formed with the power to raise money, levy troops, and issue currency, "would thirty or forty millions of people submit their fortunes into the hands of a few thousands?" Certainly not.

And why did the small-state men continue to harp on the notion that the large states had some common interest that would make them combine to destroy the economies or societies or local customs of the small states? "In point of manners, Religion and the other circumstances which sometimes beget affection between different communities, they were not more assimilated than the other States." Was a combination to be expected from the "mere circumstance of the equality of size? . . . Experience rather taught . . . [that] among individuals of superior eminence and weight in society, rivalships were much more frequent than coalitions."

As usual, Madison was right—as far as he went. What he neglected even to mention were the localists' concerns about liberty, about the *absolute* good of self-rule.

Dr. Franklin requested the floor. Speaking with his customary mixture of seriousness, humor, and suasiveness, he said that the small progress the convention had made in the past four or five weeks—despite the good attendance and "continual reasonings with each other"—was, he thought, "a melancholy proof of the imperfection of the Human Understanding." Indeed, said Franklin, the delegates seemed to feel keenly "our own want of political wisdom, since we have been running about in search of it. We have gone back to ancient history . . . And we have viewed Modern States all round Europe, but find none of their Constitutions suitable to our circumstances."

What was to be done? Surely, Franklin said to a room filled with prickly rationalists along with a complement of Catholics and Quakers and other Protestants, he thought it time for the delegates to consider "humbly applying to the Father of lights."

"I have lived, Sir, a long time, and the longer I live, the more convincing proofs I see of this truth—*that God governs in the affairs of men.* And if a sparrow cannot fall to the ground without his notice, is it probable that an empire can rise without his aid?"

Under the circumstances, said Franklin, he thought the delegates ought deeply to consider bringing in a member of the clergy to lead them in prayer.

Although the worldly Franklin may have made his proposal only as a way of gently chiding the delegates, Sherman, the devout New England Puritan of humble background, seconded the motion with sincerity.

But the delegates were no more of one mind about God than they were about central or local power. They babbled a bit. One or another of the delegates averred that they ought not to spread public alarm by asking for a minister at this point, that such a suggestion might have been in order at the beginning of the convention but seemed out of place at the moment.

And then, at last, one of the members put an end to it with a rigorously practical remark. The convention, he said, had no money to hire a preacher.

14

ANARCHY, AND THE TURNING POINT

BY NOW, AS THE DELEGATES themselves realized, the convention had broken down completely. The Madisonians and the Shermanites had reached a true stalemate, and neither side could budge the other. Clearly, a hard political deal was called for. Toward the end of June and into the first days of July, the more moderate delegates began to turn on their most obstinate colleagues—on Madison and Wilson on the one side, and Paterson on the other—to persuade them to accept some compromise. The tone of the debates changed. William Samuel Johnson of Connecticut spoke in a conciliatory way, trying to soothe the disputants, and get them each to accept a little of the other's point of view.

Franklin spoke in his best homespun manner. "When a broad table is to be made," said Franklin cozily, "and the edges of the planks do not fit, the artist takes a little from both, and makes a good joint. In like manner here both sides must part with some of their demands, in order that they may join in some accommodating proposition."

But Madison replied like a man cornered and determined to give no quarter. If the local-power men insisted on holding to their position, said Madison, he could foresee that all that would come of it would be the dissolution of the Confederation. And he took the occasion to warn his fellow delegates "to ponder well the consequences of suffering the Confederacy to go to pieces."

Once the Confederation was broken up, each state would begin to have anxieties about the intentions of its neighboring states. As a result of these anxieties, each state would soon enough commence to adopt "vigorous and high toned governments." And then it would be not only that the large states would be threatening to the small states, but that the "vigorous" governments of the small states themselves would be "fatal to the internal liberty of all." Such was usually the cost to liberty when states allowed themselves to be in a constant condition of tension or war. "The same causes which have rendered the old world the theatre of incessant wars, and have banished liberty from the face of it, would soon produce the same effects here.

"The weakness and jealousy of the small States would quickly introduce some regular military force against sudden danger from their powerful neighbors. The example would be followed by others, and would soon become universal. In time of actual war, great discretionary powers are constantly given to the Executive Magistrate. Constant Apprehension of War has the same tendency to render the head too large for the body." This was why republics must always hate war: Whatever happened on the battlefield, they always lost their liberty, in part if not in whole—and if the state of tension was permanent, so, too, was the loss of liberty.

"A standing military force, with an overgrown Executive, will not long be safe companions to liberty. The means of defense against foreign danger have always been the instruments of tyranny at home. Among the Romans it was a standing maxim to excite a war" as a ruse to keep the people enslaved. Should the states separate entirely from one another, these would be the consequences, and anyone who had been accessory to such historic consequences "could never be forgiven by their Country, nor by themselves."

Oliver Ellsworth, who had largely gone his own way in the convention, siding on some issues with the centrists, on others with the localists, refused to be panicked into agreement with the large states. Ellsworth was a man who held prayer meetings each morning in his household and studied the Bible daily; his library was half made up of theological books. Once he had reasoned his way to a conclusion that sat well with his conscience, he held to it.

The country, insisted Ellsworth, was "partly national; partly federal. The proportional representation in the first branch was conformable to the national principle . . . An equality of voices [in the senate] was conformable to the federal principle." He trusted that a compromise could be made on these grounds. But if no compromise could be made, then he, too, feared they had met not only in vain "but worse than in vain." America, he thought, would be cut in two. The danger to the small states would be dreadful. And yet the "power of self-defense was essential to the small States." It could not be taken from them. "Nature had given it, to the smallest insect of the creation" said Ellsworth, perhaps in the only moment of recognition the convention gave to its constant companions of the summer. Let the convention not attempt too much, he warned the Madisonians. "Let a strong Executive, a Judiciary and Legislative power be created; but let not too much be attempted, by which all may be lost."

Madison was beside himself with this constant insistence that the small states had something they needed to protect from the depredations of the large states. What was it? Had it not been thoroughly demonstrated in previous debate that no difference of interest existed between large and small states? Evidently there was no way to get the small states to abandon this idea except by jarring them out of it—and so Madison set about to do just that. If the small states insisted on recognizing some difference among the states, then let them meditate on this one: The real and great division of interests in the United States, said Madison with fierce precision, "lay between the Northern and Southern, and if any defensive powers were necessary, it ought to be mutually given to these two interests."

He himself, said Madison, with chilling, almost vengeful, realism, had sometimes wondered how this mutual guarantee could be made; and he had come upon an idea: Let one branch of the legislature be elected proportionally by the whole number of free inhabitants, and let the other branch be elected proportionally by the whole number of both free inhabitants and slaves. Let one branch, in short, be devoted to defending the rights of the slave owners. In this way, the north would have the advantage in one house, the south in the other.

It was an absolutely outrageous suggestion, as Madison well knew; and he can only have made it as a way of shocking the other delegates, and showing just how bad this debate could get.

In fact, however, the debate could get even worse—and did at once. If the local-power men were determined not to compromise, said Rufus King, he wanted them to know that some of the centrists were determined not to compromise, either. In fact, in his own mind, he was prepared "for any event, rather than sit down under a Government founded on a vicious principle of representation and which must be as short-lived as it would be unjust." For "any event"? Did King threaten war?

Suddenly, in reply, declarations of war came thick and fast. Jonathan Dayton, of Paterson's New Jersey delegation, was the first to his feet: "When assertion is given for proof, and terror substituted for argument, he presumed they would have no effect however eloquently spoken." For his part, he considered the Virginia Plan "a novelty, an amphibious monster, and was persuaded that it never would be received by the people."

Luther Martin, equally stout in refusing to be intimidated by King's threat, declared he would "never confederate" if it could not be done on just principles.

Gunning Bedford of Delaware, frank as usual, lashed out at the centrists. The centrists wished to persuade the localists that the large states were not motivated by avarice or any other dangerous passion. But all political societies possess ambition and avarice. "Will not the same motives operate in America as elsewhere? If any gentleman doubts it," said Bedford, putting into question for the first time the honor of his fellow delegates, "let him look at the votes. Have they not been dictated by interest, by ambition? Are not the large States [with their claims to western lands to be ratified by their domination of a new national government] evidently seeking to aggrandize themselves at the expense of the small? They think no doubt that they have right on their side, but interest has blinded their eyes. Look at Georgia. Though a small State at present, she is actuated by the prospect of soon being a great one [by the exploitation of western lands]. South Carolina is actuated both by present interest and future prospects . . . North Carolina has the same motives of present and future interest. Virginia follows."

Given the Madisonian structure of government, a few large states could vote into their own state treasuries, or into the hands of their favored land companies (in which certain leading public figures might have personal interests), the whole fortune to be made from western lands.

"Give the opportunity," declaimed Bedford, "and ambition will not fail to abuse it. The whole history of mankind proves it." So, then: "will the smaller States ever agree to the proposed degradation of them?" Never. "We have been told with a dictatorial air [by Rufus King] that this is the last moment for a fair trial in favor of a good Government. It will be the last indeed if the propositions reported from the Committee go forth to the people."

He was under no apprehensions, said Bedford; indeed, he could threaten with the best of them. He could threaten with war and with foreign troops. "The large States dare not dissolve the confederation," Bedford thundered. "If they do the small ones will find some foreign ally of more honor and good faith, who will take them by the hand and do them justice."

Rufus King replied at once. He could not sit by "without taking some notice of the language of the honorable gentleman from Delaware [Mr. Bedford]. It was not he [King] that had uttered a dictatorial language. This intemperance had marked the honorable gentleman himself. It was not he who with a vehemence unprecedented in that House had declared himself ready to turn his hopes from our common Country and court the protection of some foreign hand. This too was the language of the Honorable member himself . . . For himself, whatever might be his distress, he would never court relief from a foreign power," though, in truth, Bedford had seemed to threaten a *native* military hand.

On that note, with insults left hanging in the air and tempers still riled, the gavel was banged down, not a moment too soon, and the delegates adjourned to cool off at the local taverns. It was June 30, a Saturday.

By this time, certainly, a compromise was desperately needed to keep the convention from shattering apart entirely. No progress was being made on the convention floor. The time had come for some completely pragmatic deal to be made backstage to break the deadlock. And possibly some such deal was made, because two days later, on Monday, when the convention resumed, everything had changed.

Just what brought this change about, no one knows. A story exists to explain the event, but for all anyone knows, it was wholly made up and cannot be believed. It has been passed down to us by one of Rutledge's biographers, who says he got it from a New England newspaper, a source other scholars question. And yet if the events it tells of did not take place, something like them must have.

That evening, so the story goes, in the taproom of the Indian Queen Tavern, two men willing to compromise had supper: John Rutledge—a centrist, though one who saw some advantages in states' rights—played host at a private supper with the very pious and practical Puritan Roger Sherman, a localist but not a diehard.

Rutledge, while he defended the interests of South Carolina and of his ruling group there with single-minded intensity, was not an uncomplicated man. Unlike so many of the other delegates at the convention, who were on their way to bankruptcy, Rutledge had already been there—or nearly so. At the age of twenty-one, having just returned from law studies in England to find the family fortune completely mortgaged, he had taken over the direction of his family's affairs, and he recovered everything and more. "He fronts a fact more quickly than anyone I ever knew," one of his legal clients said of him; and that ability to deal in hard realities was always with him.

He always went his own way, and kept his own counsel. To the great surprise of his family, he married the sister of a friend with whom he had studied in England—a woman who brought no dowry with her. He married her with no announcement, and no big wedding; and he was devoted to her throughout their marriage. She was a Grimké, and two of her nieces would be among the leading antislavery activists of America. She herself gave up all her slaves before she died. John, who had started out with sixty slaves as a young man, owned twenty-eight at the time of the Constitutional Convention, and only one at the time he died. He never defended the morality of slavery, and he never attacked it; he talked always only of practicalities.

When he had first arrived in Philadelphia for the convention, he stayed with James Wilson, and there can be no doubt that his closeness to Wilson was a significant fact at the convention. He remained with Wilson for three weeks, until his wife came to Philadelphia to be with him (he was one of the few men to have his wife with him for the summer), and they moved together into the Indian Queen.

At the Indian Queen on the evening of June 30, according to our story, amidst the temptations of pipes and bowls, cards and dice, rum and beer and brandy and Madeira, Rutledge, knowing Roger Sherman's habits, carefully eschewed offering his guest either tobacco or spiritous liquors. And, before supper began, Rutledge asked Sherman to say grace. Sherman bowed his head, and prayed for ten minutes. We are not favored with an account of what the two men said to each other over dinner. We can only guess, based on what was about to happen in the convention, that in return for South Carolina's tilt in favor of Sherman's senate proposal, Sherman gave Rutledge some assurance that Connecticut would not threaten the slave trade, and would use its best efforts to bring its neighbor Massachusetts along with it.

But perhaps South Carolina alone did not have the power to deliver a majority vote along the lines Sherman wanted. To be certain of the vote, Sherman wanted to be able to count on another state that had been siding with the Madisonians. Halfway through supper, Hugh Williamson of North Carolina arrived at the table. A sharp-witted man in his early fifties, Williamson had not been heard from in the convention thus far, but after this weekend he would speak up more frequently. Williamson was a man acquainted with all sorts of adventure. He was a theologian, a physician, a businessman, a mathematician. A good friend of Ben Franklin's, he had, in fact, collaborated with Franklin on a number of electrical experiments, and was the author of many scientific papers, including his famous "Experiments and Observations on the Gymnotus Electricus, or Electric Eel." He had been in Boston harbor, waiting for his ship to set sail, at the time of the Boston Tea Party, and was the first to take the news to London, where he told the Privy Council that the colonies would revolt if British policy was not changed. At the time the Declaration was signed, Williamson was in Holland; when he sailed for home, his ship was captured, and he escaped in a small boat.

In the convention, Williamson had tended to be cautious about the powers with which the central government was endowed; he had favored an executive elected by the legislature, and he had favored a plural executive; but he was in favor, over all, of a stronger central government. Presumably he and Rutledge had already talked about the issues over which Connecticut and South Carolina were to make a deal, and Williamson had concurred.

Whether or not this dinner meeting took place over the weekend, we do know that on Monday, July 2, when the delegates reconvened, Rutledge's South Carolina colleague General Pinckney took the floor. It seemed, said the general, that the convention was exactly evenly divided on the question of giving each state an equal vote in the senate. Neither side could convince the other of the correctness of its position. They had reached the point where a purely political solution was called for: The time had come for a compromise. He recommended, under the circumstances, that a committee be appointed to work out a compromise and report back to the convention.

Sherman took the floor. "We are now at a full stop," he said, in agreement with General Pinckney, and nobody, he supposed, "meant that we should break up without doing something." A committee, he said blandly, as though he had no thought just how such a committee might sort things out, would be "most likely to hit on some expedient."

Now an avalanche of agreement swept through the convention. The Madisonians deserted their leader, and the moderate localists deserted Paterson and went over to Sherman.

Gouverneur Morris agreed with Pinckney's suggestion. He had been absent from the recent sessions of the convention, having had some business in New York, but when he returned to find the convention at a standstill, he thought a committee was essential.

Edmund Randolph deserted his fellow Virginians: He, too, declared himself in favor of committing the issue before them to a committee to seek a compromise.

Caleb Strong of Massachusetts—whether on his own or because one of the Connecticut men had talked to him—declared himself in favor of sending the issue to committee.

And Hugh Williamson of North Carolina declared: "If we do not concede on both sides, our business must soon be at an end."

Perhaps James Wilson smelled a rat. Certainly he and Madison were suddenly losing control of the convention. Wilson objected: If the delegates proposed to establish a committee, thus what lines? On the lines of one delegate from each state being a member of the committee? What then? They would decide the issue of state equality according to the very rule of voting that was at issue. This was nothing short of parliamentary theft. (The rules of voting that had been established at the very beginning of the convention—indeed, that the Virginians had persuaded the Pennsylvanians to adopt—of letting each state have its customary one vote rather than establish a new form of proportional voting, had finally come to betray the centrists at the most crucial moment.)

Madison rose. He, too, opposed appointing a committee. Such committees, said Madison, desperately looking for arguments against them, rarely produce anything but delay. Any scheme of compromise, in any case, "that could be proposed in the Committee might as easily be proposed in the House." And anyway, whatever the committee recommended would still constitute "merely the *opinion* of the Committee" and would not necessarily influence the decision of the house.

And then Madison and Wilson were deserted by another delegate from Massachusetts: The ambivalent Elbridge Gerry declared himself in favor of commitment. "Something must be done," said Gerry, as though apologetically, "or we shall disappoint not only America but the whole world."

And so, despite their best efforts, Madison and Wilson found themselves almost alone on the floor of the convention. On the other side, proving themselves equally obstinate as it came down to the end of the debate, were a few men who clustered around Paterson. When at last the delegates took a vote, they agreed overwhelmingly to refer the issue to committee to seek a compromise. The vote was nine to two in favor, with only Paterson's New Jersey delegation and Dickinson's Delaware delegation holding out to the end. The Virginians had deserted Madison, the Pennsylvanians had deserted Wilson.

To Sherman and Rutledge and Ben Franklin and some of the others, this was a great and crucial victory. To Paterson on the one side and Madison and Wilson on the other, it was certainly a signal of defeat. The New Jersey Plan had been refused; but the Virginia Plan was about to be decimated. The delegates had evidently done the worst possible thing of all: They had demolished the old Confederation, and they had failed to put a good new government in its place.

And so the convention took a recess—ironically enough, to celebrate that moment of erstwhile unity and triumph when many of these same men had set themselves on this apparently disastrous course: the Fourth of July.

15

THE FOURTH OF JULY

ON THE MORNING of the Fourth of July, Washington rose to a day of bell ringing and cannon firing, crowded streets and marching with fife and drum. He made his way through the crowds to an oration "at the Calvinist church." As he noted in his diary: "Why should we travel back to antiquity for examples of the dignity of conduct and sentiment inspired by a republican form of government—we have beheld the citizens of the United States raised by their personal interest in the government of their country to a pitch of glory which has excited the admiration of half the globe." It was a good enough speech, delivered by a young law student named James Campbell (Washington misheard his name, thought it was Mitchell), who made a tolerably good impression on his fellow Philadelphians. Like so many orators that day, young Campbell called for a strong new central government, "but," he said boldly, in the (approving) presence of Washington, "may every proposition to add kingly power to our federal system be regarded as treason to the liberties of our country."

The general emerged from the church to more crowds and marching. All over the country, this same scene was being repeated. The newspapers the next day would report on festivities and orations in some thirty towns around the country. (Most of the speeches dwelt on the sad state into which America had fallen and the need for a strong, efficient central government, or so at least the newspapers, which tended to be owned and edited by centrists, reported.) Everywhere, the Cincinnati took a prominent part in the celebrations. In Philadelphia, Washington himself attended a dinner with the state Society of the Cincinnati at the Sign of the Rainbow, a tavern run by Henry Epple, a former officer.

At the end of the day, after the parades and the artillery salutes, the bowls of punch and the bottles of Madeira, the toasts and the reminiscences of former comrades in arms, the general made his way once again to the home of the Powells, where he had his customary afternoon tea.

And soon enough, like Cincinnatus, the very model of the servant of the republic, he was back attending to his principal business: "Dear George: . . . How does your Pompkin Vines look? and what figure does the pease, Potatoes, Carrots and Parsnips make? Does your Turnips come up well, and do they escape the Fly?

". . . P.S. Keep the Shrubberies clean. What have you done to the Gravel Walks, or rather what remains to be done to them."

The Reverend Manasseh Cutler of Ipswich, Massachusetts, a portly, charming man of infectious enthusiasm, was on the road when the Fourth of July came around—just passing through New Haven, Connecticut, where the town fathers had planned to celebrate the day with a military parade, an oration in the brick meeting house, a public dinner in the state house, and a public ball in the evening. Cutler was invited to stay for the festivities, and under ordinary circumstances he would have, but he was a man in a hurry. He was a patriot, who loved the Fourth of July as much as anyone, but he was also a businessman, with business to attend to. He was on his way first to New York, and from there to Philadelphia. He had some urgent lobbying to do, even before there was yet a new government to lobby.

Cutler, an ex–army chaplain who had dabbled in medicine, law, and botany as well as religion, was the founder of a newly incorporated business, the Ohio Company, which was interested in investing in a piece of America's greatest common treasure: the lands of the west, the sale of which by the Congress would be able to wipe out the entire federal debt, finance much of what any new government might wish to undertake, and make scores of men rich. These lands, above all, were the fortune the Americans had in common, to hold and share, or divide; and many Americans were intensely interested in them.

What Cutler wanted out of the Congress in New York was the right to buy a million and a half acres of land for the same number of dollars, most of the acres reserved for his company, some of them earmarked for private investors—that is to say, for sale at bargain rates to politicians and other influential people.

The lands of the west were vast. Some were claimed by individual states. Virginia had long claimed territories that would become Kentucky and West Virginia; North Carolina had claimed what would become Tennessee; Georgia had claimed what would be Alabama and Mississippi. Gradually, these states were ceding their claims to the Confederation—Virginia ceded a large piece of territory to the Union in 1784—but some states held on. North Carolina would not cede Tennessee until 1790. Georgia would not let go of Alabama and Mississippi until 1802.

The lands that concerned Cutler at the moment, however, did belong to the Confederation: the so-called Northwest Territory, which stretched from the Appalachians all the way out to the Mississippi. Eventually, five states would be made from these uncommonly fertile lands: Ohio, Indiana, Illinois, Michigan, and Wisconsin. And the central government hoped to pay all its bills from the sale of these lands to men like Cutler, who would in turn sell them off to individual settlers. (There was some urgency in selling these lands: Settlers were already moving into some of them, and once they had taken possession, they tended to dispute the right of any government to tell them they now needed to buy from speculators the land that they had cleared and started to farm.) Cutler was eager to have an authoritative central government to guarantee the title to the lands he was buying: He wanted no trouble with conflicting claims, with squatters, or with Indians.

Other investors in land, however, were not quite so eager to see an authoritative central government. A well-connected Georgian about to speculate in Mississippi lands might well prefer a friendly local government to a distant authority. Thus, the fortune in western land fueled the same old conflict between centrists and localists—with that fierce old incentive, profit.

Meanwhile, settlers poured west. In 1775, it was said that there were 150 men and no women in Kentucky. By 1790, there were 73,677 people, including more than 12,500 slaves. Flatboats and covered wagons could be seen every day taking families west to push out the Indians, chop down the trees, clear the land, and settle in to an adventure of freedom and individualism, hard work and heavy drinking, real social and economic egalitarianism, coonskin caps and fringed leggings, exposure to all the ravages of nature and of coping alone, and the exhilaration and triumph of making one's own destiny. For these men and women, the intricacies of a finely balanced government, functioning amidst the complexities of high finance and international trade, would never have much appeal. They settled on lands they had bought from men who claimed to own them, before it was altogether clear who would sort out land disputes if they arose.

Some of the confusion over lands—at least the lands of the northwest—was resolved when Cutler passed through New York. There he handed out promises to congressmen for some of the acreage he was about to buy. And there the Congress passed the Northwest Ordinance, which went far to regularize the government of the territory under the central government. The Northwest Ordinance established, among other things, a bill of rights—a promise on the part of the old colonies to guarantee such common-law rights as trial by jury and freedom of religion to the new states—and also, such was the pressure in America already against slavery, to guarantee that there would be no slavery in these new states. In establishing this set of rules to govern the Northwest Territory, the ordinance also secured Cutler's investment.

When Cutler arrived in Philadelphia, then, his job was largely done—and his acres had been dealt out. He had secured his lands with a law that the men at Philadelphia were hardly likely to overturn. All Cutler needed to do was tactfully proselytize on behalf of a strong central government, one that would keep the promise that Congress had just given, and provide stability for his investors. Nearly everyone at the convention was passionately interested in this business of land. General Washington would die possessed of 41,000 acres of frontier lands. James Wilson was deeply, disastrously, in debt over western land speculations. It was investments in western lands that would finally send Robert Morris to debtors' prison.

The moment Cutler arrived in town, he went to the Indian Queen, where, after a cup of tea, a wash, and a sprucing up by the local barber, he sent a note in to Caleb Strong, from his home state of Massachusetts. Cutler had never met Strong, but Strong was an easily approachable man, without pretension, and he had evidently heard of the reverend. Strong invited Cutler at once into the chambers of the delegates, and introduced him to Strong's Massachusetts colleague Nathaniel Gorham (who was about to enter into partnership to purchase essentially all the lands in New York State from present-day Binghamton west), to Madison, to Mason and Mason's son who was there at the time, to Hugh Williamson of North Carolina, to Rutledge and Charles Pinckney and several others. "I spent the evening with these gentlemen," the ebullient Cutler wrote in his diary, "very agreeably" They stayed up until one-thirty in the morning, talking land and Massachusetts politics. And everyone evidently agreed that Cutler was a most charming fellow, a natural raconteur, and a man full of much fascinating information.

Early the next morning, Cutler and Strong took a stroll over to call on yet another delegate from Massachusetts, the businessman Elbridge Gerry. Gerry had rented a house on Spruce Street for the course of the convention, because he had brought his new wife, and their baby, to Philadelphia with him. "Few old bachelors," Cutler noted in his diary, ". . . have been more fortunate in matrimony than Mr. Gerry. His lady is young, very handsome, and exceedingly amiable . . . I should suppose her not more than 17, and believe he must be turned of 55. They have been married about eighteen months, and have a fine son [evidently Cutler didn't ask: it was a daughter] about two months old, of which they appear both to be extravagantly fond." He was surprised, said Cutler, "to find how early ladies in Philadelphia can rise in the morning, and to see them at breakfast at half after five, when in Boston they can hardly see a breakfast table at nine without falling into hysterics." He remarked on it to Mrs. Gerry, who replied crisply that she had always risen early and found it conducive to her health, and that it was "the practice of the best families in Philadelphia."

After breakfast, Cutler took a grand tour of the city, stopping here and there to drop off letters of introduction to various leading men of the city. He called on Dr. Rush and exchanged gossip about botany and then went on to Charles Willson Peale's, where he was escorted into a large room full of "curiosities." There, a Dr. Clarkson, who had accompanied Cutler, saw a man standing, pencil in hand, apparently making a sketch. Clarkson turned to Cutler: "Mr. Peale is very busy," said Clarkson, "taking the picture of something with his pencil. We will step back into the other room and wait till he is at leisure." Then, just as they entered the other room, they saw Peale coming toward them. Clarkson "started back in astonishment."

Mr. Peale, he said, "how is it possible you should get out of the other room to meet us here?"

Peale smiled. "I have not been in the other room for some time," he said.

"No!" said Clarkson. "Did I not see you there this moment, with your pencil and ivory?"

"Why, do you think you did?"

"Do I think I did? Yes. I saw you there if ever I saw you in my life."

"Well, let us go and see."

And of course, to the immense delight of Cutler, Peale revealed a wax statue of himself—and "I beheld two men, so perfectly alike that I could not discern the minutest difference."

Altogether Cutler had a wonderful day. He ended the afternoon, accompanied by Gerry, with a call on Dr. Franklin. "We found him," said Cutler, "in his Garden, sitting upon a grass plat under a very large Mulberry, with several other gentlemen and two or three ladies. There was no curiosity in Philadelphia which I felt so anxious to see as this great man, who has been the wonder of Europe as well as the glory of America." Cutler expected he would sit silently in awe of the great man, speak only when spoken to, answer questions put to him as though they were questions from a monarch. "But how were my ideas changed, when I saw a short, fat, trunched old man, in a plain Quaker dress, bald pate, and short white locks, sitting without his hat under the tree." Franklin rose to greet Cutler, "took me by the hand, expressed his joy to see me, welcomed me to the city, and begged me to sit myself close to him. His voice was low, but his countenance open, frank, and pleasing."

Although Franklin had no personal interest in land speculations, he was endlessly curious about the west, and about the ways of the world. The other men around the mulberry tree turned out to be delegates to the convention. The doctor brought out his extraordinary two-headed snake to show to Cutler and talked about its uniqueness—his theory was that it was a species all its own—and about the difficulty it would have if it were traveling among bushes and one head chose to go on one side of the stem of a bush and the other head chose to go on the other side, and the particular problem it would face if "neither of the heads would consent to come back or give way to the other." He was about to go on with a story that all this reminded him of—"to mention a humorous matter that had that day taken place in Convention"—when the other men present reminded him of the rule of secrecy, and he had to be silent. God alone knows just what Franklin was trying to say to Cutler—or whether Cutler understood what Franklin was saying to him—but a possibility does suggest itself.

If Franklin was speaking in a parable, as he so often did, he might have been saying this to Cutler: On the business of land investments, the convention—like the two-headed snake— had different thoughts. For some, an interest in land investments would be best served by a strong central government; others' interests would be best served by strong local governments. Clearly, if the snake was to get around the bush, some meeting of the minds needed to occur, some agreement to compromise. And to the extent that Cutler might urge any solution on the convention, it would be in his interest to urge this compromise.

The other men at Franklin's, said Cutler, were preoccupied with political talk, but the doctor wanted to talk philosophical matters, and so directed most of his conversation to

Cutler. "I was highly delighted with the extensive knowledge he appeared to have of every subject, the brightness of his memory, and clearness and vivacity of all his mental faculties . . . his manners are perfectly easy, and everything about him seems to diffuse an unrestrained freedom and happiness. He has an incessant vein of humor, accompanied with an uncommon vivacity, which seems as natural and involuntary as his breathing."

The next morning, Cutler was up before five o'clock and on his way out to the edge of town, where he met Strong, Colonel Mason and his son, Williamson, Madison, and Rutledge, among others, to take a tour of the famous Bartram's garden. Bartram's garden was one of the great wonders of eighteenth-century America. Planted originally by John Bartram, and cared for at the time Cutler passed through by John's son William, it contained hundreds of specimens of trees, shrubs, flowers, and plants of all sorts—magnolias and tulip trees, catalpas, sassafras, laurels, wild grapevines, and all kinds of treasures utterly unknown to European visitors.

The gentlemen found Bartram hoeing in his garden, "in a short jacket and trowsers, and without shoes or stockings. He at first stared at us, and seemed to be somewhat embarrassed at seeing so large and gay a company so early in the morning." But Cutler put him at east with a flow of botanical talk, and soon enough Bartram was giving the visitors a guided tour of his rarest specimens.

From Bartram's garden, Cutler went on to an inn, to a tour of the hospital, to the library at Carpenters' Hall, to the State House—and everywhere he went he recorded his pleasure, his curiosity about the novelties he saw, the beautiful views, the handsome buildings, the graciousness of his hosts. Finally, when it came time for him to get back to New York to make certain that the Congress had completed its work without a hitch, and he returned to the Indian Queen to pack his bags and say farewell to Gorham and Mason and Williamson and the others, Gorham expressed his sorrow that Cutler was leaving and said "he could not conceive how I came to be in so great demand in Philadelphia, as I had never been there before, for that there had not been ten minutes in the day but somebody was inquiring for me, or letters or packets were left."

And so Cutler swept back out of town, having left, so far as we know, no shares of acres behind, but (if he did what Franklin might conceivably have been urging him to do) having spread the notion that there was money to be made if only the men in Philadelphia would finish the work of establishing a strong, stable central government—by way of a suitable compromise.

16

THE GREAT COMPROMISE

WHEN THE CONVENTION gathered again on the morning of July 5, Madison had already heard rumors of the work the committee had done over the recess and he was not happy about it. In fact, it was garrulous old Dr. Franklin—so underestimated by so many of the younger delegates—who had done the dirty work. Usually as quiet in a committee room as he was in the convention, Franklin was nonetheless—as founder of the American Philosophical Society, as a member of the committee that wrote the Declaration of Independence, as ambassador to France, where he got millions from King Louis XVI to support a republican revolution, as president of the Pennsylvania Executive Council—not inept when it came to politicking. Not for nothing had the French called him a crafty old chameleon. And it was he who had come up with the wording of a compromise proposal that the committee had accepted.

The committee submitted Franklin's words to the full convention: Let the house be based on proportional representation, with one member for every forty thousand inhabitants; and let the senate have one vote per state; to sweeten the deal, let the house have sole control of all money bills, without giving the senate the power even to alter or amend them.

Madison was disgusted. Not only was the very idea of compromise objectionable to him, but this particular compromise struck him as absurd. Giving the house control of money bills was a worthless provision, he said. Such a provision did

200

not mean that the house would control the purse strings. Both bodies would still need to pass on other measures of legislation, and the senate would simply veto an endless string of bills—until the house made money bills to conform to the senate's wishes. What, then, did such a provision accomplish?

So, said Madison, the committee had done nothing. Its members simply offered the convention the same dilemma it had had before the holiday, of satisfying either the centrists or the localists. For his part, he would not hesitate to choose his side. In truth, he would be happy to see the small states go their way. The large states would join together, and he was confident that in the future, "by degrees," the small states would come along to join the Union.

Gouverneur Morris joined ranks with Madison. He had come to the convention, he said pointedly to the localists, not as the representative of some narrow state interests; he had come, he thought, as a representative of America; truly, "he flattered himself he came here in some degree as a Representative of the whole human race." Now, what would be the consequences, he asked, if the small states clung to their ideas of local power and the large states were forced to make a union on their own? The small states would probably form together in a group too; and there would be "noise" and dissension. The two sides would inevitably resort to "the sword" to settle their differences.

"The scenes of horror attending civil commotion can not be described, and the conclusion of them will be worse than the term of their continuance. The stronger party will then make traitors of the weaker; and the Gallows and Halter will finish the work of the sword. How far foreign powers would be ready to take part in the confusions he would not say." These possibilities of strife were inherent in the localists position; what stubbornness kept them from seeing the logical conclusion to the position they took?

Colonel Mason was upset by these immediate threats from Madison and Morris. The colonel had served on the committee over the Fourth of July, and as the major author of the first written constitution of modern times and of its bill of rights, he was not accustomed to having his best efforts simply ignored. Although the report of the committee might be liable to some objections, said Mason, "he thought it preferable to an appeal to the world by the different sides." He was not prepared to sit back and watch the whole country be torn apart. If these men could not resolve this conflict, who ever would? He was obliged to say that it could "not be more inconvenient to any gentleman to remain absent from his private affairs than it was for him; but he would bury his bones in this city rather than expose his Country to the Consequences of a dissolution of the Convention without anything being done."

During the next several days, the atmosphere in the convention would not improve. The debates would spill out of the sweltering convention hall and—as more committees were appointed to work out compromises to the compromises—into sweltering committee rooms and then into the private and public rooms of the city's taverns.

On the evening of July 6, General Washington attended a dinner of a number of convention delegates at City Tavern, which was several blocks from the Indian Queen and down toward the river. No doubt Washington conferred with his colleagues on convention strategy; and no doubt the Virginia contingent was no longer as jaunty as it had been even a few days before. The most extreme localists were not carrying the convention, but neither were the Madisonians, and Washington was slipping toward one of the deepest glooms of his career. Hamilton had gone back to New York in a funk, thoroughly undone because Lansing and Yates always outvoted him in the New York delegation. Washington wrote him there: "I *almost* despair [Washington's italics] of seeing a favorably issue to the proceedings of our Convention, and do therefore repent having had any agency in the business."

And then, in this atmosphere of confusion, ragged tempers, heat, and despair, Gouverneur Morris, whose self-confidence always seemed to sustain him, took charge of the debate on behalf of the men of order and proposed several fresh ideas.

Morris had taken some time to warm to this task of framing a constitution, but he had hit his stride by now. It had taken Madison to draft a plan, but once an outline existed, Morris proved himself a dazzling commentator. Altogether, before the convention was finished, Gouverneur Morris would take the floor 173 times, more than any other member. "He does not allow the conversation to flag," a Dutchman once said of him.

Pacing the convention hall dramatically, his six-foot frame drawn up to a princely bearing, his head held high, his peg leg resounding against the bare wooden floor, a sarcastic remark about to roll off his protruding lower lip at any moment, he struck on one passage after another, coming at the constitution from a dozen different directions. No one knew where he might pounce next. "He is very callous," it was said of him, "and prides himself on being so; but he is vain, and unaware of it."

At first Morris's ideas would seem to be a digression that led the convention on a long, elaborate detour. But in the end that detour would bring the delegates to the compromise they found so elusive.

Morris started by tossing aside all the arguments Madison and Wilson had been painstakingly building for weeks. It was absurd, he said in his expansive, high-handed way, in all this talk of proportional representation, to think of basing representation on numbers of people. In fact, said Morris, correctly conceived, representation ought rather to be based on wealth. To be sure, he said dismissively, "life and liberty were generally said to be of more value than property." But really, "an accurate view of the matter would nevertheless prove that property was the main object of Society."

The "savage" state, Morris declaimed with lofty perspective, was more favorable to liberty than the civilized society, and "it was preferred by all men who had not acquired a taste for property." The savage state with all its glorification of liberty was only renounced by men for the higher goal of attaining property, "which could only be secured by the restraints of regular Government." Voting ought to be apportioned according to property.

Had the delegates thought, Morris went on, recalling a point Madison had made earlier, what would happen when the time came that the lands to the west were settled and new states carved out; when these new states would have thousands and thousands of voters—rude frontiersmen all—able to outvote the original colonies?

If one apportioned representatives on the basis of population, the time might come soon when the west would have a big influence in the new government. Surely the men of the eastern seaboard did not relish such a prospect. And surely, Morris assumed, they would not simply give their power away to people they didn't know and couldn't trust, to legislate they knew ot what laws—put the preponderant political power of the country into the hands of a lot of rude frontiersmen and other western rabble, men without property, background, commercial or social ties to bind them to the interests of the east. But it would not be easy to avoid such a nightmare if one gave the west its fair share of the vote based on population.

Fortunately, there was a way to avoid this dreadful possibility. The eastern states were more developed than the west, and were likely to remain so for some time to come; if legislators were apportioned according to wealth, the east would naturally dominate the west (and by the time the west was developed, it, too, would be populated by a social class with interests similar to the people of the east coast).

Morris's ruminations cut across the old lines of debate and rearranged some alliances in an instant. All the unsolvable conflicts—those between north and south, east and west, even big and little, centrist and localist—would be dissolved in a single common interest: property.

Rufus King, whose mind, sharp as it was, was not as nimble as Gouverneur Morris's, was able, nonetheless, to follow along behind Morris and do some practical calculating. Congress had already laid out the Northwest Territory into five states, and specified that as soon as any new state had a population equal to the population of the smallest of the thirteen original states, that new state could claim admission to the Union. Delaware had a population of only 35,000. If the southwestern territories were also to become states very soon, then in a short time, as King did his arithmetic, ten new states could be added to the Union, ten new votes in the senate—representing no more population than the population of Pennsylvania—giving the west control of the senate and, if their population increased quickly, ultimately giving the west control of the house as well.

Morris had panicked delegates sufficiently that they appointed a committee at once to look into his proposal. The committee was composed of Gouverneur Morris, John Rutledge, and Edmund Randolph, and of Rufus King and Nathanial Gorham from Massachusetts.

The committee members returned in just a couple of days with their report. The house, they said, should consist initially of fifty-six members, of which New Hampshire should have two, Massachusetts seven, Rhode Island one, Connecticut four, New York five, New Jersey three, Pennsylvania eight, Delaware one, Maryland four, Virginia nine, North Carolina five, South Carolina five, and Georgia two. Such an apportionment gave official recognition to the relative strength of the states as they seemed to be at the moment. And the legislature should have the power to alter the number of its members from time to time—so that those who held the power would ever after determine how that power was to be redistributed, or not. (There was not much sense of principle in this, or even much sense of a systematic attempt to base representation on either population or wealth: The committee had gone right to the heart of the matter and begun to haggle over relative power, leaving it to others to find rationalizations for their numbers.)

No doubt the delegates all started in on their arithmetic. With representatives allocated in this manner, the northern states would have thirty-one votes, the southern states twenty-five—not an objectionable ratio, depending on how north was divided from the south. The small states, if North Carolina was counted among them, had twenty-two, or slightly more than a third—which could be significant in any votes requiring a two-thirds majority. Wealth had been taken into account in some vague fashion—at least the "wealth" that the south possessed in its slaves. The numbers of the south's representatives were determined by reference to the total population of whites and three-fifths of blacks. And since it was left to the legislature to decide when and by how much to add new members, the east held sway over the west. It was an interesting proposal.

A number of the delegates made some throat-clearing speeches, and then Paterson expressed what must have been on everyone's mind. This business of taking both population and wealth into consideration, he said, was very vague. It was not clear just what advantage certain northern states were given on the basis of some theoretical wealth, but as far as the southern states were concerned, they clearly picked up some advantage in the arrangement, for the basis of calculating wealth was odd in the extreme. The committee had evidently counted slaves into the balance as representing southern property. And so, presumably, a man of Virginia had his vote augmented to the extent that he owned slaves. A touch of cynicism pervaded the scheme. It seemed odd to Paterson that slaves were thus somehow represented in the national government when they were not represented in the states to which they belonged.

Other men of the northeast were troubled in another way. If the country was not divided simply into north and south, but rather into northeast, midatlantic, and deep south, then the states of the northeast had only fourteen votes, while the deep south had twenty-one, which seemed greatly out of balance.

Altogether, it was agreed, the report of the committee of five was imperfect. And so the convention appointed another committee, a committee of eleven, to go over again this business of the number of representatives to be allotted to each state.

The committee of eleven took just one evening to work up their report, and they presented it the next day to the full convention. The revised plan called for a house of sixty-five members. None of the committee members had budged much from their previous positions. One more representative had been given to New Hampshire, one more to Massachusetts, one to Connecticut, one to New York, one to New Jersey, two to Maryland, one to Virginia, and one to Georgia. In this way, the four northeastern states picked up three votes, the four southern states two. If the country was divided into northeast, midatlantic, and deep south, the northeast had seventeen votes, the deep south twenty-three.

It was hardly a dramatic shift, but Rutledge took to whittling away at the north immediately. He moved that New Hampshire be reduced by one vote; it was neither populous nor rich and was not entitled to more than two representatives. General Pinckney seconded the motion.

Rufus King replied in prickly defense of the committee report. Whereas a strict north/south division of the country might seem to give a preponderance to the north, the delegates could see that the four states of the northeast, with 800,000 population, had almost one-third fewer representatives than the four southern states, which had only 700,000 population (in fact, the population of the south was almost 950,000 whites and more than 500,000 blacks). The southern states deserved no more representatives than they had.

General Pinckney did not see it quite the same way. If the regulation of trade, for instance, was to be given to the general government, then the four southernmost states would be at the absolute mercy of the midatlantic and northern states, who could outvote the south at will: The wealth of the south would be in the hands of the north, to manipulate by way of trade laws. The southerners would be reduced to mere suppliers of tobacco and rice, mere overseers of plantations, whose business was determined entirely by trade laws written by northerners.

And then Colonel Mason suddenly tore into the whole arrangement that was being based on Morris's nortions. Mason had evidently been bothered from the beginning by this talk of establishing some permanent way for these men who framed the government to ensure that their kind would continue to control it. And now he turned on the idea. According to the committee report, Mason noted, reapportionment in the future would be left to the legislature. In that case, what if, in the future, population shifted so that instead of a majority in the north there would be a majority in the south? Would the legislators of the north voluntarily vote to give away power by increasing the number of southern legislators? Of course not. No more than the easterners as a whole thought they would give up power to the west.

"From the nature of man we may be sure that those who have power in their hands will not give it up while they can retain it. On the contrary we know they will always when they can rather increase it." So what would happen? Say, for the sake of argument, that one-fourth would govern three-fourths. What would the three-fourths do? They would complain. And "they may complain from generation to generation without redress." Was this the way to constitute a government?

The provision was presumably put in so that the east could forever dominate the west. But did that make sense, either?

Would the west complain less than anyone else if they were not given just representation? Indeed, would they even apply to join the Union under such unjust conditions? No, said Mason, if western states were to be brought into the Union at all, "they must . . . be treated as equals, and subjected to no degrading discriminations. They will have the same pride and passions which we have, and will either not unite with or will speedily revolt from the Union, if they are not in all respects placed on an equal footing with their brethren."

Both Hugh Williamson of North Carolina and Randolph of Virginia agreed with Mason: A census must be taken periodically, and the numbers of legislators revised according to a simple mathematical formula, so that nothing was left to the discretion of future legislators.

In that case, said General Pinckney swiftly, he would have to insist that blacks be counted equally with whites in determining population.

Wealth, said the slave-owning Pierce Butler of South Carolina, coyly backing up the general, was produced by the labor of people. And people produced equal amounts of wealth whether they were black or white. Since wealth "was the great means of defence and utility to the Nation," then slaves must be considered "equally valuable to it with freemen." Therefore, it followed that "an equal representation ought to be allowed for them in a Government which was instituted principally for the protection of property, and was itself to be supported by property."

Now Gouverneur Morris was exercised. His proposal, deftly taken up by the southerners, had been completely twisted into a device to give undue power to the south. If the southerners, said Morris, were to insist that blacks be counted as whole men for an estimation of wealth, the people of Pennsylvania would simply revolt: They would not for a minute tolerate "being put on a footing with slaves."

At the same time, he must take exception to Mr. Mason's remarks about doing justice to the western states. Westerners would certainly "not be able to furnish men equally enlightened to share in the administration of our common interests. The Busy haunts of men—not the remote wilderness— was the proper School of political Talents. If the Western people get the power into their hands they will ruin the Atlantic interests." As for the objection to leaving the legislature to determine its membership in the future, surely "their duty, their honor, and their oaths" would ensure that they would do the right thing, and adjust their membership in a just fashion.

Madison was surprised, he said, twitting Morris, to hear such an expression of confidence in the honor of men coming from a member who on all previous occasions had argued so strongly about the fundamental "political depravity of men."

But, said Madison, Gouverneur Morris's reasoning "was not only inconsistent with his former reasoning, but with itself." At the very same time Morris urged his southern colleagues to have confidence in the future goodwill of the northerners, "he was still more zealous in exhorting all to a jealously of a Western majority. To reconcile the gentleman with himself, it must be imagined that he determined the human character by the points of the compass."

The truth, said Madison, "was that all men having power ought to be distrusted to a certain degree"—men of the future as much as men of the present and past, easterners as much as westerners. The numbers of representatives ought not to be left to legislators of the future, but permanently fixed by some fair rule in the constitution. And "with regard to the Western States, he was clear and firm in the opinion that no unfavorable distinctions were admissible either in point of justice or policy": No area of the country could justly or as a practical matter be allowed to dominate another, just as, for the security of all, no group or faction or set of interests could be allowed to dominate the whole country. The numbers of representatives, said Madison, ought to be fixed by population.

As Wilson listened to the debate, a solution to the impasse finally became clear to him. Evidently, he said, the delegates had the grounds for a compromise right under their noses if they would simply tie together three elements that had emerged in the debate but had not yet been linked—namely, representation, population, and—the issue Morris had raised—wealth, or, as Wilson preferred to redefine it, taxation.

If taxation was placed in the formula instead of wealth, a very interesting set of possibilities emerged. It was a matter of longstanding tradition that taxation and representation ought to go together. Indeed, that had been one of the great rallying cries of the Revolution. Let them go together in this instance— let representation be based on taxation, and let taxation be based on population. Thus, for example, the south could count their slaves as part of their population, pay higher taxes, and have more votes in the legislature. But the votes would be based on taxation, not on slave population directly.

Yes indeed, said General Pinckney, this was a possible formula. And the south would be happy to pay higher taxes in order to have more votes. However, if it was to be the constitutional formula for voting, then the south would want the recognition of slaves to be specifically written into the constitution, as part of the southern basis of representation, so that the south need not fear that a legislature would eliminate slaves in computing representation in the future. The property in slaves, said General Pinckney to the delegates who had just been extolling the merits of wealth, "should not be exposed to danger under a Government instituted for the protection of property."

With that, Wilson's patience snapped at last. The most preposterous and monstrous "principles" were being advanced to defend mere interests. The notion that the ownership of slaves was somehow justified by appeal to the sanctity of property was more than Wilson could any longer bear. He could not agree, said Wilson, that simple greed, in the form of the wish to own property, much less property in slaves, could be elevated to the status of a moral right or made the very goal of politics. The ownership of property might be a fact of human society, it might be an understandable human appetite, it might even be seen as an expedient foundation in certain instances for political liberty; but it was hardly the proper end, "the sole or the primary object of government and society." Such an idea was far too reductive. On the contrary, politics, the art and science of government, ought in the end to be put in the service of some aspiration more worthy of a life on earth; in Wilson's own view, "the most noble object" of human endeavor, the only true object of society, was "the cultivation of the human mind"—and the delegates ought to turn their attention to framing a government that would serve that end.

As for matters of designing a workable basis for representation, Wilson left the moral plane and return to his down-to-earth thought on linking representation and taxation. He thought, Wilson said, that "less umbrage" would be taken by northerners on the whole issue if the rule of representation "should be so expressed as to make [slaves] indirectly only an ingredient in the rule, by saying that they should enter into the rule of taxation: and as representation was to be according to taxation, the end would be equally attained."

With that, indeed, all sorts of issues were rearranged, all sorts of interests protected, and all sorts of appearances saved. The southerners could count their slaves without having to say whether their were people or property. The northerners need not worry over the issue of whether slaves were identified as people or property. The south would have a large share of votes, but they would pay for that share. The large states would be made to pay, as the south was, for their larger voting power. The east dominated the government at first but not forever. Under Wilson's proposal, a census was to be taken periodically; both taxation and representation would be based on the results of that census; and blacks would be counted in on the three-fifths ratio.

This was the moment on which the whole convention turned. The delegates flocked to Wilson's proposal. It was an enormous success. In truth, as he discovered in a matter of moments, it was a greater success than Wilson even quiet hoped, or wanted. For not only did the delegates accept this basis for voting, but the Shermanites came back in a surprise move to tack onto Wilson's idea their old proposal for a senate that equally represented the states, and so make—by way of this intricate combination of desires—a great compromise that would settle, in one grand provision, all the most crucial issues that had been tormenting the convention. Suddenly the delegates were presented with a remarkable conjunction of issues, and a potent one. This was the constellation of issues for which the convention had been searching.

With Wilson's proposal slotted in, a Sherman's idea for the senate put with it, the delegates now had before them a motion that, in its entirety, contained these specifics: that votes would be apportioned in the house according to direct taxation, that direct taxation was to be based on population, that population was to be based on all numbers of free citizens and three-fifths of blacks; that the states were to have equal votes in the senate; and that the house would have sole control of money bills. It was a stunning gathering up of interests, and it was brought at once before the convention for a vote on July 16.

On this, which would come in retrospect to be called the Great Compromise, the voting blocs split—disintegrated is really the word. Massachusetts divided—Elbridge Gerry and Caleb Strong voted in favor of the compromise; King and Gorham stayed with the Madisonians and voted against it. Connecticut voted for the compromise, as did New Jersey, Delaware, Maryland, and North Carolina. Madison's Virginia voted against it, as did Wilson's and Morris's Pennsylvania (thinking in part of the interests of the large states, in part of the embarrassment over the issue of the blacks). South Carolina—with some of its delegates siding with Madison, and some still wanting blacks to be counted whole—voted against it. In the end, however, the Great Compromise was approved by the exceedingly narrow margin of five in favor, four against, and one divided. From this narrowly approved compromise all else would very quickly follow; around it, all provisions would be fitted into place: Both the centrists and the localists would be given their due in the new government.

Edmund Randolph, the man who had proposed the Virginia Plan so many weeks before, took the floor to try to stop the stampede that gave the localists their provision on the senate. He was not at all pleased, he let his colleagues know. This vote that had just been taken, said Randolph, had "embarrassed the business" most extremely. He had actually come to the convention that morning with some propositions to make that might have been reassuring to the localists, but he saw now that they were determined in their course, wrong as it was. Under the circumstances, he thought it might be best for the convention to adjourn, to enable the Madisonians to consider "the steps proper to be taken in the present solemn crisis of the business, and the small states might also deliberate on the means of conciliation."

To adjourn? Indeed, said Paterson in his best high-handed manner, he thought it was "high time for the Convention to adjourn." And not only should the convention adjourn; it ought also to rescind "the rule of secrecy" so that "our Constituents" might be "consulted"—that is to say, so that Paterson could tell the world just how unprincipled these Madisonians were: When they had finally lost a vote, they said they quit.

General Pinckney, his sense of easy joviality gone, was alarmed. He wished to know, said the general, whether Mr. Randolph meant to call for a permanent adjournment—that is, an adjournment *"sine die,* or only an adjournment for the day." If Randolph meant to adjourn for more than a day, then the general must inform his colleagues that he would be returning at once to South Carolina, and that he would not return. In short, as far as he was concerned, the convention would be over.

Randolph was shocked. He had never meant to propose an adjournment *sine die,* he said, and was sorry that his meaning had been "so readily and strangely misinterpreted." He had in view, he said temperately, merely an adjournment "till tomorrow, in order that some conciliatory experiment might if possible be devised, and that in case the smaller States should continue to hold back, the larger might then take such measures, he would not say what, as might be necessary."

Paterson peremptorily seconded the motion for adjournment until the next day—"as an opportunity seemed to be wished by the larger States to deliberate further on conciliatory expedients." The small states, that is to say, would have nothing more to consider in the way of conciliatory expedients.

A vote was taken. The convention, obviously confused, divided exactly in half on the question whether to adjourn until the next day. Anxiety shot through the delegates again: Did half the delegations really mean they wished to terminate the convention forever?

Jacob Broom of Delaware, who had said almost nothing in the course of the convention, now appealed to his fellow delegates. He thought it his duty, he said, "to declare his opinion against an adjournment *sine die.* "Such a measure he thought would be fatal."

At last, grudgingly, Elbridge Gerry rose to admit that he had voted against adjournment until the next day, because he saw no new ground for conciliation. Nonetheless, "as it seemed to be the opinion of so many States that a trial should be made, [Massachusetts] would now concur" in an adjournment for a day.

In the end, John Rutledge's voice was heard. At first he had seen no need for adjournment, Rutledge said, because he saw no chance of compromise. The localists were fixed in their position. They had "repeatedly and solemnly declared themselves to be so." And the centrists were equally fixed in their position. Nonetheless, said Rutledge—and one could almost feel the ground shift as Rutledge hesitated, about to throw his weight over to the side of compromise, to desert Madison, to close the deal on this great piece of bargaining—for his own part, he conceived "that although we could not do what we thought best in itself, we ought to do something."

With that, no doubt with considerable excitement spreading among the delegates, the convention was adjourned until the following day. That night at the Indian Queen and at City Tavern, in parlors and rooming houses all over town, the politicking must have been furious. The results of it would show the next morning.

In the morning, at the State House, a group of the centrists gathered in caucus to sort out just how to respond to this latest, perhaps conclusive, development in the convention. Oddly enough, someone, probably Wilson, subverted the meeting before it had even begun—by inviting a few of the localists to sit in as observers. Madison understood the implications of that invitation at once: The localists would see that the centrists were divided, and so, destined to be defeated. Why Wilson would have done such a thing, if indeed it was Wilson who did it—whether he did it mistakenly, without thought, or consciously, to subvert Madison's stubborn refusal to give in—is impossible to know. The effect of the invitation, however, was quite clear.

Some of the centrists thought the demands of the localists were not so pernicious; others thought it more important to have some constitution rather than none at all. In any case, it was evident to the observers present that the centrists were no longer able to come up with a common strategy. The presence of the localists, as Madison had seen at once, was the death kneel for the centrist coalition. All the rest was merely "vague conversation." At that moment, Madison gave up and accepted the Great Compromise, and the contradictory impulses of the men of order and the men of liberty became forever linked together in the constitution.

PART IV

PART IV

17

THE PRESIDENT

With the acceptance of the Great Compromise, nearly every-thing else—at least in broad outline—began to fall quickly into place. As though to signal the end of weeks of wrangling and frayed tempers, the hot weather broke, and a cool breeze wafted through the windows of the State House. The local-power men, feeling protected by the senate, became wonderfully agreea-ble—and as Madison sat back morosely, they rushed forward to grant large powers to the new central government. Indeed, some of them began to propose measures that went beyond the ideas of the centrists. Gunning Bedford, who had been such an obstinate opponent of the Madisonians, proposed now, with the convert's zeal, that the national legislature be granted enormous, unencumbered powers: "to legislate in all cases for the general interests of the Union, and also in those to which the States are separately incompetent." Gouverneur Morris, perhaps scarcely able to believe his ears, quickly seconded the motion, and the delegates easily voted the provision into place.

All the great questions, it seemed, had been settled; and nothing remained but to make the matters of detail conform to the grand plan. But of course, some of these little details were awfully nettlesome. As soon as the issue of the presidency was raised again, for instance, the delegates fell into a swamp of confusion.

The Virginia Plan had called for an executive elected by the national legislature. It was a good plan, a parliamentary plan, and when the delegates had first considered it, it seemed an excellent way to keep the president from becoming too monarchical. On reconsideration, however, the plan did leave open the possibility that the executive would be rendered too dependent on the legislature—and therefore so weak as not to be an effective check against the threat of legislative tyranny.

How, the delegates wondered, could the president be made independent if he was appointed by the legislature? One could appoint him for a long term, of course, so that he would in time grow independent of the legislators who had appointed him—but then he might grow to be a virtual king. Or one could forget this election by the legislature and have him elected by the people—but if he was elected by a majority of the people, that would give the advantage to the large states again, and to the north. He could certainly not be appointed by the state legislators, since that would throw power back to the states again. If he was appointed by electors specially chosen for the purpose, who then would elect the electors? But if he could not be chosen for life, and could not be chosen by the legislature, or by the people, or by the states, or by electors, how was he to be created at all? It was into this confusion that the delegates now fell amidst a blizzard of proposals.

And what of the possibility of reelection? Would that make a president behave better—in the hope of being rewarded—or make him even more subservient to the legislature, or the states, or whoever was given the power to reelect him? And if he was not eligible for reelection, would that make him more honest, or simply more determined to exploit his position quickly, while he enjoyed it?

Gouverneur Morris, no friend of democracy, had a surprising proposition: The executive must be elected by the people at large. If he was elected by the legislature, "it will be the work of intrigue, of cabal, and of faction: it will be"—Morris reaching for the most horrible comparison he could conceive—"like the election of a pope by a conclave of cardinals."

Colonel Mason, friend of the people, was equally surprising: "It would be as unnatural to refer the choice of a proper character for chief Magistrate to the people, as it would to refer a trial of colours to a blind man." What the colonel had in mind was that the people were to distant from one another to

know the qualities of a man from a different locale well enough
to judge him intelligently.

A popular election, Elbridge Gerry joined in, was "radically vicious. The ignorance of the people would put it in the
power of some one set of men dispersed through the Union and
acting in Concert to delude them into any appointment." (What
Gerry had in mind was that a popular election would fall into
the manipulative hands of the Society of the Cincinnati.)

The danger of "cabal" worried all the delegates—the
thought that a small group would get together to promote a
candidate, tie that candidate to their personal interests, drum
up such support for him as to overwhelm any opposition, and
so thwart the republican system altogether by putting it in the
service of this little group. They worried that such a cabal might
be formed among members of the national legislature, if the
legislature elects the executive; or among special electors, if
they had a chance to meet together and scheme before they
voted; or among the executives of the state governments, who
might become a group of professional politicians who would
always dictate their choice to the country. They knew of political parties, of course: Parties, or "factions," existed in England—and the Americans despised them as vehicles of special
interest that frustrated the will of the people. The delegates to
the convention were determined to design a system that could
function without parties, that would be available directly to
citizens, without any such intervening and distorting mechanism. They were determined, too, to make sure that the president not become the captive of a military establishment such
as the Cincinnati, or of a cabal of businessmen or some other
group of the rich or powerful. (They never dreamed of the pernicious effects of the cost of election campaigns in the twentieth century, and the way candidates would be made dependent on groups of contributors, who constitute a peculiarly
modern form of faction or cabal.)

To avoid the evil designs of cabals, some thought there
was no way to avoid appointment by the national legislature.
Then, if the executive was given a long term in office, and was
not eligible for reelection, he would be sufficiently independent.

But, said Gouverneur Morris, if the executive was not eligible for reelection, that would destroy "the great motive to good behavior, the hope of being rewarded by a re-appointment. It was saying to him, make hay while the sun shines."

To get around that objection, the executive might be made eligible for reelection, but given a shorter term—although in that case, the executive would be dependent forever on the legislature.

The delegates sank into more complexities: If one didn't want an executive dependent on the legislature, then was it right for the delegates to provide for the impeachment of the president? Would he not be the pawn of the legislature if he had always to fear impeachment?

(On the other hand, if he was not subject to impeachment, would he not resort to any means whatever "to get himself reelected?")

Gouverneur Morris had a way around these objections. If the executive's term was short, he would be out of office soon enough in any case; and then, if he was not reelected, that would be his impeachment.

Gerry was shocked to hear such a sentiment. A good magistrate will not fear the prospect of impeachment, said Gerry; a bad one ought to be kept in fear. He hoped, he said, "the maxim would never be adopted here that the chief Magistrate can do no wrong."

"Guilt," Randolph chimed in, "wherever found, ought to be punished. The Executive will have great opportunities of abusing his power; particularly in time of war when the military force, and in some respects the public money, will be in his hands. Should no regular punishment be provided, it will be irregularly inflicted by tumults and insurrections."

History, said Dr. Franklin, echoing the other two, argued for the practice of impeachment. "What was the practice before this in cases where the chief Magistrate rendered himself obnoxious? Why recourse was had to assassination, in which he was not only deprived of his life but of the opportunity of vindicating his character. It would be the best way therefore to provide in the Constitution for the regular punishment of the Executive when his misconduct should deserve it, and for his honorable acquittal when he should be unjustly accused."

"No point," concluded Colonel Mason firmly, "is of more importance than that the right of impeachment should be continued. Shall any man be above Justice? Above all shall that man be above it who can commit the most extensive injustice?"

Gouverneur Morris, repentant, rose to declare that his mind had been changed by the debate. He was not "sensible of the necessity of impeachments."

And so the delegates turned back to the means of electing this impeachable president. One of the difficulties with a popular election, said Madison, was that it favored the northern states over the southern, because slaves of the southern states could not vote. The device of electors might obviate this difficulty—since the apportionment of electors could be weighted, just as the apportionment of the house of representatives was, to give greater influence to the south.

The delegates chased this idea of electors around for a while. They considered how the electors might be apportioned, and whether they ought to be elected by the state legislatures—to give some weight, again, to the individual states. When the centrists objected to that, it was then proposed that the electors be chosen by the national legislature—and so the delegates had come full circle to the difficulty of having the national legislature pick the president.

Thus it was proposed, again, to make the president ineligible for reelection, so that he wouldn't be dependent on the national legislature for reelection—and thus it was objected, again, that if the president was not eligible for reelection, he would have no reward for good behavior.

So in desperation, the delegates proposed that the president be appointed by the national legislature but, to make him independent, serve for a term of ten years. Luther Martin suggested eleven years. Elbridge Gerry suggested fifteen years. Rufus King suggested—sarcastically—twenty years. Such, said King in exasperation, "is the medium life of princes."

Having circled all the way to the beginning, the delegates were stumped. For his part, said Mason, as he looked over the progress of the debate, he was led to conclude that an election by the national legislature, as originally proposed, was the best.

"If it was liable to objections it was liable to fewer than any other." He did think, though, that the president ought to be ineligible for a second term. The great officers of the state, said Mason, and particularly the chief magistrate, "should at fixed periods return to that mass from which they were at first taken, in order that they may feel and respect those rights and interests, which are again to be personally valuable to them." The Virginia constitution had a chief executive elected by the legislature, and dependent on it, and not eligible for reelection for four years—so that he was returned to private life to see how it was.

Dr. Franklin concurred: it was imagined by some people, said Franklin, that returning a magistrate to the people somehow degraded him. This, the doctor said, "was contrary to republican principles. In free governments the rulers are the servants, and the people their superiors and sovereigns. For the former therefore to return among the latter was not to *degrade* but to *promote* them—and it would be imposing an unreasonable burden on them to keep them always in a State of servitude and not allow them to become again one of the Masters.

On that note, the convention agreed to have an executive chosen by the legislature, for a term of seven years, to be ineligible for reelection, and to be impeachable for simple malpractice or neglect of duty. Few of the delegates were entirely happy with this arrangement, and they had not heard the end of it. But once again, the wisdom of the convention was to have a chief executive similar to a prime minister in a parliamentary system, an instrument of the legislature, very limited in powers, and easy to get rid of—on grand head of state able to claim special powers and privileges, no one who would be too easy a prey to some cabal or other.

This completed the delegates' debate on the newly accepted, compromised Virginia Plan. Now, as they all knew, the compromise plan would have to be gone over and fleshed out in detail—to have all the powers of the legislature and executive spelled out, all the qualifications for office rationalized, and a myriad of other small points resolved. Such work was too nitpicking for the convention to thrash out as a whole, and so they appointed a Committee of Detail, composed of John Rutledge, Edmund Randolph, Nathaniel Gorham, Oliver Ellsworth, and James Wilson. And for the next two weeks, while the Committee of Detail met every day to draw up a final, detailed constitution to present to the convention, some of the other delegates set out on an expedition toward Valley Forge to go fishing.

18

✢

DETAILS

THE COMMITTEE OF DETAIL met daily—at the State House, and
probably in James Wilson's study too, and over at the Indian
Queen. Rutledge was the chairman, and he took advantage of
his position by opening the proceedings with readings from
portions of some of his favorite documents. Rutledge had always admired the Iroquois Indians, particularly their legal
system, which gave autonomy to each of the six Iroquois nations for their internal affairs but united them for purposes of
war. The first text Rutledge read was taken from a piece of
parchment that was a replica of the Iroquois Treaty of 1520,
which began: "We, the people, to form a union, to establish
peace, equity and order . . ." He commended the phrasings to
his colleagues—and so, in some part, the preamble to the new
constitution was based on the law of the land as it had been
on the east coast before the first white settlers arrived.

Little is known of the proceedings of the Committee of Detail. No record of their conversations was kept; and all that
survives from which to piece together a notion of how they did
their business is several drafts of the constitution as they now
wrote it up. First there is a draft in the hand of Edmund Randolph, on which are a set of corrections in the hand of John
Rutledge. Then there is another draft, this one in the hand of
James Wilson—and once again corrections in the hand of Rutledge.

They worked efficiently. The outlines of the constitution

226

had been settled by the convention as a whole, and the Committee of Detail evidently spent little or no time debating those issues again. They fleshed out the broad principles in large part by picking and choosing appropriate passages from familiar documents. The Articles of Confederation provided most of the wording for the new constitution, followed by the state constitutions and, to a far lesser extent, the New Jersey Plan, and even Charles Pinckney's plan.

This was, once again, the sort of atmosphere that was congenial to Rutledge. Usually he knew what someone was going to say before the other finished speaking, and his interruptions earned him a reputation for rudeness; but then he could be so quick-witted and ingratiating and cheerful to talk to that he was usually forgiven. He was the consummate committee man, able to shape a conversation without anyone quite noticing that he was doing it—and reserving for himself, with the merest flick of a small correction, the last word. He was no good, in any case, at writing out the first words: In all his years in politics, he rarely wrote a complete sentence. When he did, he showed a poor grasp of grammar.

In some instances, Randolph's first draft went into considerable detail in its provisions; in other instances, he simply indicated what sort of provision was required in a certain place and left it to other committee members to help him fill in the particulars. And occasionally he would jot down a reminder to himself and his colleagues about just what sort of work they were about—such as the note that two things must be kept in mind at this stage of the work: "1. To insert essential principles only, lest the operations of government should be clogged by rendering those provisions permanent and unalterable, which ought to be accommodated to times and events. and 2. To use simple and precise language, and general propositions, according to the example of the (several) constitutions of the several states. (For the construction of a constitution necessarily differs from that of law.)" If for nothing else, Randolph deserved the gratitude of his colleagues for knowing that a constitution must outline broad principles, not detailed statutes.

Randolph then jotted down the structure of the government, filled in some detail about the powers of the several branches, and slotted into their appropriate places provisions such as the power of impeachment.

Wilson evidently took this document, then, with Rutledge's corrections, and some extracts from the New Jersey Plan and other texts, and worked them up into a single harmonious draft beginning with the phrase "We the people of the States of New Hampshire, Massachusetts . . ." and so forth, a document with a preamble and twenty-three articles, divided into forty-three sections. The first two articles were introductory; the next seven—easily the largest part of the document—dealt with the Congress; just one article dealt with the executive; just one dealt with the judiciary; and the remaining twelve articles dealt with such matters as interstate privileges, admission of new states, the guarantee to the states of republican governments, provision for future amendments, and ratification.

Provisions for the powers of Congress, far from being innovations, were taken directly from the Articles, sometimes verbatim, provisions that the Articles had in turn sometimes picked up from colonial charters, sanctified by long and deep tradition and the test of many years' experience in America and in English history.

The New York constitution of 1777, of which Gouverneur Morris had been one of the principal authors, provided the model for the chief executive, in the specification of his powers and duties, and in the means of succession in the event of his death or removed from office.

Here and there, the committee filled in points on which the convention had been silent or contradictory. When it came to qualifications for membership in Congress, the committee named citizenship and residence, but left it up to the legislature to decide whether any property qualifications were to be added. On the qualifications for voters, the committee specified that they should be the same in each state as were the qualifications to vote for the most numerous branch of each state legislature. In this way, the committee avoided judging among all the different usages current in the states, and relied on time to produce uniformity.

In several instances, the committee stepped onto very dangerous ground. The proposal that the national legislature be empowered to legislate for the general interests of the Union was tossed aside. Instead, a list of seventeen specific powers was drawn up. And then that list, meant to serve as a limitation on Congress, was rendered useless at once by the addition of an unlimited provision to "make all laws which shall be necessary and proper for carrying into execution the foregoing powers, and all other powers vested by this Constitution in the government of the United States, or in any department or officer thereof." The phrase was first written in Rutledge's hand, penned into Randolph's first draft.

The boldest innovation of the committee came in two provisions apparently insisted on by Rutledge, and perhaps Randolph (provisions made essential to the south by virtue) of what Rutledge had just done with the powers of Congress). The first was that any navigation act would have to be passed by a two-thirds vote of both houses of Congress. The reasons for such stipulation on navigation acts would have been clear to the other delegates: Before the Revolution, Britain had required that all American goods be shipped in British-built, British-owned vessels. Now the south, which had no shipping industry to speak of, feared that the north would impose a law stating that all shipping must be in American—that is to say, northern—ships. And so, by way of the navigation laws, the north would control the economy of the south; indeed, of the whole country. But if a two-thirds vote was required on navigation laws, the south could protect itself with the representatives it had bargained for in the house. (The usefulness of that edge of slightly more than one-third of all representatives began to be seen already—buttressed by a senate that equally represented the states.)

The second provision put in by the Committee of Detail under Rutledge's watchful eye was this: "No Tax or Duty shall be laid by the Legislature, on Articles exported from any State; nor on the emigration or Importation of such Persons as the several States shall think proper to admit; nor shall such emigration or Importation be prohibited." This is to say, there could be no interference with the slave trade—either directly, by way of laws passed affecting the trade itself, or indirectly, by way of navigation laws.

Thus finished with a detailed draft of the constitution, the committee sent it around to the print shop of Claypoole and

Dunlap, the trustworthy publishers of the *Pennsylvania Packet*, who plunged into their cases of type and composed seven handsome pages of text, with fine broad margins where delegates could make notes; and they printed up about sixty copies, which they delivered to Rutledge to present to the convention on the morning of August 6.

As the delegates reconvened at the State House on the sixth, they were probably bemused to see that a few newcomers had just arrived in town—far too late to do anything of consequence. Among others, the two delegates from New Hampshire, Nicholas Gilman and John Langdon, had finally gotten to Philadelphia. Gilman was a young man, aged thirty-two, who had worked his way up in a career as a professional politician—more noticed for the company he kept than for his own abilities. Langdon came from an old and well-to-do family, and had joined the revolutionary movement at the very beginning. In these past few months, the New Hampshire legislature had not been able to bring itself to pay the expenses of its delegation to Philadelphia (as all the other states did); finally it was Langdon who defrayed the expenses for both of them out of is own pocket so that he could be in on the event.

The arrival of the new delegates was not, however, the only change that the conventioneers would have noticed as they reassembled. Yates and Lansing of New York were gone, having left in the midst of the debate over the Great Compromise, once they realized they had lost all hope of preventing some form of agreement. Hamilton had returned—at the urging of General Washington, and perhaps with the thought that, with Yates and Lansing gone, he could play a significant role again. But even now, back in Philadelphia, because he did not on his own constitute a quorum of his delegation, he could not cast the vote on behalf of New York, and seemed a bit subdued.

He had arrived in town in the same coach as Elbridge Gerry, who had taken advantage of the break in debates—as had a number of other delegates—to have a little vacation. Gerry had gone up to New York with his young wife and baby, and he missed them already. "How is my dearest girl," he wrote his wife, "her little Pet [their daughter], and family Friends. An answer to such questions as these is more interesting to me than all the delusive prospects of pleasure or Happiness from other Quarters." When he arrived in Philadelphia and got ready for bed, Gerry noticed that he had left behind in New York his "comforter," the miniature of his wife that he always carried with him, and dropped a hint that Mrs. Gerry send it to him.

The weather was hot once more in the city. Luther Martin had also taken advantage of the break to leave Philadelphia for a respite, and when he rode into Philadelphia on horseback—as Gerry wrote his wife—Martin "nearly fainted when he dismounted on account of the Heat" (and, possibly, on account of what he had been drinking at the taverns along the way).

Back at their worktables in convention, the delegates turned their attention to the report of the Committee on Detail—impressed no doubt by the fact that they were now moving into the final phase of their labors. The structure was in place; all that remained was to pick at nits. And yet, as they went over the nits, from time to time the delegates turned up an issue of basic principle.

For instance, in the report of the Committee of Detail, the question of a property qualification for officeholders had been left up to the first national legislature to decide. That was all well and good, but as Charles Pinckney pointed out, if the first legislature should be composed of rich men, "they might fix such qualifications as may be too favorable to the rich; if of poor men, an opposite extreme might be run into." For his own part, Pinckney was quick to say that he was opposed to an "undue" aristocratic influence in the constitution. Nonetheless, he thought members of the government "should be possessed of competent property to make them independent and respectable." He thought the president ought perhaps to have a "quantum of property" worth at least one hundred thousand dollars (a stunning sum of money in those days), "in like proportion for the members of the National Legislature." And he proposed a phrase in the constitution calling for members to have "a clear unencumbered Estate" of a certain amount.

"A clear unencumbered Estate": There was a phrase to make men think. For whose estate was unencumbered? Certainly not Robert Morris's. Certainly not James Wilson's. Certainly not George Washington's. Debts and mortgages were the way of the land—except, perhaps, in the south, where several generations of planters had passed down inheritances that left a number of plantation owners eligible, under Pinckney's formula, for the presidency and for federal judgeships.

Dr. Franklin did not hesitate a moment to pour scorn on Pinckney's suggestion. The doctor expressed his dislike "of everything that tended to debase the spirit of the common people. If honesty was often the companion of wealth, and if poverty was exposed to peculiar temptation, it was not less true that the possession of property increased the desire of more property. Some of the greatest rogues he was ever acquainted with," said Franklin, "were the richest rogues. We should remember the character which the Scripture requires in Rulers, that they should be men hating covetousness."

Pinckney's proposal was shouted down by so general a chorus of noes that a vote was not even called for.

The Committee of Detail had suggested that for a man to be eligible for the senate, he must have been a citizen of the United States for four years before his election. Gouverneur Morris moved to revise that to fourteen years. An awkward sensation passed around the room among the recent immigrants.

Once again, the advocate of charity and democratic instinct was Franklin, who allowed that he would be very sorry to see anything like "illiberality" inserted into the constitution. The people of Europe were friendly to the United States, said Franklin, and had been during the war. Even in England, the United States had many friends. And "in every other country in Europe all the people are our friends. We found in the Course of the Revolution that many strangers served us faithfully—and that many natives took part against their Country." When foreigners looked around for a place in which they might find greater happiness than in their native lands, and turned to the United States, "it is a proof of attachment which ought to excite our confidence and affection."

Perhaps it was Franklin who, with those words, gave courage to James Wilson. In his ever noticeable Scottish burr, Wilson acknowledged that he spoke "with feelings which were perhaps peculiar," mentioning the circumstance of his not being a native, and the possibility, "if the ideas of some gentlemen should be pursued, of his being incapacitated from holding a place under the very Constitution which he had shared in the trust of making."

Gouverneur Morris showed himself splendidly indifferent to his colleague Wilson's feelings: "The lesson we are taught is that we should be governed as much by our reason, and as little by our feelings as possible. What is the language of Reason on this subject? That we should not be polite at the expense of prudence." There was, Morris went on cheerfully, "a moderation in all things. It is said that some tribes of Indians carried their hospitality so far as to offer to strangers their wives and daughters. Was this a proper model for us? He would admit them to his house, he would invite them to his table, would provide for them comfortable lodgings," said Morris, milking the homily for all he could, "but would not carry the complaisance so far as to bed them with his wife."

Some said that the best sort of people would emigrate to the United States and bring their fortunes with them; but Morris was elaborately unimpressed with that argument. "As to those philosophical gentlemen, those Citizens of the World, as they called themselves, he owned he did not wish to see any of them in our public Councils. He would not trust them. The men who can shake off their attachments to their own Country can never love any other."

When it came to setting a citizenship requirement for the senate, however, the delegates voted down Morris's highfalutin suggestion for a fourteen-year requirement. So, right away, undaunted, unembarrassable, Morris moved a thirteen-year requirement. And that, too, was voted down. General Pinckney moved a ten-year requirement. That was voted down. At last the delegates agreed to a nine-year requirement. As for the house, the delegates voted a requirement of seven years' citizenship.

Finally, they turned to the question of who was to be qualified to vote for all these elected officials. Gouverneur Morris raised the issue. The right of suffrage, he said, ought to be restricted to freeholders. (This restriction went very far indeed: in seven states, every male taxpayer could vote; elsewhere, property qualifications were moderate.)

What, asked a shocked Colonel Mason, will the people say "if they should be disenfranchised" by this new constitution—

if they should have voting rights that they currently possessed taken from them? "There is no right," Pierce Butler was quick to add, "of which the people are more jealous than than of suffrage."

To Colonel Mason, the proposal for a property qualification turned everything on its head. The true idea, said Mason, "was that every man having evidence of attachment to and permanent common interest with the Society ought to share in all its rights and privileges. Was this qualification restrained to freeholders? Does no other kind of property but land evidence a common interest in the proprietor? Does nothing besides property mark a permanent attachment? Ought the merchant, the monied man, the parent of a number of children"—the old man's mind no doubt went back to his children, not all of whom stood to inherit substantial property—"whose fortunes are to be pursued in their own Country, to be viewed as suspicious characters, and unworthy to be trusted with the common rights of their fellow Citizens?"

Madison was of two minds. He thought that in the future, a great majority of the people might be without landed or any other sort of property, and they might combine to vote wealth into their own hands. Nonetheless, in the end, he did think that the convention ought to agree to a provision that the people would find acceptable.

Then, one more time, Ben Franklin spoke on behalf of the ordinary people: The delegates might have all sorts of fears and fancies, all sorts of theories about how a restricted vote would or would not protect liberty and property, and advance or inhibit the growth of aristocracy. But Franklin brought the conversation back down to daily life. The convention should be careful, he said, not to adopt measures that would "depress the virtue and public spirit of our common people; of which they displayed a great deal during the war, and which contributed principally to the favorable issue of it." The doctor reminded his colleagues of the "honorable refusal" of American seamen who were captured and put in British prisons during the war "to redeem themselves from misery or to seek their fortunes by entering on board the Ships of the Enemies to their Country" (as, in fact, the British seamen had, turning against Great Britain in midwar to side with the colonies). This phe-

nomenon proceeded, said Franklin, "from the different manner in which the common people were treated in America and
Great Britain." And that loyalty and love of country was a
treasure that no government ought to throw away lightly if it
wished to survive.

Very much later, Franklin's instincts about "public spirit"
would be extended as an argument in favor of economic egalitarianism: If income is redistributed just enough to give
everyone a stake in the success of the society as a whole, then
everyone will work for the success of the society and not be at
war with it.

Whatever the merits of that argument, the strictly political (and non-marxist) reason for economic egalitarianism—for
eliminating poverty and diminishing great wealth, for drawing everyone toward the middle class—is that everyone is safest when there are no great concentrations of power in society,
when economic power, like all other power, is dispersed as
widely as possible, and when no groups are left outside the
polity. Certainly, such would be the safest of all possible arrangements for the middle class.

In any case, said Franklin, he doubted that the elected—
that is, the delegates to this convention—had any right "to
narrow the privileges of the electors."

With that, the proposal of Gouverneur Morris was voted
down resoundingly.

Doubtless the delegates would have been happy to leave
the whole business of suffrage there. Certainly they had tried
very hard to avoid—and so far had largely succeeded in avoiding—the issue that was inextricably tied into this debate on
suffrage, and that threatened, if it got out of hand, to tear the
convention entirely apart: the issue of slavery.

19

SLAVERY

RUFUS KING, the bright young Massachusetts lawyer who was usually so strictly practical, and was never one to stir up passions idly, raised the issue, without seeming to realize just how disruptive it could be. He was bothered by the pair of provisions that the Committee of Detail had inserted into their final draft of the constitution: that no law could be passed that threatened the slave trade in any way, and that any navigation law required a two-thirds majority for passage.

What, said King, returning the debate to first principles, were the great objects of this central government they were establishing? First, to provide defense against foreign invasion. Second, to provide against internal sedition. What, then, was the effect of these provisions about slavery on the whole government?

"Shall all the states then be bound to defend each; and shall each be at liberty to introduce a weakness which will render defence more difficult? Shall one part of the United States be bound to defend another part, and that other part at liberty not only to increase its own danger, but to withhold the compensation for the burden?"

There was so much "inequality and unreasonableness in all this," said King, that "no candid man" could undertake to justify it to the people. He had hoped that some compromise would have been reached on this subject—at least that some time limit would have been placed on the importation of slaves into the United States. But to let slaves continue to be imported into the United States, and then, on top of that, to let their presence cause the south to have increased representation in the legislature, was outlandish.

Roger Sherman, who had joined forces with the south, now showed that he could be counted on under fire. No slave owner himself, he was coldly pragmatic. He regarded the slave trade, Sherman said, "as iniquitous." Nonetheless, the issue of representation had been settled "after much difficulty and deliberation," and he did not now think himself "bound to make opposition."

As the debate drew in more and more of the delegates, none spoke with as much clarity, or ferocity, as Gouverneur Morris—the man of property, the man who believed government existed fundamentally to protect property, the man who loved to show how callous he was, the man who never spoke for the rights of the underclass—who proceeded to speak violently against slavery. Representation, he said flatly, should be apportioned according to the number of free inhabitants in each state, and he moved that the word "free" be inserted in the provision before the word "inhabitant." He would never concur, he said, speaking without the least reserve in a gathering full of slave owners, "in upholding domestic slavery. It was a nefarious institution. It was the curse of heaven on the States where it prevailed."

Compare, said Morris, the free regions of the middle states, "where a rich and noble cultivation marks the prosperity and happiness of the people, with the misery and poverty which overspread the barren wastes of Virginia, Maryland, and the other States having slaves." Travel through the whole of America and one would find that the country varied with the appearance and disappearance of slavery. "Proceed Southwardly," said Morris to his southern friends, "and every step you take through the great regions of slaves presents a desert increasing with the increasing proportion of these wretched beings.

"Upon what principle is it that the slaves shall be computed in the representation? Are they men? Then make them Citizens and let them vote. Are they property? Why then is no other property included? The Houses in this City are worth more," Morris declared to Pinckney and Rutledge and Butler, "than all the wretched slaves which cover the rice swamps of South Carolina."

What finally did the issue come down to? "That the inhabitant of Georgia and South Carolina who goes to the Coast of Africa, and in defiance of the most sacred laws of humanity tears away his fellow creatures from their dearest connections and damns them to the most cruel bondages shall have more votes in a Government instituted for protection of the rights of mankind than the Citizen of Pennsylvania or New Jersey who views with a laudable horror so nefarious a practice."

And what was proposed as the compensation to the northern states "for a sacrifice of every principle of right, of every impulse of humanity? They are to bind themselves to march their militia for the defence of the southern states; for their defence against those very slaves of whom they complain. They must supply vessels and seamen, in case of foreign Attack. The Legislature will have indefinite power to tax them by excises, and duties on imports: both of which will fall heavier on them than on the Southern inhabitants; for the bohea tea used by a Northern freeman he will pay more tax than the whole consumption of the miserable slave, which consists of nothing more than his physical subsistence and the rag that covers his nakedness.

"On the other side the Southern States are not to be restrained from importing fresh supplies of wretched Africans, at once to increase the danger of attack, and the difficulty of defence; nay they are to be encouraged to it by an assurance of having their votes in the National Government increased in proportion . . . For what then," asked Morris, "are all these sacrifices to be made?"

A silence fell on the house. No one rose to answer Morris. At last Jonathan Dayton of New Jersey, the youngest man in the room, who had done so little to merit attention in the course of the convention, rose to second Morris's motion to insert "free" before the word "inhabitants." He did not have much hope that the motion would pass, explained Dayton, but he seconded the motion "that his sentiments on the subject might appear [in the record], whatever might be the fate of the amendment."

Roger Sherman responded with perfect control. He did not regard "the admission of the Negroes"—he did not use the word "slave"—"into the ratio of representation as liable to insuperable objections. It was the freemen of the Southern States who were in fact to be represented according to the taxes paid by them, and the Negroes are only included in the Estimate of the taxes. This was his idea of the matter."

On that chilly note, a vote was called on the motion, in the hope that the business of slavery could be put to rest in the convention. The motion to insert the word "free" before "inhabitants" was voted down ten to one.

But this was not to be the end of the debate on slavery. Although it cannot be said that there was much support in the country as a whole for the abolition of slavery and the slave trade, the issue did gnaw at the consciences of a few of the delegates. And at the same time—and more important for the moment—some of the delegates saw an immediate political use to be made of the issue.

That old coalition of local-power men—Dickinson and Luther Martin, joined by young John Francis Mercer, who had just arrived late from Maryland—along with such new allies as Gerry and Colonel Mason, stirred once more when the issue of slavery was raised. Some of the men, Mason for one, seem to have been moved by the purest of principles. But others saw an opportunity to use slavery in one last effort to split apart the coalition of centrists brought together by the Great Compromise.

The localists gathered some allies among the other disgruntled delegates, and they began to meet in the evenings to plot and counterplot. "Mr. Gerry," said Luther Martin, "was the first who proposed this measure to me." Gerry and Mason and Martin met, as Martin recalled, with "the delegates from New Jersey and Connecticut, a part of the delegation from Delaware, an honorable member from South Carolina, one other from Georgie and myself."

Luther Martin, who had done so badly as an advocate for the local-power men in his earlier harangue, was the one who brought up the issue to the full convention. Certainly, said Martin, the privilege of importing slaves—indeed, of encouraging their import by not taxing the traffic—was "inconsistent with the principles of the revolution and dishonorable to the American character to have such a feature in the constitution."

Rutledge was quick to slap down this question of principles. He did not see, Rutledge declared, how the importation of slaves could be encouraged by the fact that there was to be no tax on the traffic. Nor was he apprehensive of any insurrections on the part of the slaves, but he would "readily exempt the other States from the obligation" to protect the southern states from such uprisings should they occur. The hardest of political considerations was riding on this question. Religion and humanity, said Rutledge, had nothing to do with it. "Interest alone," said the head of the South Carolina delegation, who was even then quietly divesting himself of his own slaves, "is the governing principle with Nations." If the delegates wished to debate the slavery issue, there was only one question in it to be debated: "whether the southern states shall or shall not be parties to the Union." With that, Rutledge sat down.

The men of Connecticut showed their mettle now. Having been central agents in arranging the Great Compromise, they were not about to let it be broken apart by these insinuating questions of morality. Oliver Ellsworth spoke for them. "Let every state import what it pleases," said Ellsworth coolly. "The morality or wisdom of slavery are considerations belonging to the States themselves." Connecticut stood firm with the south.

Sherman came stiffly to the support of his colleague. He disapproved of the slave trade, he said; yet, since the states had the right to import slaves at the moment, and "as the public good did not require" that right to be taken from the states, and since "it was expedient to have as few objections as possible" to the new scheme of government, Sherman thought it best, on the whole, "to leave the matter as we find it."

Colonel Mason boiled over with outrage. "This infernal traffic," said the colonel, would end in the worst possible disaster for America. "The present question concerns not the importing States alone but the whole Union." True enough, Virginia and Maryland had already prohibited the importation of slaves. North Carolina had done the same "in substance." But all that would be in vain if South Carolina and Georgia were at liberty to carry on. "The Western people are already calling out for slaves for their new lands; and will fill that Country with slaves if they can be got through South Carolina and Georgia." And the evils of slavery were legion. "Slavery discourages arts and manufactures. The poor despise labor when performed by slaves. They prevent the immigration of Whites, who really enrich and strengthen a Country. They produce the most pernicious effect on manners. Every master of slaves is born a petty tyrant."

The institution of slavery, as Colonel Mason said, like other great moral errors that a nation commits, like lack of compassion for the destitute, like behaving toward other nations or peoples without regard for the good opinion of mankind, brings "the judgment of heaven on a Country. As nations cannot be rewarded or punished in the next world they must be in this. By an inevitable chain of causes and effects providence punishes national sins by national calamities."

The delegates were chastened by this, or stirred up, or thrown on the defensive. Oliver Ellsworth was the first to reply. As he had never owned a slave, he said pointedly to the slave-owning colonel, he "could not judge of the effects of slavery on character." He said, however, that if it came to a consideration of slavery in a moral light, then certainly "we ought to go farther and free those already in the Country."

Then, too, Ellsworth suggested caustically, some gentlemen from Virginia might have more an economic than a moral motivation for opposing the slave trade. "As slaves also multiply so fast in Virginia and Maryland that it is cheaper to raise than import them, whilst in the sickly rice swamps foreign supplies are necessary," if the delegates only outlawed the slave trade without outlawing slavery, "we shall be unjust towards South Carolina and Georgia. . . .

"Let us not intermeddle," said Ellsworth. "As population increases poor laborers will be so plentiful as to render slaves useless. Slavery in time will not be a speck in our Country. Provision is already made in Connecticut for abolishing it. And the abolition has already taken place in Massachusetts. As to the danger of insurrections from foreign influence, that will become a motive to kind treatment of the slaves."

"If slavery be wrong," declared young Charles Pinckney, suddenly casting himself in the role of classicist, "it is justified by the example of all the world." He cited Greece and Rome and other ancient societies. "In all ages one half of mankind have been slaves."

The older Pinckney, the veteran of many a political war in Charleston, spoke more resignedly. Even if he and "all his colleagues" were to sign the constitution and use "their personal influence" on behalf of a prohibition of the slave trade, "it would be of no avail towards obtaining the assent of the Constituents. South Carolina and Georgia cannot do without slaves." And would not. The question was simply whether there was to be a Union or not. And if it came to that, the general was ready to pay hard cash to assuage the moral qualms of his colleagues. With a degree of easy cynicism, he suggested they refer the clause about the slave trade to a committee along with the provision on the import tax, and see whether or not an understanding might be worked out. For his part, said the general, he thought an equal tax on slaves and other imports would be only right.

Rutledge seconded General Pinckney's motion. Gouverneur Morris, quick to turn the screws on the southerners, suggested that this same committee also consider the clause on export taxes and the clause on navigation laws. An export tax might be made to favor the north; the navigation laws favored the south; both might become part of a deal on the slave trade.

In the midst of all this, Sherman, in a sort of delayed moral reaction to the whole debate on slavery, suddenly wanted to draw a fine line on the issue of the slave traffic. He did not wish to prohibit it, and he did not want to tax it. For if the importation of slaves were taxed, that would throw the whole thing out into the open and make "the matter worse, because it implied [slaves] were *property*"—an acknowledgment Sherman could not make openly.

No one dealt with Sherman's small moral panic. The pragmatic thing was done. The clauses were referred to committee to work out a compromise, and while the committee did so, the delegates wrangled over lesser issues.

"I am exceedingly distrest," Gerry wrote to his wife, "at the proceedings of the Convention—being apprehensive, and almost sure, they will not if altered materially lay the foundation of a civil War."

Madison took sick. His notetaking fell off by a third, though he struggled to continue to attend every session and to keep his record of the debates. The work, as he later told his secretary, almost killed him.

By this time, it seems, the work, and the anguish of settling for something imperfect or even wrong—whether that anguish focused on the slave trade or not—had begun to take its toll on many of the delegates.

"I never was more sick of anything than I am of conventioneering," Gerry wrote. Indeed, he was suspicious of everything by this time, and even thought his letters to his wife were being opened and read by his political opponents. "There are a set of beings here capable of every kind of villainy to answer their purposes, and I think they need not open this letter to know my opinion of them: but if that measure is necessary, they have my permission."

On August 25, the committee reported out its compromise: Navigation acts would no longer require a two-thirds majority to be passed—this was the gift to the shipping interests of the northeast; the slave trade would be continued, but only until the year 1800—this was the gift (hedged by the time limit) to the southern states; and the slaves imported would be subject to a tax just like any other import—this was the price the south agreed to pay.

And so the Gerry-Mason cabal, far from shattering the coalition made by the Great Compromise, had only forced the coalition to bind itself even more closely together by virtue of another, and this time more unsavory, compromise.

General Pinckney moved at once to alter the compromise, to allow the south to import slaves past the year 1800, until the year 1808. Madison all but gagged. "Twenty years," said Madison with quiet resignation, "will produce all the mischief that can be apprehended from the liberty to import slaves." But Pinckney's motion passed. Only Paterson's New Jersey, Quaker Pennsylvania, Mason's and Madison's Virginia, and Dickinson's Delaware voted against it.

That the framers built a flaw of monstrous proportions into the constitution is certainly clear in hindsight. It was clear enough to Colonel Mason and some few others at the time. It was, and is, equally clear that there was no national passion against slavery in the eighteenth century, no widespread moral objection, and, as was said at the time, no possibility of union without it. Such strong antislavery advocates as Dr. Benjamin Rush of Philadelphia actually thought that the ban on importing slaves after 1808 made the constitution an antislavery document.

And yet, clearly, the constitution did not eliminate slavery—the delegates did not even try to set a clear limit to its life span—but rather left it to bring further tragedy on the country. Surely Mason was right in trying to draw a larger lesson at the convention: that politicians make great national tragedies inevitable when they sacrifice moral imperatives to immediate practical needs, when they forget that morality is simply the accumulated folk knowledge about how to get along in human society over the long term.

Gouverneur Morris, determined to tar the men who had forced this measure through the convention, moved to record the names of those with whom the compromise had been made. He suggested that the provision be amended to state that importation of slaves would not be prohibited "into North Carolina, South Carolina, and Georgia." He wished it to be known, he said, "that this part of the Constitution was a compliance with those States."

But Colonel Mason came to the defense of his fellow southerners. He was against naming the states, said the colonel, "lest it should give offence to the people of those States. And Roger Sherman, still bothered by the agreement he had made, suggested that the word "slaves" not be used, but that some term of description be put in its place. (The word "persons" was substituted.)

Sherman was bothered, too, about taxing the import of these persons, and so "acknowledging men to be property." But that, said the practical Rufus King tersely, was "the price" that must be paid. And with that the debate was ended.

20

THE POWERS OF CONGRESS

THE DELEGATES WERE LOOKING for an end to their labors. They began to appoint more and more committees to speed up their work. Speeches became shorter. Votes were called more peremptorily. Matters of principle were dropped, not raised again, given up.

And yet they had still to go back and look over a most important matter: the powers they were giving Congress. However impatient they were to put an end to the convention, they must give Congress at least a brisk review.

Congress, it was agreed, was always the first topic of conversation, the foundation of the new government, the locus of its primary powers, the embodiment of the republican principle, the battleground over which centrists and localists had fought; yet not all of its powers had been settled on.

They started with several lists of powers—one that Madison presented to the convention, another that Pinckney dropped on the table (possibly, at least in part, filched from Madison, picked up in conversations back at Mrs. House's), four suggestions from Gerry, a couple of suggestions from Rutledge and Mason, and an additional short list of civil rights from Pinckney. Most of them are ordinary stuff, and were familiar to the delegates, having come from the Articles:

To coin money;
To fix standard weights and measures;

To dispose of unappropriated lands of the United States;

To regulate affairs with the Indians;

To grant charters of incorporation;

To secure to literary authors their copyrights;

To grant patents for useful inventions;

To borrow money, and emit bills on the credit of the United States.

Such powers were routine affairs and merited little or no debate. Two other powers, however, did merit debate—and got a good deal of it: the power to control the magnitude and use of the military, and the power to provide for the general welfare.

By far most of the members of the convention were against establishing any large standing army; all agreed that a standing army drained the resources of the nation, tended to drag the nation into war, to fight wars of conquest or enterprise rather than defense, and so threatened to exert a fatal influence from day to day on the republic. Gerry said bluntly that he thought "an army dangerous in time of peace and could never consent to a power to keep up an indefinite number."

Yet some force, the delegates agreed, was necessary to repel sudden invasion, and to put down insurrections. Gerry proposed that the constitution specify that the military be kept to the barest minimum necessary for defense, that "there shall not be kept up in time of peace" more than a certain number of troops—say, two or three thousand.

As Gerry might have anticipated, a military man was there to question his proposal. General Pinckney asked whether no more troops "were ever to be raised until an attack should be made on us." Preparations for war, Jonathan Dayton added, "are generally made in peace; and a standing force of some sort may, for ought we know, become unavoidable."

Grudgingly, Gerry had to yield to these concerns. And yet the delegates agreed with him enough about the dangers of a permanent military establishment that they determined that no appropriation of money for the military "shall be for a longer Term than two Years." If not limited in numbers, the military could at least be limited in its life span, so that it could not go on indefinitely without the possibility of Congress eliminating or curtailing it, if they had the wit to do so. The delegates

could not conceive—such were the limitations of an eighteenth-century politician's imagination—that the Congress,
oblivious of the lessons of history, would one day not only
allow the buildup of an enormous military establishment,
but be too timid or dishonest even to insist that it be efficient.

Then the delegates turned their attention to that ragtag
bunch of civilians who served in their state militias. If some
uniform standards of training and discipline were enforced, the
country could have a citizens' military force to rely on rather
than being solely dependent on a large standing army. (There
was something wonderful in a citizens' army: If defense required their participation, and they refused to participate if a
war seemed unmerited to them, that alone would provide a
check on a too venturesome, or panicky, government.) Colonel
Mason moved that Congress be empowered to make laws reg-
ulating the militias.

Madison suggested that the national government be entitled to appoint the general officers of the militias and the states
appoint the lesser officers.

That, said Sherman, was "absolutely inadmissible." If the
people were so far asleep as to allow their officers to be appointed by the national government, "every man of discern-
ment would rouse them by sounding the alarm to them." The
people, or their local representatives, must be allowed to elect
their own officers.

Gerry, evidently vibrating in every nerve, stuttered out his
consternation. The convention, he said, was "pushing the experiment too far. Some people will support a plan of vigorous
Government at every risk. Others of a more democratic cast
will oppose it with equal determination. And a Civil war may
be produced by the conflict."

But, said Madison, since the greatest danger to liberty came
from a standing army, it only made sense to provide for a good
militia, and to have it so organized that it could provide for
the national defense—and with that argument the delegates
finally agreed. They gave Congress the power to organize, arm,
and discipline the militia, and to govern such parts of it as
might be employed in the service of the national government.
They reserved to the states they right to appoint their officers,

but provided that they train the militias "according to the discipline prescribed by Congress."

And then, having provided a military force, Congress was given the ultimate power of state, the power to make war. It required little debate. The delegates could scarcely conceive where else the power to commit the blood and treasure of the nation to war could be lodged except among the direct representatives of the people and of the states.

Young Pinckney objected. He thought the proceedings of the house of representatives would be "too slow," that the house would be too numerous "for such deliberations," and that the power ought to be lodged soley in the senate. But Pinckney's colleague from South Carolina Pierce Butler thought that the same objection obtained with the senate as with the house, and that the president ought to have the power to take the nation to war. The president, Butler was touchingly sure, would not commit the nation to war except when the nation would be content to support it.

Gerry was amazed. He had never expected "to hear in a republic," he said, "a motion to empower the Executive alone to declare war," to give to any single individual—one to whom the delegates would not even give the power to raise taxes or regulate interstate commerce—the power to put at risk thousands or millions of lives, or even the very existence of the nation.

Gerry and Madison had a more sensible suggestion to make. The house ought to be able to declare "war"; the president ought to have the power to repel "sudden attacks," though not to go on to wage war. Sherman agreed, and clarified the Madison-Gerry suggestion: "The executive should be able to repel and not to commence war."

Colonel Mason spelled out the delegates' concerns in even more detail. He was against "giving the power of war to the Executive," because he was not to be safely trusted with it. In general, said Mason, he was in favor of "clogging rather than facilitating war; but for facilitating peace." With this all the delegates could agree. And so the warmaking power was given to Congress, and to Congress was given the power to starve the military financially, to "clog" the warmaking power—should they have the courage and understanding to do so—and to keep the new nation from the habit of military ventures, which are always the death of a republic and its freedoms.

Finally, as they came to the end of their review of congressional powers, the delegates agreed to give Congress the power "to make all laws necessary and proper for carrying into execution the foregoing powers"—all the powers that were specified, as well as the power, generally, to "provide for the common Defence and general Welfare of the United States." These were broad and sweeping powers, adopted, it seemed, almost casually.

In one form or another, in one context or another, these phrases had come up again and again in the convention. It had been proposed to give Congress the power to assume state debts that had been taken on for the general welfare, or to defray all expenses "incurred for the common defense and general welfare." Often it seems to have been an explanatory phrase: Taxes were to be raised "for the common defense and general welfare of the United States." Occasionally the phrase seemed to stand on its own—as an additional power of Congress, as something Congress ought to attend to in addition to all its other duties. A certain ambiguity clung to the phrase, and it was not quite resolved. At one point, when Gouverneur Morris was drafting a provision, he separated the general-welfare clause from all the others with a semicolon—establishing it as an independent power. On reconsideration, Roger Sherman got the semicolon struck out. But it is not at all clear that the other delegates, who took for granted the predominance of Congress in this new government, understood the stakes that some pedants would claim were riding on this semicolon. And when they adopted a provision in its final form, without the semicolon, there can be no doubt that they meant the common defense and other general welfare to be the two great concerns of Congress, and that the Congress ought to have the power to perform its duties.

21

THE PRESIDENT AGAIN

NONE QUESTIONED who the first chief executive of the United States was to be. All the delegates agreed on this if nothing else. But who was to succeed Washington, and how he was to be chosen, remained a complete mystery.

Rumors of the troubles the convention was having over the office of the president spread beyond the convention hall, and one bit of gossip particularly stirred up the country. It was said that the delegates were thinking of establishing a monarchy, and that they had sent to the bishop of Osnaburgh to see if he would be interested. The bishop of Osnaburgh was, in fact, the duke of York, the second son of King George III. So inflammatory was that rumor that the members of the convention decided to leak its own rumor for the first and only time to the press—a task that Franklin probably performed: "Tho we cannot affirmatively tell you what we are doing; we can, negatively, tell you what we are not doing—we never once thought of a King." (Well, almost never.)

Toward the end of August, the hot and weary delegates appointed a Committee of Unfinished Business—which included Sherman, Madison, Gouverneur Morris, Dickinson, Williamson, and Rufus King among its members—to gather up all the postponed matters that had been accumulating during the summer. Of all these postponed matters, the business of the presidency stood out among a litter of minor nuisances—and finally, on September 4, the solution that the committee reported to the convention was stunning. Point by point, the plan proposed by the committee systematically answered every question the delegates had raised about the presidency.

What the committee proposed was that the president be elected for a term of four years, that each state appoint, "in such manner as its Legislature may direct," a number of electors, specifically not members of the state legislatures, equal to the whole number of senators plus members of the house of representatives. The electors would vote for two persons, at least one of whom would not be from their own state. The list of votes would then be transmitted to the senate. If one person had a clear majority, he would be president. If no one had a clear majority, the senate would choose the president from among the top five candidates.

The intricacies of the plan require a little unraveling: That each "state" was to appoint electors gave power at once to the states in the election of a president. That the states appoint electors in such manner as its legislature might direct allowed the possibility of a popular vote without forcing it. That the electors were not to be members of the state legislatures gently removed with one hand part of the influence given to the state legislatures with the other hand. That the number of electors should be equal to the number of a state's senators and representatives gave the advantage to the large states, and weighted the system to give extra votes to the south. That the electors were required to vote for at least one man from another state guaranteed that the front-runner would not always automatically be a man from the largest state. That the senate would choose the president from among the top five candidates gave the last advantage to the small states, which had leverage in the senate.

One other set of provisions was crucial. In voting, the electors would meet in their own states, not gather at some central place—which would prevent them from getting together in a cabal and bargaining and plotting for their own interests, the way modern political parties do. The system was designed, in short, to work without political parties—unlike the British system, for instance, which is based on the idea of a governing and an opposition party. The American system was meant to have the possibility, at least, of the people operating directly on their government, without any party standing between the people and the government and compromising or bartering or simplifying their wishes—pursuing the aims of the party at the expense of the aims of the people. The constitution might not be able to prevent political parties from coming into being, but it would at least make it possible to exist without them— and to establish the principle that political parties, far from being sacrosanct or indispensable, were always to be held in deep suspicion.

The delegates were at first so taken aback by the intricacy of this plan that they hesitated to do much more than ask some exploratory questions.

But Madison—who had presumably disagreed with the majority on the committee—cut at once, for any who did not grasp it, to what he saw as the worst flaw in the plan. It would be extremely rare, said Madison unhappily, for any single candidate to emerge from his process with a clear majority, and so the election would invariably be thrown into the senate, which would choose the president from a list of five candidates. In effect, the large states would nominate, and the small states, in the senate, would elect.

Gouverneur Morris agreed—and saw nothing wrong with it. The virtues of the plan, said Morris, were that it got around a legislative appointment, it got around the possibility of intrigue and cabal, it got around the old inconvenience of making the president ineligible for another term, so that he would not be too dependent on the legislature, and it even brought the people in on the election.

Colonel Mason was unimpressed. The committee had done excellent work in avoiding the dangers of cabal and corruption, he said but it had simply thrown the election into the senate; "nineteen times in twenty the President would be chosen by the Senate, an improper body for the purpose."

Wilson was hesitant. "It is in truth the most difficult of all [subjects] on which we have had to decide," said Wilson; and he had himself "never made up an opinion on it entirely to his own satisfaction." On the whole, however, he thought it might be better to refer the final vote to the house of representatives rather than the senate—to keep the election closer to the people (and more to the advantage of the large states)—and to confine their final vote to less than five candidates.

Gradually, the full implications of the committee's plan began to come clear to the delegates, and to disturb them. The president, being effectively chosen by the senate, could eventually get together with the senate in combination against the house of representatives. Since he would be eligible under this plan for reelection, and since, as the incumbent, he would probably always appear among the top five candidates on the electors' list, he could become fixed for life as the chief executive under the auspices of the senate.

"We have," said Edmund Randolph, "in some revolutions of this plan made a bold stroke for Monarchy. We are now doing the same for an aristocracy . . . a real and dangerous Aristocracy."

No wonder that champion of aristocracy Gouverneur Morris, who had been a member of the Committee on Unfinished Business, was such a defender of this new mechanism for electing the president.

As the delegates considered how this system would work in detail—that is to say, how many members of the senate would be required to carry the election among the candidates—they became even more startled. If the senate consisted of twenty-six members, and a quorum consisted of a majority of the membership—that is, of fourteen members—and if a majority vote of that quorum elected the president, then eight senators would choose the president.

Now that the implications of the idea had become vividly clear to the delegates, Colonel Mason ceased to hold back. He would prefer, said Mason, "the Government of Prussia to one which will put all power into the hands of seven or eight men, and fix an Aristocracy worse that absolute monarchy."

Elbridge Gerry had an odd sort of compromise to suggest. If the president should be elected originally by the senate, then, when it came time for reelection, if no candidate had a clear majority, the house of representatives could select the president. Rufus King liked the idea. He thought it would "satisfy particular members."

If particular members, said George Read testily, were to be constantly catered to in all their little preferences, there would be no end of alterations.

On the whole, said Hamilton, he liked the plan for electing

the president, although he had to agree with the others that it did give the power of the appointment to the senate. What was the remedy for that? He saw none better than "to let the highest number of ballots, whether a majority or not, appoint the President. What was the objection to this? Merely that too small a number might appoint. But as the plan stands, the Senate may take the candidate having the smallest number of votes and make him President."

Hamilton's suggestion was fair enough, but he had forgotten just how intricate this electoral plan was, and how many interests it was designed to satisfy. If a mere majority or plurality of votes elected the president, that would leave the advantage with the large states; the point of throwing the election into the senate was to enable the small states to check the influence of the large states.

Let the vote be referred to the house, Roger Sherman suggested, to the people's branch of the legislature instead of to the senate. This, along with the provision that states have electors chosen by popular vote, would introduce a second "democratic" element into the formula. But then, to give weight to the states once again, and especially to protect the small states, let the members of the house vote by state.

As the delegates turned the plan over and over again in their minds, they concluded that the Committee on Unfinished Business had in fact met almost all their needs. By taking Roger Sherman's proposal—to refer the final choice to the house but to have the house vote by state—they were satisfied that they had perhaps not the best system but the best they could devise. The president, in rising to his office, would be the creature of so many different constituencies that he would not be able to favor one small faction over all the others; he would be least likely under this plan to be the creature of a faction or a party; he would not have to stand for the common good, but it had been made as hard as possible for him to stand against it.

The vice-president, then as always, was an afterthought. He was someone to succeed to office should the president become incapacitated. And the plan before the convention provided that he would be whoever happened to come in second in the balloting. Adopted without extensive debate, it was a

remarkable provision, and showed how completely the delegates assumed this government would work smoothly without
a party system. In fact, the vice-president might in practice be
whoever had been the president's leading opponent in the election, quite possibly a man of different views entirely. No matter; he was only there to carry out the legislature's laws.

(Within only a few years, this perception of the executive
was to change. Directly after the close of the convention, two
factions emerged in the country: predictably enough, those who
believed in a strong central government and those who believed in strong local governments. The two factions developed
into strong political parties—the centrists led by Washington
and Hamilton and John Adams, the localists led by Jefferson,
who was elected president in 1800. In 1804, an amendment
was passed: Votes were henceforth to be cast distinctly for
president and distinctly for vice-president. The party slate was
born.)

Having constituted the election process in a way that was
finally satisfying to them, the delegates turned to consider the
powers they wished to give to the president. The first thing
they did, now that they had constituted a well-fettered chief
executive, was to slice some powers away from the too powerful senate and give them to the president. The powers both
to make appointments and to conclude treaties were taken from
the senate and given to the president "by and with the advice
and consent of the senate." The delegates got stuck on one point
over the power to conclude treaties. The provision before them
called for the consent of two-thirds of "the members present"
of the senate on any treaty. Madison suggested that two-thirds
be required on any treaty "except treaties of peace," which the
country ought to be able to conclude with less difficulty than
other treaties.

When the convention agreed to that provision of Madison's, he then proposed that two-thirds of the senate ought to
be able to conclude a treaty of peace on their own, without the
president, to make it possible for the country to make peace
even though the president may wish to make war. "The President," said Madison, "would necessarily derive so much power
and importance from a state of war that he might be tempted,
if authorized, to impede a treaty of peace."

Nathaniel Gorham was not impressed with Madison's reasoning. Since the legislature could deny the president funds to carry on the war, it was already in the hands of the legislature to stop the president from continuing a war. Madison's provision was not necessary.

Pierce Butler sprang to Madison's defense, insisting that his provision was an essential security "against ambitious and corrupt Presidents. He mentioned . . . the artifices of the Duke of Marlborough to prolong the war of which he had the management."

But Madison and Butler lost on that idea.

Colonel Mason then introduced a pet idea of his, that the president have a privy council, which would act as something of a restraint on him. Not even the most despotic governments were without such a council, said Mason. "The Grand Signor himself had his Divan." Mason suggested that the council be appointed by the house or the senate—which would adjust the office ever so slightly back toward a parliamentary system.

But the delegates voted it down. There was an impatience now with new suggestions, and—unfortunately—an eagerness to settle what was already on the table and get finished. Had the delegates been able to see two centuries into the future, they would very likely have spent a few more hours searching for ways to fetter the chief executive.

Rufus King returned to Madison's suggestion that a two-thirds majority of the senate not be required on treaties of peace. He thought two-thirds ought to be required; as his colleagues Gerry had said, "in treaties of peace the dearest interests will be at stake, as the fisheries, territory, etc." That ought to require the approval of more than a simple majority. The convention agreed with King and Gerry, and voted down Madison's proposal.

Colonel Mason returned to the provision on impeachment. "Why is the provision restrained to Treason and bribery only?" asked Mason. "Treason as defined in the Constitution will not reach many great and dangerous offenses. . . . Attempts to subvert the Constitution may not be Treason." He thought the delegates ought to add "or maladministration." Gerry seconded his motion. "So vague a term," said Madison, "will be equivalent to a tenure during pleasure of the Senate." Colonel

Mason withdrew "maladministration" and substituted "other high crimes and misdemeanors."

Under these circumstances, said Madison, the president will be far too dependent on the senate. On the contrary, said High Williamson, "there was more danger of too much lenity than of too much rigour towards the President." The other delegates agreed with Williamson and made the president removable for mere misdemeanors.

Gradually, now, the debate wound down to trivia. A sense overcame the delegates that the major elements of the constitution had all been settled. Nothing was left to debate. The talk went on desultorily awhile longer, and then the convention drew itself up and appointed its last committee, the Committee of Style—to take all the provisions and agreements and compromises and phrasings and put them together in a proper order and write them up in a crisp style: in short, to write the final draft of the constitution. Five members were appointed to the committee: the practical Rufus King, the mastermind Madison, the conciliatory Connecticut delegate Johnson, and the two great prose stylists in the hall, Gouverneur Morris and Alexander Hamilton.

22

FINISHING TOUCHES AND FINAL
OBJECTIONS

ON THE COMMITTEE OF STYLE, while Hamilton and Madison sat back with the other committee members, it was Gouverneur Morris who took pen in hand to write up the final draft of the text of the constitution. One would have expected Morris to write a document full of rhetorical flourishes, of elegant, exquisitely balanced phrases, perhaps even of sly wit; but the text that he produced was, in fact, eloquent in its spareness. There were no lofty opening sentiments about the rights of man, no grandiloquence about the historical moment. The phrases that were later to take on such resonance—powers "necessary and proper," powers for the "general welfare"—were familiar, homely phrases from earlier American constitutions. The form of government, the separation of powers, the republican principles, were not declaimed, only provided. The language—though it would certainly be subject to later interpretation and misinterpretation—was as simple and direct and broad as admirers of classical Greek could make it.

All the twenty-three articles, and innumerable little amendments and instructions that had been referred to the committee, were distilled to seven articles. The whole vexing question of ratification was simply removed from the constitution and put in a letter to Congress—saying that the convention recommended having Congress pass the document along to state ratifying conventions—and so, in this quiet, understated way, the idea was eased along as a mere convenient thought rather than an issue of the constitution itself.

Even the constitution's handsome preamble ("We the people of the United States, in order to form a more perfect Union, establish justice, insure domestic tranquillity, provide for the common defence, promote the general welfare, and secure the blessings of liberty to ourselves and our posterity, do ordain and establish this Constitution for the United States of America") was in the nature of an exposition of the basic job to be done rather than an invocation to greatness.

The fine phrase "We the people" was a solution to the ticklish question of just who was to ratify the constitution. The preamble prepared by the Committee of Detail had begun "We the people of the States of New Hampshire, Massachusetts, Rhode-Island . . ." and so forth—an awkward preamble if Rhode Island and some other states refused to ratify the document. If the space had been left blank, to be filled in with the names of the states after they had ratified, that would have called attention to the question of how many states ought to be necessary to ratify. The phrase "We the people" simply eliminated the problem with a graceful wave of the hand— and, to be sure provided a nice invocation of the collective wisdom and consent of the people. That, at least, seemed characteristic of Gouverneur Morris.

The word "nation" never once appeared in the document, which showed a finely honed sensitivity to the lingering unease of the small-state men, but the words "United States" were used liberally: there could be no mistake that this document was meant, above all, to gather the thirteen states into a single polity, henceforth indissoluble.

When the committee reported out its final draft (once again neatly printed up by Claypoole and Dunlap), the delegates needed only four days, from Wednesday the twelfth of September to Saturday the fifteenth, to review the committee's work and pronounce it satisfactory.

At first a few of the delegates were eager to show themselves conciliatory to the grumblers. Hugh Williamson of North Carolina, upset by Randolph's qualms, suggested striking out the clause that required a three-fourths vote of both senate and house to overrule a presidential veto, and substituting instead a requirement for only a two-thirds vote. He had himself proposed the three-fourths provision, he said, but he had since been convinced that he was mistaken, that a three-fourths vote put too much power in the hands of the president. Roger Sherman, the great patron of compromise, agreed.

Gouverneur Morris, friend of a "high-toned" government, sprang to the defense of the three-fourths rule, saying that the thing to be feared was not a deficiency of laws but an excess of them, and that in any case, mathematically the difference was trivial; the difference amounted in one house to only two members and in the other to not more than five. Little knowledge of arithmetic, retorted Colonel Mason, "was necessary to understand that three-fourths was more than two-thirds."

Randolph was placated. The provision was changed to two-thirds. But not much more was done to mollify disgruntled men like Randolph. The delegates were much too impatient to want to consider any more measures of conciliation. Votes were called. New ideas were put down.

Colonel Mason, author of the renowned Virginia Bill of Rights, said he wished that the constitution were provided with a bill of rights, and he would be happy to provide one in a few hours. Elbridge Gerry agreed.

Astonishingly enough, Roger Sherman opposed the idea. The state declarations of rights "are not repealed by this Constitution," said Sherman, "and being in force are sufficient." If a list of rights was enumerated, Sherman argued, it might appear that the framers positively meant to exclude some rights that they had just inadvertently overlooked (or they might be forced by a few states to exclude something most states already had and cherished). All powers not specifically granted to the government were, in any case, reserved to the people. A bill of rights was not necessary—since the basic rights of the Magna Carta and the common law were so deeply ingrained in America—and might do more harm than good.

Colonel Mason was surprised, and no doubt offended, that his offer to draft a bill of rights was so summarily dismissed. The laws of the United States, said the colonel, "are to be paramount to State Bills of Rights"—and so presumably would overrule such state laws, leaving citizens without protection.

But the convention was in no mood to listen. It was just such flourishes as a bill of rights that the Committee of Style had avoided. A bill of rights, said Mason, "would give great quiet to the people." No matter, the proposal for a bill of rights was voted down by the convention unanimously.

In other ways, smaller ways, the delegates could not resist tinkering with the document. The power to appoint the treasurer, for instance, was taken from Congress and given to the president, which neatened up the separation of powers. And a clause was inserted forbidding the president to receive any "emolument" other than his salary from the United States, which foreclosed the possibility of individual states vying with each other to buy the chief executive's favor.

The matter of who was to control certain forms of patronage was distributed between the executive and legislative branches when Congress was given the power to "vest the appointment of such inferior officers as they think proper" in the president, or in the courts, or in the heads of departments.

In the end, small defeats were handed out to a number of the delegates. Hugh Williamson tried to get the number of members of the house increased, in order to increase the popular base of the legislature, and he failed. Rutledge and Morris tried to insert a provision whereby any officer who had been impeached would be temporarily suspended from office, and they were defeated. Franklin tried to give Congress the power "to cut canals," and was defeated. Madison and Pinckney tried to give Congress power to establish a university, and were defeated. New Hampshire's Langdon tried bigheartedly to give more congressional seats to Rhode Island and North Carolina, and was defeated.

Most of the delegates accepted their defeats with equanimity, but not Randolph, Mason, and Gerry. As Randolph looked over the completed work of the convention, he still felt that "indefinite and dangerous power" had been given to the central government. It gave him genuine pain, he said, to find himself differing from his colleagues "on the close of the great and awful subject of their labours." In conscience, he would not accommodate himself to the constitution that they had made together. There was only one way he could see that would allow him to give his support to the constitution, and that was if provision was made for the states to propose amendments as the constitution went through the ratification process and then, once all the proposed amendments had been put forward, another convention would be called to compose the final constitution. Should this proposal be disregarded, said Randolph, it would be "impossible for him to put his name to the instrument."

The delegates had talked of this business of ratification before, during the time that the Committee of Style had been meeting. The majority of the delegates then spoke against the notion of taking the plan to the Congress sitting in New York for its approval. That, they said, would be certain death. The Congress would vote by states, and according to its rules, Rhode Island alone could veto the whole plan. Some delegates suggested that the state ratifying conventions might be allowed to propose amendments; but the majority objected to that as certain to produce a complete deluge of irreconcilable amendments that would make ratification impossible.

To Randolph, however, the idea that the Philadelphia convention could circumvent Congress, could circumvent the need for the approval of all thirteen original parties to the Articles, and, beyond all that, could refuse to entertain amendments proposed in the ratification process, was intolerable. If no change was made in this proposal, said Randolph, he would be obliged to dissent from the whole constitution. It was his idea that the state conventions should be at liberty to offer amendments to the plan—and that these should be submitted to *a second general convention.*

A second general convention, with another set of delegates, another set of plans, another set of debates: It is a wonder that Randolph wasn't hooted down for his suggestion. Wilson was astonished that anyone seriously proposed referring the constitution to Congress, when they all knew that Rhode Island would oppose it; the delegates of New York had already shown themselves so opposed that they had not even stayed through the whole convention. "After spending four of five months in the laborious and arduous task of forming a Government for our Country, we are ourselves at the close throwing insuperable obstacles in the way of its success."

Still, Randolph was not pacified. In his view, the cumulative effects of the provisions the convention had voted into place had finally, bit by bit, given altogether too much power to the central government. He felt that the rights of his own state were not adequately protected. And he could not support and promote "the establishment of a plan which he verily believed would end in Tyranny."

Colonel Mason followed immediately on Randolph's heels. Mason had written out, on his Claypoole and Dunlap copy of the constitution, some notes about his objections to the document. Above all else, said Mason, this constitution that they had made in these past several months had, unaccountably, no declaration of rights; and, since the constitution was to supersede all state constitutions, it put at jeopardy all of Americans' fundamental rights. That objection, and that alone, was solid ground for not signing the document they had all produced.

Second, because the numbers of the members of the house of representatives were so few, "there is not the substance but the shadow only of representation, which can never produce proper information in the legislature. . . . the laws will therefore be generally made by men little concerned in, and unacquainted with their effects and consequences."

Third, the senate was to have the power to alter money bills, although the senators, since they would be elected by the state legislatures, "are not the representatives of the people or amenable to them." This control of the purse strings, along with the senate's power in the appointment of ambassadors and other officers, in making treaties, in trying impeachments, and the senators' influence on and intimate connection with the executive, "will destroy any balance in the government, and enable them to accomplish what usurpations they please upon the rights and liberties of the people." Here, certainly, was the basis for the growth of an aristocracy.

As for the court system, the federal judiciary was to be constructed and extended so as "to absorb and destroy the judiciaries of the several States." This was a plan said to have the benefit of a uniform system of laws. But what would be the result? The law courts would be rendered "as tedious, intricate, and expensive, and justice as unattainable by a great part of the community as in England." Altogether the courts were so designed as to enable "the rich to oppress and ruin the poor."

As if all this were not enough, the president was not supplied with a constitutional council, "a thing unknown in any safe and regular government." What would be the result of this? The president would inevitably "be unsupported by proper information and advice, and will generally be directed by minions and favorites."

As for the legislative branch provided by this constitution, the Congress, "under their own construction of the general clause . . . may grant monopolies in trade and commerce, constitute new crimes, inflict unusual and severe punishments, and extend their power as far as they shall think proper." What, then, was the use of any other provision the framers had made in the constitution? The state legislatures would have nothing to protect their own powers, and the people nothing to protect their rights.

There was nowhere in the constitution a declaration of any kind for "preserving the liberty of the press, or the trial by jury in civil cases, nor against the danger of standing armies in time of peace," no bill of rights to protect those fundamental rights of the people for which they had fought since the Magna Carta, and for which they had just suffered the agony of revolution.

Altogether, said Mason, the constitution was not a democratic instrument at all; it set up a government of the privileged few to rule over the many, and left the many with almost no means whatever to alter the government to take account of their needs and rights. "This government," said Mason, "will set out a moderate aristocracy: it is impossible at present to foresee whether it will, in its operation, produce a monarchy, or a corrupt, tyrannical aristocracy; it will most probably vibrate some years between the two, and then terminate in the one or the other."

"This Constitution," declared Mason, "had been formed without the knowledge or idea of the people. A second Convention will know more of the sense of the people, and be able to provide a system more consonant to it. It was improper to say to the people, take this or nothing." As it was, said Mason, he could not put his name to the document, and when he returned to Virginia, he would give it neither his support nor his vote there. Only if the delegates provided for a second convention would he sign.

Elbridge Gerry rose in support of Randolph and Mason, to give his list of objections to the document. Among other things, he said, he objected to the duration and reeligibility of the senate, as a method of election certain to encourage aristocracy. He objected to the number of representatives allotted to Massachusetts as not sufficient. He objected that three-fifths of blacks were to be represented "as if they were freemen." He objected that under the congressional power over commerce, monopolies might be established. But all these objections were minor, said Gerry, and he could dismiss them, "if the rights of citizens were not rendered insecure." And those rights had been rendered insecure by the power of Congress to make whatever laws they "may please to call necessary and proper," to raise armies and money without limit, and to establish a tribunal without juries. Under the circumstances, he thought the best that could be done was to provide for another convention after the people had had a chance to digest this proposed instrument. For his part, he could not sign the document as it was.

No one replied to Gerry. No one any longer cared to bother. And all, in any case, were preoccupied with their own private anguish about the document they were about to accept. Franklin disliked the document, thinking it cheated democracy. He had favored, along with Randolph and Mason and Gerry, having a second convention. Hamilton had frankly expressed his dislike for the constitution, thinking it not nearly aristocratic enough. Gentleman John Francis Mercer of Maryland, among others, had walked out. Nearly everyone had had to give up some cherished object, and to accept some despicable provision.

Indeed, as one looked around the hall, it was impossible to find anyone who was entirely happy with the document. And it was easy to find delegates who openly detested it, or only settled for it out of fatigue or despair of doing better. "I wish," General Washington wrote to Patrick Henry, "the Constitution which is offered had been made more perfect, but I sincerely believe it is the best that could be obtained at this time."

Edmund Randolph's motion to call for a second convention was brought to a vote, and the delegates shouted it down without even a roll call. And then, with that last obstacle removed from their way, the great question was put on the summer's work as a whole, whether "to agree to the Constitution as amended," and all the states voted at once: "Ay."

Suddenly the work was finished. The last vote was cast. The delegates consented to rest with what they had done. The session had run late, until six o'clock in the evening. It was Saturday, the fifteenth of September. The delegates adjourned to allow time for a copyist to engross the text in a fine hand on four large pieces of parchment.

23

THE SIGNING

ON MONDAY MORNING, the seventeenth of September, the delegates converged on the State House for the last time. The summer heat had abated. It had rained over the weekend, leaving the city clear, cool, and fresh. Forty-one of the sixty-one delegates appointed to the convention were there for the last ceremony of the reading and signing of the document. John Dickinson, worn out by the long summer of debates, had left over the weekend, asking George Read to sign for him. Hamilton sat alone at the New York delegation's table. Ellsworth had gone back home to tend to business, leaving Johnson and Sherman there on behalf of Connecticut. Gorham and King of Massachusetts were there, Paterson and Livingston and Wiliamson and Daniel of St. Thomas Jenifer and the latecomers Langdon and Gilman were there. All the Pennsylvanians were in their seats. All four South Carolinians were in attendance. Washington, Madison, and Judge Blair were there. And the three dissenters—Randolph, Mason, and Gerry—were there to withhold their signatures.

The engrossed constitution was read aloud to the delegates, who listened to the familiar words in silence. At the end, Dr. Franklin rose. He had a speech in his hand, but since it was a long speech, and he found it hard to stand for long, he asked James Wilson to read it out for him.

"Mr. President," Franklin's speech began, "I confess that there are several parts of this constitution which I do not at present approve, but I am not sure I shall ever approve them: For having lived long, I have experienced many instances of being obliged by better information or fuller consideration, to change opinions even on important subjects, which I once thought right, but found to be otherwise. It is therefore that the older I grow, the more apt I am to doubt my own judgment, and to pay more respect to the judgment of others."

It was, evidently, to be Franklin's last effort to bring his fellow delegates together into some sense of shared community, to bring them to accept the work they had done so that they could take it to the country and, in good conscience, seek its approval.

He doubted, said Franklin, whether any other convention that the country was capable of assembling would be able to make a better constitution. For "when you assemble a number of men to have the advantage of their joint wisdom, you inevitably assemble with those men, all their prejudices, their passions, their errors of opinion, their local interests, and their selfish views. From such an Assembly can a perfect production be expected?"

Thus, said Franklin, he consented to the constitution "because I expect no better, and because I am not sure that it is not the best."

As for the opinions he had of the constitution's errors, "I sacrifice them to the public good." He would not voice them outside the walls of the State House. For, "if every one of us in returning to our Constituents were to report the objections he has had to it, and endeavor to gain partisans in support of them, we might prevent its being generally received."

He wished, said Franklin, that those members of the convention who still had objections to the constitution "would with me on this occasion doubt a little of his own infallibility—and to manifest our unanimity, put his name to the instrument." To make it easier for each man to do this, and still be true to his own conscience, however, Franklin had a sly suggestion. He suggested that the constitution have a phrase added to the end: "Done in Convention, by the unanimous consent of the States . . . In Witness whereof we have hereunto subscribed our names." Thus the delegates would not have to say that they unanimously approved of the constitution, but would only attest to the fact that the state delegations voted unanimously in approval.

Gorham of Massachusetts immediately took the floor and said that if it was not too late, and with the thought of making the constitution less objectionable to some of the members present, he would propose amending the clause about representation in the house of representatives to specify that the number of representatives "shall not exceed one for every thirty thousand inhabitants" rather than one for every forty thousand. In this way, the membership of the house would be increased.

At that moment General Washington rose, and made his only speech to the convention. He wished, said the general briefly, that this proposed alteration might be made. "The smallness of the proportion of Representatives had been considered by many members of the Convention an insufficient security for the rights and interests of the people." As late as it was for proposing amendments, he thought this one of such consequence, involving as it did the principle of democratic representation, "that it would give much satisfaction to see it adopted."

There was no further debate. The measure, with Washington's approval, was adopted unanimously.

And then Edmund Randolph, no doubt feeling remorse at having set himself apart from so many of his close colleagues, apologized for refusing to sign the constitution, and retreated from his retreat from it. He did not mean, he said, by this refusal to sign, "that he should oppose the Constitution without doors. He meant only," he said evasively, "to keep himself free to be governed by his duty as it should be prescribed by his future judgment."

Gouverneur Morris was less patient than Franklin. He had objections too, said Morris, but "considering the present plan as the best that was to be attained, he should take it with all its faults. The majority had determined in its favor, and by that determination he would abide." The great question was not whether or not this was the best possible government of all, but "shall there be a national government or not?" And if there was not, certainly there would be general anarchy.

As the delegates once again began to show their irritation

with one another, Franklin stepped back into the debate. Nothing was more important, in Franklin's view, than to keep friends, and to keep peace. He began by trying to conciliate Randolph, assuring him that he had not had him in mind in his previous remarks. When he had drawn up his speech, said Franklin, he did not know that any particular member would refuse to sign the constitution. He had "a high sense of obligation to Mr. Randolph for having brought forward the plan in the first instance, and for the assistance he had given in its progress." He would not think to judge Randolph harshly now—although he did wish the member from Virginia would "yet lay aside his objections, and, by concurring with his brethren, prevent the great mischief which the refusal of his name might produce."

Still Randolph refused to sign, as did Mason, and Gerry. And so the convention voted (ten in favor, none opposed, one divided) to have the delegates sign the document in a manner that attested to the fact that the states unanimously approved it—against the firm opposition, ironically enough, of the very man who had opened the convention with the presentation of the Virginia Plan.

The original parchment copy of the document was so prepared and then set out on the small baize-covered table at the front of the room, next to the silver inkstand. The delegates formed up to come to the table to sign the document. It was past three o'clock in the afternoon, and the sun had moved so that it cast its light satisfyingly over the table and the parchment. The delegates arranged themselves geographically, beginning with New Hampshire and going south through Massachusetts, Connecticut, and New York, down to Georgia.

Franklin had to be helped slowly to the front of the room, and it was said that he wept as he signed. Whether or not that was true, certainly the old man could not resist a small fit of sentimentality was he looked up to see the presiding officer's chair, on which a bright sun happened to be painted. As the last of the delegates were signing the document, Franklin turned to several colleagues who were standing near him and remarked that painters had always found it difficult, in their art, to distinguish a rising from a setting sun. He himself, said Franklin, had often wondered, as he gazed at the speaker's chair during the debates, worrying over the course that the convention was taking, whether this sun was rising or setting. "But now at length I have the happiness to know that it is a rising and not a setting Sun."

After the last member had signed, the parchment document was dispatched by stagecoach to New York and to Congress. The delegates voted, unanimously, to adjourn *sine die*, and as Washington recorded in his diary, "The business being closed, the members adjourned to the City Tavern," Philadelphia's most genteel tavern, for dinner at the hands of cooks experienced in both the French and English manner, and, no doubt, for lashings of Madeira, port, punch, and brandy.

None of the delegates lingered in Philadelphia. Some left that very night. Some rushed up to New York, where Congress was in session, to make certain that their handiwork got the proper sort of attention and approval. Messrs. Claypoole and Dunlap were rewarded at last for their discretion: Having the constitution in hand, they were allowed to be the first to print it, in their newspaper, the *Pennsylvania Packet*. Within the next few days, all the other Philadelphia papers had picked it up; and in the next two weeks, papers around the country published the document, often in special editions.

Washington left the day after the delegates' last celebration at City Tavern, at about one o'clock, accompanied in his carriage by Judge Blair. They journeyed back across the bridge at Gray's Ferry and down to Chester, where they spent the night, then off late in the morning (held up by rain), retracing in reverse Washington's trip to Philadelphia, lodging at Head of Elk on the Elk River. There, crossing the river, they had a narrow escape. Because of the previous night's rainfall, the river was too swollen to ford safely, and the only bridge was, as Washington said, "old, rotten, and long disused." His choices were to stay an extra day until the river had calmed down, or take the bridge. Washington and Judge Blair got out of the carriage and sent it on across the bridge. The bridge gave way, and one of the horses fell through. The second horse was about to follow, and the carriage after it, but the men rushed forward, helped by some people from a nearby mill, and pulled the carriage and the horses out, and up on the far side of the river.

Washington was home in three more days, to his great relief. He arrived at Mount Vernon on September 22 at sunset,
as he recorded in his diary, "after being absent 4 months and
14 days." The next day he spent with his family; friends came
to dinner; and the day following he was back on his horse,
riding out to Dogue Run and Muddy Hole to check on the wheat
and the rye, to see how well the plows were working in field
number six, and to oversee the labor of farmhands in the New
Meadow.

In Philadelphia, of the delegates who had come from out
of town, only Madison stayed on—postponing for several days
his return to New York, and to the sessions of Congress there,
in order to work away in his room at Mrs. House's. There, in
solitude once again, surrounded by his histories and papers,
working meticulously by candlelight, he sent off several copies
of the constitution to a few of his close friends, along with his
notes on his own evaluation of the work.

He felt still the blow of having lost, by virtue of the great
compromise, everything he had prepared for so many months
to achieve. Madison believed that the recognition the convention had given to the states in the senate would empower the
states to keep the central government from ever being supreme. As he wrote to Jefferson, "the plan, should it be adopted,
will neither effectually answer its national object nor prevent
the local mischiefs which everywhere excite disgust against the
state governments." And he saw little to redeem his failure.

Ironically enough, of all the delegates who attended the
Constitutional Convention, it was Madison who, in the years
to come, would undergo the most dramatic change of mind. As
the delegates had all assumed, Washington would indeed become the first president; and as many had feared, Washington
and Hamilton and the other centrists who joined Washington's
administration, and those who followed in 1796 in the administration of John Adams, began to build a very high-toned central government on the foundation of the constitution. In truth,
by the late 1790s, when troubles with the French sent anxieties
of possible war through the country, the central government
passed three quite high-handed laws. The first of these was the
Naturalization Act of 1798, which revised the required period
of residency for citizenship from five to fourteen years. The

second was the Alien Act, which gave the president the power to expel foreigners by simple executive order. And the third was the Sedition Act, which took a nasty step past rooting out conspirators and made it a misdemeanor to speak or write against the president of Congress "with the intent to defame" or even to bring them "into contempt or disrepute." Twenty-five men were arrested under this law, and ten were convicted, including several newspaper editors and a congressman.

What was to stand against such patently unconstitutional laws? The answer came at once from James Madison, who wrote what came to be called the Virginia Resolves: Nothing could stand between the citizens and an unconstitutional federal government but the states, declared Madison. He clung still to the Union; he did not argue for the right of individual states to stand between the government and individual citizens; but he did argue that the states together had the right to declare laws void. Having fought to the very end against giving any residual powers to the states in the constitution, he now turned to the states to preserve the elusive balance of power he had tried to demolish.

In his opposition to the Alien and Sedition laws, Madison was joined by his old friend Jefferson (who wrote the Kentucky Resolves, which argued that an individual state *did* have the right to interpose itself between a citizen and the federal government). Together Madison and Jefferson launched a campaign against what seemed to them a dangerous tendency toward a too powerful central government. When Jefferson was elected president in 1800, thousands of ordinary people throughout America felt the country had been returned to them. And Madison began to acquire the reputation that he has had ever since, of being one of America's strongest defenders of local self-rule and liberty against a too strong central government. He had, at last, embraced the Great Compromise.

EPILOGUE: RATIFICATION

THE INITIAL REACTION to the constitution was one of surprise, even shock. It was one thing to write a constitution, and quite another to have it accepted. When the constitution was first broadcast across the country, it seems fair to say, the majority of the people were completely against it. "The greatness of the powers given" to this new government, declared the renowned Revolutionary hero Richard Henry Lee of Virginia, "and the multitude of places to be created, produce a coalition of monarchy men, military men, aristocrats and drones, whose noise, impudence, and zeal exceed all beliefs." To say, said Lee, "as many do, that a bad government must be established, for fear of anarchy, is really saying, that we must kill ourselves, for fear of dying."

Here was a central government far too strong, with a president sure to grow to royal proportions, a senate already constituted with the lineaments of aristocracy, and a house of representatives that was, as Colonel Mason said, "not the substance, but the shadow only of representation," or as Lee declared, "a mere shred, or rag of representation." There was no bill of rights in this constitution; there was an unlimited power for the central government to levy taxes. What, many of the veterans of the American Revolution wondered, had they fought the war for?

Before the opposition could quite gather its forces, however, the plan was slipped dexterously past Congress. Madison,

William Samuel Johnson of Connecticut, Rufus King, Nathaniel Gorham, Langdon and Gilman of New Hampshire, were all in New York to help push it through Congress and on to the special ratifying conventions that the plan called for. Only eight days after the new constitution was presented to Congress, a vote was called. Of those who were present to vote, nearly a third had been delegates to the Constitutional Convention, and the momentum they gave to its passage through Congress was irresistible. Richard Henry Lee objected to this unseemly haste, which seemed to smack of stampeding the Congress before its members had had a chance to digest the proposal.

The resolution that sent the constitution along to the state legislatures, calling on the states to summon special ratifying conventions, opened with the words "Resolved unanimously." This was a nasty piece of trickery, said Lee, giving the impression that the Congress had some sort of unanimously positive feeling for the new plan; there was nothing unanimous about Congress's reaction to the constitution except their agreement to pass it on to the states.

What was possibly even a nastier piece of trickery was that the defenders of the constitution had taken to calling themselves federalists. In truth, "federalists" were people who believed in the federal form of government provided by the Articles of Confederation. Partisans of the constitution, who believed in a strong national government, ought honestly to have called themselves nationalists. But the designation federalist had a long and familiar tradition, and Americans loved it; so the pro-constitution forces absconded with the word, insisting that they meant they favored a strong and efficient federal government; and the true federalists were reduced to calling themselves antifederalists.

Jefferson, in Paris, was showered with copies of the constitution by Madison, Washington, Franklin, and others of his friends and colleagues. Elbridge Gerry managed to rush the first copy to him, with a few prejudicing remarks about it. Jefferson looked over the plan dispassionately and concluded that its lack of a bill of rights was a deep fault. He hoped, Jefferson wrote to Madison, with the sensibility of an Olympian, that "the first 9 conventions may receive, and the last 4 reject [the constitution]. The former will secure it finally, while the latter will oblige them to offer a declaration of rights in order to complete the union. We shall thus have all its good, and cure its principal defects."

Those who had spent the summer in the caldron of Philadelphia were not as detached as Jefferson. Even before the text of the constitution had reached the Congress in New York, Franklin had appeared before the Pennsylvania state legislature, and prodded one of his colleagues to read the document aloud to the Assembly.

The Assembly, as it happened, was in its closing days, getting ready to adjourn and to have its members stand for a new election. The framers of the constitution wanted the Assembly, before it adjourned, to set up elections to a ratifying convention. One of the framers proposed a motion to that effect.

Robert Whitehill, a backcountry man, whose farm lay out beyond the Susquehanna River near Harrisburg, rose on the floor of the Assembly. Whitehill had been one of the authors of the Pennsylvania constitution of 1776, which had provided for a one-house legislature, annual elections, and election of the president of the Supreme Executive Council by the legislature—a model democratic system, now about to be buried under the new federal constitution. Whitehill opposed the motion, charging its defenders with a lack of candor in trying to jam the constitution through before the people had had a chance to become acquainted with it.

But the friends of the framers held a majority in the Pennsylvania Assembly, and they insisted, by a margin of forty-three to nineteen, on bringing the issue of ratification to a vote on the floor that very afternoon. Then, just after taking that vote, they adjourned until four o'clock.

During the recess, Whitehill and the gathering band of opponents of the constitution, most of them western Pennsylvanians, supporters of the old radical Pennsylvania constitution of '76, agreed on a strategy to stop the framers. The Assembly consisted of sixty-nine members; a quorum of forty-six was required for the Assembly to conduct business. Whitehill's antifederalists, by staying away from the afternoon session, could keep a quorum from appearing in the Assembly hall and so force an adjournment.

When the Assembly resumed that afternoon, a roll call

showed only forty-four members present, and so the following morning, the Assembly dispatched the sergeant at arms to round up missing members. The sergeant at arms returned soon enough with the news that the missing members refused to attend the session. The Assembly adjourned, with the partisans of the constitution angered by Whitehill's ruse.

The next day the Assembly gathered for yet another session. Again a quorum was missing. Again the sergeant at arms was sent out to gather up the missing members. By this time, the resolution of the Congress in New York (which called for state legislatures to summon ratifying conventions) had arrived in Philadelphia, and the sergeant at arms went out with this resolution authoritatively in hand. He was backed up by a group of the framers' supporters, who went along with him, raising a ruckus as they careened from tavern to tavern, stirring up partisans on both sides.

Eventually, the little self-appointed posse came upon two of Whitehill's men ensconced in their lodgings. The resolution of Congress was read to the recalcitrant members. Still the members refused to budge. And so the unofficial posse swarmed into the rooms, took hold of the two Assembly members, and dragged them, protesting, back through the streets of Philadelphia and into the Assembly hall. There a large group of local artisans, always dependably hostile to country men, and especially to westerners, crowded around—shouting and mocking the out-of-towners, following them into the Assembly hall, jamming the doors, and blocking any chance of escape. The two westerners were unceremoniously shoved forward, their clothes torn, their faces, it was said, "white with rage." One of the westerners, keeping his mind clearly focused on the Whitehill strategy, offered to pay a fine for his absence, but the crowd laughed him down. And when he turned to make his escape, the crowd shouted out, "Stop him!"—and he was turned back into the room. With their quorum assembled, the Pennsylvania legislature duly voted—with only two votes against the motion—to set the first Tuesday in November as election day for delegates to the Pennsylvania ratifying convention.

The strong-arm tactics of the federalists aroused terrific passion, and although the federalists controlled most of the newspapers, the editor of Philadelphia's *Independent Gazetteer* took up the cudgels against the federalists and published a series of attacks written under the byline Centinel. According to Centinel, Pennsylvanians had "the peculiar felicity of living under the most perfect system of local government in the world"—now about to be replaced by "the supremacy of the lordly and profligate few." These few were attempting to stampede the people into accepting their new scheme by saying there was "no alternative between adoption and absolute ruin." This, said Centinel, was "the argument of tyrants." These conniving aristocrats tried to dignify their cause by dressing it up with the presence of Washington and Franklin. "I would be far from insinuating that the two illustrious personages alluded to, have not the welfare of their country at heart; but that the unsuspecting goodness and zeal of the one has been imposed upon, in a subject of which he must be necessarily inexperienced . . . and that the weakness and indecision attendant on old age has been practiced on in the other."

Centinel was joined by some others in criticizing the constitution—most notably by one of the very framers, Colonel George Mason, who published his list of objections in the *Pennsylvania Packet*. The story circulated widely that Mason had declared that he would sooner cut off his right hand than put his signature to the constitution.

This defection, among other goads, brought James Wilson out of his study and into the garden on the south side of the State House to address a public meeting. Public speaking was not Wilson's strong suit. His manner, his "lordly carriage," was so naturally offensive to most people that one federalist newspaper writer labored to explain that Wilson *had* to hold his head as he did in order to keep his spectacles from falling off his nose. But he spoke with his customary close reasoning, and his audience evidently listened closely.

The greatest, and most commonly heard, charge against the constitution, said Wilson, was that it lacked a bill of rights. but in the constitution, every right that was not specifically granted to the central government was reserved to the states. To have drawn up a list of particular rights would only have duplicated what was already in the state constitutions. Strictly speaking, Wilson's arguments were true: All rights not specifically given the federal government were reserved to the states and the citizens. But Wilson's opponents knew that reasoning of this sort was too abstract for comfort.

As for the omission of a provision for trial by jury in civil cases, said Wilson, the usages of the various states so differed as to make a uniform law impossible. As for the issue of a standing army, the power of direct taxation, and other matters, Wilson explained the reasoning of the Constitutional Convention in each case. His speech was superb; it only lacked an attempt to deal with the central complaint of the anitfederalists—that the new constitution set a federal government above a state government that was, in Pennsylvania's case at least, more democratic. He tried to get around that difficult issue simply by tarring his opponents. "It is the nature of man," said Wilson, "to pursue his own interests in preference to the public good." And so he was not surprised that so many men opposed this new constitution, since it threatened to eliminate lucrative state offices which they currently held and otherwise affected their "schemes of wealth and consequence."

For their part, the antifederalists struck back at Wilson with the locally familiar charge that he "has always been strongly tainted with the spirit of *high aristocracy;* he has never been known to join in a truly popular measure, and his talents have ever been devoted to the patrician interest."

And to that a federalist writer replied with a recipe for an "Antifederal Essay." The correct ingredients were these: *"Well-born,* nine times— *Aristocracy,* eighteen times— . . . *Negro slavery,* once mentioned— *Trial by Jury,* seven times— *Great Men,* six times repeated—MR. WILSON, forty times—and lastly, GEORGE MASON's *Right Hand in a Cutting Box,* nineteen times— put them all together, and dish them up at pleasure."

If the antifederalists tended toward exaggeration and violence in their diatribes, the federalists tended toward condescension and contempt in theirs. But since Philadelphia was a cosmopolitan, commercial port city—and so a federalist one— the defenders of the constitution had the clearest advantage in mob action. Roving bands of supporters of the new constitution roamed the streets, banging on doors and lobbing rocks through windows. They did little real damage, though they tried to spread as much fear as they could. When the antifederalists demanded the arrest of the disorderly gang that attacked one lodging place of their fellows, the city administration—a federalist lot—failed to find any of the unruly mob.

When at last elections were held for the ratifying convention, the antifederalists had managed to elect some colorful old country politicians to represent their cause—among them two native Irishmen, John Smilie, a former house carpenter; and William Findley, a weaver. Findley, a big fellow with shaggy hair and a genial, disrespectful manner, affected his own form of patrician dress. He had a fondness in particular for white beaver hats. He and his colleagues were wily politicians of long experience, deeply dedicated to frontier liberties and individualism, men far better able to cajole a crowd than James Wilson was; but their talents did not count for much. The federalists had outpolled the antifederalists in the election by a margin of two to one; and when the convention gathered on November 21, the federalists had forty-six delegates to the antifederalists' twenty-three. Men of both sides would grapple heroically with each other in debate; but when it came to voting, they would split exactly among federalist/antifederalist lines.

Unable to affect the outcome by persuasion, Whitehill resorted to parliamentary maneuvers—trying to get the convention to rearrange itself as a committee of the whole, a ruse calculated to delay the convention, to give the antifederalists time to rally opposition to the constitution. But Whitehill's motion—like all the other maneuvers of the antifederalists—was brought quickly to a vote, and voted down by a margin of two to one. Gradually, in one vote after another, the antifederalists were brought around grudgingly to the final vote—whether or not to ratify the constitution as a whole—and the state of Pennsylvania declared itself in favor of the constitution, forty-six to twenty-three.

The vote placed the crucial state of Pennsylvania in the column of supporters of the constitution—but at an enormous price. Having won by virtue of sheer power—and even of brute force—the federalists did much to damage their own cause across the country. If these were to be their consistent tactics, they might well anticipate defeat. A couple of weeks after the Pennsylvania ratifying convention, at a bonfire celebration of the new constitution, a gang of antifederalists came out of the dark armed with clubs and attacked James Wilson. Wilson fought back and was knocked to the ground, and he might have been done in had not an old soldier who was present thrown himself on top of Wilson to shield the convention's staunchest defender of popular suffrage from the blows of the people.

Yet if ratification in Pennsylvania was a bitter experience, several other states came along without any great battle. Indeed, the little states fell into line with surprising ease. After all the trouble they had caused at the Constitutional Convention, they proved now the most eager to put themselves under the protection of this strong new government. Delaware, with the support of John Dickinson and George Read, had actually preceded Pennsylvania in approving the constitution—thus, in the words of one of the Pennsylvania antifederalists, having "reaped the honor of having first surrendered the liberties of the people"—by a unanimous thirty to zero vote of its delegates to the ratifying convention. New Jersey's ratifying convention debated for a full week before voting unanimously in favor of the constitution—with Paterson leading the way. In Maryland, the elections to the ratifying convention gave such a large margin to the federalists that they did not even bother debating. They simply sat back, listened to Luther Martin and his colleagues rail at them for four days, and then called for a vote. The vote went sixty-three to eleven in favor of the constitution. Georgia voted unanimously in favor. Connecticut came along with somewhat more thoughtfulness and ambivalence, voting in favor of ratification by 128 to forty.

Even so, as these federalist victories piled up, several key states of the Union—Massachusetts, Virginia, and New York— all of them crucial to the success of the new plan, had yet to be heard from. And each, in its way, was to prove very difficult. To assist the federalist cause in the resistant political atmosphere of New York, a series of essays commenced to appear in the newspapers, signed with the pen name Publius, that argued in favor of adopting the new constitution—essays that would come to be known collectively as *The Federalist*. It had been Hamilton's idea to turn out these essays, with which he hoped to overwhelm the New York opposition. And overwhelm the opposition he did, publishing eighty-five essays in all, one every two or three days, for a period of six months, essays that considered the proposed constitution from every angle of dispute, answered its opponents' objections, and explained the principles on which the constitution rested.

To help him write some of the essays in this rhetorical tour de force, Hamilton recruited Madison—who had, of course, been at the convention every day that summer, and knew the plan inside out—and John Jay, who had not been in Philadelphia, but was a learned lawyer (who would become the first chief justice of the Supreme Court), and a man who shared Hamilton's admiration for the established order, for aristocracy if not monarchy.

The Federalist is, perhaps, not the best of all possible guides to just what the constitution is and is meant to be, since it was intended—to be altogether candid—as the text for a sales campaign. Moreover, it was written by one man (Hamilton) who was so opposed to the basic ideas of the constitution that he did not attend most of the sessions of the convention, who spoke rarely in the convention, and when he did speak, spoke most eloquently on behalf of aristocracy; by another (Jay) who was not at the convention at all and whose Anglophilia would have predisposed him to a far more aristocratic scheme than the one that conventioneers finally framed; and by a third (Madison) who had a view of a necessarily unfettered supremacy of the national government that had not been accepted by the other delegates. Under the circumstances, it cannot be surprising that *The Federalist* promotes a conception of the constitution that is, among other things, more aristocratic than the consensus of those who actually wrote the document.

Hamilton opened the series with an outline of the whole project, promising that the series would cover the necessity of the Union, the deficiencies of the Confederation, the need for an energetic government, and the ways in which the proposed constitution corresponded to republican principles. Jay followed with four essays on the need for a union to cope with foreign dangers and sectional disputes—arguing, among other things, that the breadth of interests in the new government would be so great as to inhibit men's natural proclivities to go to war; that, in this sense as well as in others, the extended republic would actually give rise to public virtue.

The essays took up issues of the military, of the separation of powers, of the house and senate, of the means of election, of the presidency, and of the judiciary—all of them issues that had been debated in the convention in detail. Several of Madison's essays constituted a neatened-up version of the notes on ancient and modern confederacies that he had used throughout the convention debates. One of Madison's most famous essays, *Federalist* Number 10, spoke of the way in which factions are formed—along economic lines—which he had gone into at some length during the convention: of how the poor need to be protected from the rich as well as the rich from the poor, and how all the citizens need to be protected from the depredations of whatever factions are formed.

Nothing in *The Federalist* would have been unfamiliar to a delegate to the Constitutional Convention (except the absence of sharply conflicting views). Here were the arguments—and the references to history, to renowned political philosophers, to the examples of England and Germany and ancient Greece and Rome, to more recent and common American experience—that had been heard in Philadelphia, here expressed in classically balanced and elegant language, with perfectly honed phrases, and pruned into a coherent, if not entirely representative, vision.

The Federalist was not without its critics. The antifederalists were particularly incensed that Publius alleged that they wanted several separate confederacies, which was simply not true. And one friendly observer, even as he praised *The Federalist*, said he could not understand why Publius had taken such pains to argue what seemed so evident, that a strong, efficient government was better "than the States disunited into distinct, independent governments, or separate confederacies." But General Washington pronounced himself pleased with the essays, saying he thought no other public presentation of the arguments in favor of the constitution was "so well calculated . . . to produce conviction on an unbiased mind." And Jefferson thought *The Federalist* was "the best commentary on the principles of government which ever was written."

The essays were reprinted in the newspapers and magazines around the country, though not very widely reprinted:

Twenty-two publications printed at least one of the essays, but only six journals reprinted six or more of them. Although they received wide circulation in book form, what was crucial about the writings of Publius was not that they were a great popular success but that they circulated among those men who were taking part in ratifying conventions across the country, and gave partisans of the constitution the best arguments they could use in favor of the new plan.

Such arguments were essential—and proved crucial—in the state of Massachusetts, whose ratifying convention of 350 members gathered on January 8, 1788, in Boston's Brattle Church, with a narrow but distinct majority opposed to the constitution.

The Massachusetts convention had among its delegates some of the famous old figures of the Revolution, including the radical democrat Sam Adams, and John Hancock, who was enormously popular and enormously powerful. Because he was so sensitive to the ways the political breezes were blowing, he was able to side with the rich Boston merchants and with Daniel Shays at the same time. (Hancock stayed away from the early sessions, claiming that his gout was too severely painful to let him leave home—holding back on purpose, his critics said, waiting until the outcome of the convention was certain so that he would be sure to be on the winning side.)

Unlike Pennsylvania, the ratifying convention that was assembled in Boston was not stacked with federalists; among the members of the convention were not only a fair sampling of farmers from the western parts of Massachusetts but even twenty-nine men who had fought with Shays.

"Sir," said the plainspeaking Samuel Thompson to the chairman of the convention, "gentlemen have said a great deal about the history of old times" in proving the superiority of this new constitution over the old democratic ways of New England. "I confess, I am not acquainted with such history— but I am, sir, acquainted with the history of my own country." And, from that acquaintance, said Thompson, "I suspect my own heart, and I shall suspect our rulers." Too much power was granted to the distant new government, and without adequate restraints built in. He wondered at the great rush to push this constitution through to acceptance. "There are some parts of this constitution which I cannot digest: and, sir, shall we swallow a large bone for the sake of a little meat? Some say swallow the whole now, and pick out the bone afterwards. But I say, let us pick off the meat, and throw the bone away."

Massachusetts was a state full of enthusiasts for the tradition of the democratic town meeting and deeply suspicious of any republican idea of the delegation of authority to elected representatives. And opponents of the constitution filled the newspapers with attacks on "the hideous daemon of aristocracy . . . the NOBLE order of Cincinnatus, holders of public securities, bankers and lawyers, who were for having the people gulp down the gilded pill blindfolded."

The idea that a single central government, said another of the delegates, could efficiently and justly rule in every small town of such a vast continent was absurd. "You might as well attempt too rule Hell by prayer."

That the new plan called for senators to be elected for terms of six years was outrageous in the eyes of men who believed annual elections to be the most basic requirement of democracy. The senate was an aristocratical bunch, said one delegate, and the house was nothing but an "assistant aristocratical branch."

"Had I a voice like Jove," thundered Samuel Nason, a saddler and storekeeper from Maine, "I would proclaim it throughout the world—and had I an arm like Jove I would hurl from the world those villains that would attempt to establish in our country a standing army! I wish, sir, that gentlemen of Boston would bring to their minds the fatal evening of the 5th of March, 1770, when by standing troops they lost five of their fellow townsmen."

"These lawyers," said Amos Singletary, a self-taught farmer from Worchester County who had sat in the state legislature for years, "and men of learning, and moneyed men that talk so finely, and gloss over matters so smoothly, to make us poor illiterate people swallow down the pill, expect to get into Congress themselves. They expect to be the managers of the Constitution, and get all the power and all the money into their own hands. And then they will swallow up us little fellows."

This remark by Singletary drew forth at last a reply from

another fellow farmer, Jonathan Smith, a Berkshireman. "Mr. President," said Smith, "I am a plain man, and get my living by the plough. I am not used to speak in public, but I beg your leave to say a few words to my brother ploughjoggers in this house. I have lived in a part of the country where I have known the worth of good government, by the want of it. There was a black cloud that rose in the east last winter [Smith did not need to mention Shays by name], and spread over the west."

At this, another delegate rose and challenged Smith to say what he meant by the east.

"I mean, sir, the county of Bristol," said Smith. "The cloud rose there and burst upon us, and produced a dreadful effect. It brought on a state of anarchy that led to tyranny. I say, it brought anarchy. People that used to live peaceably, and were before good neighbors, got distracted, and took up arms against government."

Here another delegate rose angrily and asked what this had to do with the constitution. Sam Adams intervened, and asked that the house let the gentleman "go on in his own way."

". . . People, I say, took up arms, and then, if you went to speak to them, you had the musket of death presented to your breast. They would rob you of your property, threaten to burn your houses; oblige you to be on your guard night and day; alarms spread from town to town; families were broke up; the tender mother would cry, O, my son is among them! . . . Then we should hear of an action, and the poor prisoners were set in the front, to be killed by their own friends. . . . Our distress was so great that we should have been glad to snatch at anything that looked like a government."

When Smith saw this new constitution, "I found that it was a cure for these disorders . . . I got a copy of it and read it over and over. I had been a member of the convention to form our own state constitution, and had learnt something of the checks and balances of power, and I found them all here. I did not go to any lawyer to ask his opinion—we have no lawyer in our town, and we do well enough without. I formed my own opinion, and was pleased with this constitution. My honorable old daddy there [gesturing to Amos Singletary] won't think that I expect to be a congressman and swallow up the liberties of the people. I never had any post, nor do I want one.

But I don't think the worse of the constitution because lawyers and men of learning and monied men are fond of it."

While the debates went along in this way, freer than the debates had been in Pennsylvania, and more down-to-earth, the federalists worked behind the scenes to do all they could, short of the strong-arm tactics their colleagues had used in Pennsylvania, to influence the outcome. They were not having an easy time of it. Madison, who kept his eye on the progress of the constitution through each of the state ratifying conventions, wrote to Washington that the news from Massachusetts "begins to be very ominous."

The most crucial piece of politicking the federalists labored to bring off was to recruit John Hancock to their side, and they finally succeeded at this with the aid of Sam Adams. At first Adams had been opposed to the constitution. "I stumble at the threshold," he wrote to Richard Henry Lee. "I meet with a national government instead of a federal union of sovereign states." Adams was helped across the threshold by a shrewd plan for compromise. The constitution had been presented to Massachusetts, as to the other states, in a take-it-or-leave-it fashion. The states were not to be allowed to set any conditions to their acceptance of the constitution; they must ratify it exactly as it stood, or turn it down. But as it began to appear that the antifederalists might defeat the constitution altogether, a group of federalists got together with Adams and came up with what they called a Conciliatory Proposition—a plan to mollify the anxieties of the antifederalists, and of Adams and others. Their notion was that the constitution ought to be ratified, but with a number of "suggestions" for amendments attached to it. The suggestions would not be demands or conditions; they would simply be Massachusetts' first order of business for the new government to take up.

The Massachusetts men came up with a list of nine amendments, a list of fairly mundane concerns, including a limitation on the federal power to govern elections, and a prohibition against Congress establishing a "company of merchants with exclusive advantages of commerce." The items were not matters of great political principle; they were not a bill of rights. They were reflections of local concerns. But they were, also, a precedent: an insistence that Massachusetts would not accept a take-it-or-leave-it demand on the constitution. Massachusetts would simply go ahead and begin the process of amending the constitution. Thus, Adams and his colleagues not only broke the resistance of the Massachusetts convention to the constitution, they also provided an example for the states that would come after Massachusetts to present similar lists of suggestions. It was this example that led quickly to the Bill of Rights (which was ratified by the requisite number of states by December 5, 1791).

The group had Theophilus Parsons, a prominent Boston attorney, draw up a speech to present the Conciliatory Proposition to the convention, and then a little delegation of them called on John Hancock at his commodious home on Beacon Hill. They found Hancock languishing, his legs propped up and wrapped in flannel. The delegation told Hancock that the convention had reached the moment of decision, and that he could turn it in favor of the constitution. They told him, too, that according to the gossip, if he did join their cause he could expect their support for the next gubernatorial election in Massachusetts. Even more, they told him that it looked as though Virginia might not ratify the constitution. And if Virginia did not ratify, then Hancock would be the "only fair candidate for President" of the new United States. With that, Hancock's gout began to improve. He was carried like a hero into the convention, his legs still wrapped in flannel, and he delivered Theophilus Parsons's speech as though he had written it himself. The effect was wonderful. The convention was transformed.

To be sure, some of the antifederalists pointed out that a list of suggestions for amendments would have no binding effect. Such a set of proposals might make the men of Massachusetts feel better, but the objectionable system would remain exactly as it was. The hopes of the antifederalists would be defeated, and there would be no chance in the future to revive them.

Yet, after a few days of debate, minds began gradually to change. The question turned, in effect, on whether the process for amending the constitution seemed fair and workable, or, at least, better than the process for amending the Articles; if it did, then there seemed much less reason to oppose the constitution. Finally, a young antifederalist lawyer from Andover named William Symmes announced his change of position. He felt in his own mind, he said, that what he was doing was right. He knew that his constituents did not agree with him, but he hoped they would forgive him for what he was about to do. (As it turned out, his constituents never did see things Symmes's way; in fact, when he got back home, his neighbors made life so unpleasant for him that he had to move out of Andover.) With Symmes's change of mind, others followed.

Adams almost lost the momentum the federalists had acquired when he proposed a series of amendments to guarantee freedom of the press and the rights of conscience, to prohibit standing armies and unreasonable search and seizure. The effect of Adams's proposals was to throw the convention into a panic: If Adams thought such guarantees were necessary, then perhaps the new government did threaten to deprive the citizens of the states of their basic rights. And so Adams withdrew his motion.

In the end, when the final vote was called, the constitution was approved by a slim margin of 19 votes, 187 to 168. But then a most remarkable thing occurred. In place of the bitterness that had marked the conclusion of the Pennsylvania ratifying convention, a good deal of warm feeling was expressed in Brattle Church. Abraham White of Bristol County declared that he had opposed the constitution with all his will; but now, since a majority had decided in its favor, he would return home and work to persuade his constituents to live happily under it. Where the Pennsylvania convention had left bitterness in its wake, the Massachusetts convention left a sense—and a model for others to follow—of an agreement reached by those unique guarantors of legitimacy, the free exercise of speech and the ballot.

By June 2, when the Virginia delegates assembled at last in Richmond for their ratifying convention, eight states had voted in favor of the constitution. Only one more was needed, and it appeared that the Virginia vote could well be that one. But the Virginia delegates felt their vote was more important than simply a clinching one: Whether it was strictly true or not, the Virginians believed that there would be no Union at all without their own state, which had taken the lead in so much of the history of America, not to mention the constitution itself.

To be sure, the Virginians assembled a ratifying convention of some of the most illustrious men in the Union. Among the defenders of the constitution were Madison; George Wythe (who had had to leave the Philadelphia convention to attend to his sick wife); John Marshall (who would be chief justice of the Supreme Court, and was at the moment an intense young man of thirty-three); George Nicholas (a famous orator at the time, a rotund man whom a local caricaturist immortalized as a plum pudding with little legs); Judge Edmund Pendleton (chosen as the presiding officer of the convention, a commanding man whose presence was made even more riveting by the fact that he got about on crutches because he had injured a hip, and so rose to speak with elaborate, slow dignity). To the annoyance of Richard Henry Lee, his cousin Light Horse Harry Lee was to be found among the federalists too. And of course, the presence of General Washington, though he himself stayed carefully aloof at Mount Vernon, was felt in the hall on the side of the federalists.

Among the antifederalists were Colonel Mason (dressed most severely in black silk), James Monroe (at the moment an obscure young man of thirty), Benjamin Harrison (the father of President William Henry Harrison), John Tyler (the father of another president), and Richard Henry Lee. In the back of the hall were fourteen gun-toting delegates from frontier Kentucky (a territory still in the possession of Virginia).

The antifederalist forces were led by that extraordinary speechmaker Patrick Henry. Tall and stoop-shouldered, the practiced old orator could get so wound up in the heat of debate that he would take to twirling his ill-fitting brown wig around on his head as he laid about him with rhetorical flourishes. No one was his equal for sheer thespian dazzle. He had, it was said, the powers of Shakespeare and Garrick combined—or as Madison complained, Henry could demolish, merely with a pause or a shake of the head, an hour's worth of carefully constructed debate before he had even begun to speak. In Virginia, the antifederalists were called Henryites.

By contrast, Madison was his usual retiring self. So small he could barely be seen by the spectators, so soft-spoken he could often not be heard, he fell ill finally, in the midst of these exhausting debates, as he had in Philadelphia. It is a wonder that he was able, after all these interminable months of struggle for his cherished plan, to revive; but he did bounce back after several days, and took up the debate again—and even showed some sly sense of theatrics of his own. When he rose to speak, he would hold his hat in his hand (his painstakingly prepared notes were concealed inside his hat) and speak modestly, as though some little thought had just occurred to him— which he would then convey with his customary precise logic.

Patrick Henry opened the debate in Virginia by inquiring what right had the men who wrote the constitution to begin with the words *We the people?* "My political curiosity, exclusive of my anxious solicitude for the public welfare, leads me to ask, who authorized them to speak the language of *We the people*, instead of, *We the states?* States are the characteristics and the soul of a confederation. If the states be not the agents of this compact, it must be one great consolidated national government, of the people of all the states. . . . The people gave them no power to use their name . . . You must, therefore, forgive the solicitation of one unworthy member, to know what danger could have arisen under the present confederation, and what are the causes of this proposal to change our government."

Men spoke of dreadful unrest and dangers in the future, but had there been a single instance of such unrest in Virginia? To Henry and his followers, the Madisonian cure far exceeded the disease. If some difficulties had arisen among the states, then the powers of Congress to regulate trade needed to be strengthened, and the state governments needed to be given new vigor; but surely there was no need to surrender vast powers of taxation to a central government, to organize a court system that would cause the state courts to be swallowed up by the federal courts, to establish a standing army, to create a chief executive who would enslave America, to destroy the states, which were the bastions of liberty.

The constitution, said Henry, was as "radical" a document as the resolution "which separated us from Great Britain . . . The rights of conscience, trial by jury, liberty of the press, all your communities and franchises, all pretensions to human rights and privileges, are rendered insecure, if not lost, by this change . . . Is this tame relinquishment of rights worthy of freemen? . . . It is said eight states have adopted this plan. I declare that if twelve states and a half had adopted it, I would with manly firmness, and in spite of an erring world, reject it . . . Liberty, greatest of all earthly blessings—give us that precious jewel, and you may take everything else! But I am fearful I have lived long enough to become an old fashioned fellow.

"Whither," asked Henry, "is the spirit of America gone? Whither is the genius of America fled? . . . We drew the spirit of liberty from our British ancestors. But now, Sir, the American spirit, assisted by the ropes and chains of consolidation, is about to convert this country into a powerful and mighty empire . . . There can be no checks, no real balances, in this government. What can avail your specious, imaginary balances, your rope-dancing, chain-rattling, ridiculous ideal checks and contrivances?"

(Here, it was said—such was the power of Henry to conjure—a delegate "involuntarily felt his wrists to assure himself that the fetters were not already pressing his flesh.")

The Henryites did well in the debates; their arguments were moving and impressive as they returned again and again to the theme that liberty and democracy would, under this new constitution, be sacrificed to the juggernaut of nationalism and expansive imperialism. Whether they spoke of taxation or courts or the powers of the presidency, their theme was always the same: The government of Virginia was small, responsive, free, and good; and there was no need to sacrifice it to a vision of powerful nationalism. "Look at the use which has been made in all parts of the world of that human thing called power. Look at the predominant threat of dominion which has invariably and uniformly prompted rulers to abuse their power. . . . I conjure you to remember . . . that when you give power, you know now what you give . . . The experience of the world teaches me the jeopardy of giving enormous power."

Yet from the very beginning, the Henryites were undermined by a position that Edmund Randolph took in the debate. Randolph had switched his position again since the convention. No longer opposed to the Madisonians, he favored the constitution now—and the precise way in which he expressed his approval was particularly damaging to the Henryites. He had, he said, from the very first, liked the constitution drawn up by the Philadelphia convention, providing it could be improved, by the adoption of certain amendments, before it was ratified. It seemed to him that it was essential to make these amendments before the constitution was ratified. Now, however, he had come to realize that this procedure would cause dangerous delay in adopting a new form of government, that the delay would be such that the very survival of the Union would be jeopardized. That, said Randolph, was out of the question. He would rather, he said (in a rhetorical threat that was becoming altogether common), "assent to the lopping of [his right arm] before I assent to the dissolution of the union." Now Massachusetts had come up with a different means of proceeding—to propose amendments to be adopted at a later date—and Randolph liked this idea. It was a way of leaving the constitution open to improvement by way of a perfectly acceptable voting procedure. If one trusted the way the constitution was to be thus subject to the collective will of the people, there was nothing left to oppose. Given the choice between insisting on "previous amendments"—those insisted upon before the states agreed to ratify—and risking the fate of the Union, or settling for the Massachusetts example of "subsequent amendments"—those made in the future, after all the states had ratified—Randolph did not hesitate in taking the Massachusetts example.

Thus, Randolph set the terms of the debate: Delegates were given the choice not so much whether or not they would accept the constitution, but whether or not they would insist on previous amendments or settle for subsequent amendments. The antifederalists were forced to argue for previous amendments; the federalists opted for subsequent amendments—and as the debate wore on from day to day, the antifederalists came more and more to seem like mere obstructionists, who would not trust the democratic process of the future. And so it was the vacillating Randolph who, perhaps more than anyone else, finally tipped the balance toward ratification.

It can hardly be surprising that the Henryites were furious with Randolph. Henry himself turned to Randolph at one point in the debate and said: "That honorable member will not accuse me of want of candor when I cast in my mind what he has given to the public"—this in reference to a letter Randolph had written some time before to the Virginia legislature to explain why he had not signed the constitution—"and compare it to what has happened since." What was Henry about to do? Under the code of honor that held sway in the eighteenth century, he could not accuse Randolph of dishonesty, of having been bribed, of having been offered high office in the new government in trade for his support—at least not directly. "It seems to me very strange and unaccountable that that which was the object of his execration, should now receive his encomiums. Something extraordinary must have operated so great a change in his opinions."

Randolph had no doubt what Henry meant, and he rose with him temper flaring. "I disdain his aspersions," said Randolph to the convention, "and his insinuations. His asperity is warranted by no principle of parliamentary decency, nor compatible with the least shadow of friendship: and if our friendship must fall—let it fall, like Lucifer, never to rise again." Such words could not pass without consequences. That night Henry's second called on Randolph to arrange the particulars of a duel. But friends of the two men stepped in, mollified tempers, and the matter was settled, as it was said, "without a resort to the field."

Through all this, as the two sides counted and re-counted their delegate strength—and estimated that a change of four or five votes, or three votes, or eight votes, would decide the outcome—Madison rehearsed his familiar arguments: about the weakness of confederacies as seen in ancient examples, about the need for direct taxation in place of the old system of requisitions, about the need to treat with foreign nations as a united country.

And Henry spoke of how few votes had decided the issue in Massachusetts, how great was the opposition to the constitution in Pennsylvania, how uncertain the outcome might be in New York. Enormous numbers of people opposed this constitution; there was no reason to have it rushed through to adoption, without amendments, in the face of such clear and substantial opposition.

"He tells you," Henry said of Madison, "of important

blessings which he imagines will result to us and mankind in general, from the adoption of this system. I see the awful immensity of the dangers with which it is pregnant. I see it. I feel it." As Henry went on speaking, conjuring up forebodings of the future, of the powerful government they were about to set above themselves, of the dangers to liberty and self-government that they had fought so hard to secure in the war of the revolution, of the momentousness of the decision about to be made in such haste, storm clouds gathered over the convention hall. Darkness fell, and, at last, a storm broke with terrific thunder and lighting—as though the heavens confirmed Henry's worst forebodings—and the convention had to adjourn for the day.

It was the next day that a final vote was called. To turn the vote in their favor, the federalists accepted every suggestion the Henryites put forth for subsequent amendments. The list that Henry and Mason and their colleagues prepared contained a full bill of rights and twenty other amendments calculated to trim the power of the new national government, to preserve the states, to diminish the powers of the executive and of the Congress and of the judiciary, and to preserve local rule against the tendencies of empire. The objections of the localists were, in large measure, answered.

The vote went in favor of the constitution, by a margin of eighty-nine to seventy-nine—a close vote, but a decisive victory for the federalists. The Virginians imagined that they had been the ninth, and therefore clinching, state to ratify. They found, in fact, when news arrived a few days later, that New Hampshire had beaten them to it by several days. Virginia was the tenth state to ratify.

Under the circumstances, reluctant New York had little choice but to join the Union. Hamilton had maneuvered to hold the vote in New York until after the news of the Virginia vote arrived. Thus, faced with union or ostracism, New York chose union. That, far more than the arguments of *The Federalist*, decided the issue for New Yorkers, as it had, in some degree, for many of those who finally went along with the momentum of the new plan. New York was the eleventh state to ratify. North Carolina did not come along until November of 1789.

Rhode Island, the thirteenth state, acquiesced to the inevitable, finally, in 1790, by a stubborn vote of thirty-four to thirty-two, and the United States were joined together in a common rule of law.

The rule of law thus established was not a treaty among sovereign states who might withdraw their consent when it suited them, not a set of agreements that rulers might put aside at their convenience, or when they claimed that some higher necessity required it, or that they might choose to obey in part and suspend in part, but a supreme law of the land to whom all were subject. In the absence of the principle of the divine right of kings, the constitution derived its power from the highest lawmaking authority that remained: the people themselves.

Moreover, the constitution established a rule of law born specifically of the Great Compromise, a compromise between the centrists and the localists, between the men of order and the men of liberty, between those who sought a uniform system of laws and those who sought the greatest possible self-rule, between those who appealed to the ultimate good of justice and those who appealed to the ultimate good of liberty.

To be sure, the Great Compromise did not silence debate on these great issues for all time. Political parties would form in the earliest days of the republic not only along lines of interest but also according to more abstract preferences for central or local power. The American Civil War would be fought over the very issue—whether central or local power was supreme—that had provoked the Constitutional Convention to begin with.

Many still think even today that the constitution established a system that is too highly centralized, too powerful, too expansive, too destructive of individual liberty. Many others think, on the contrary, that the central government is too constrained in its abilities to deal with its own domestic problems, even with the simplest problems of dispensing justice or caring for the helpless and destitute. The debate continues with us, not just in dishonest arguments—made in the name of liberty—that champion of injustice, special privilege, servility, and the domination of other nations, but in honest beliefs that the claims of liberty and self-government ought to override those of uniform justice; and not just in the base claims of those hoping to feed at the public trough, but in honest pleas that the claims of justice must override those of liberty.

If we look to the founding fathers and the story of the Constitutional Convention for guidance in this debate, clearly we will not find a simple choice on one side or the other of the issue, a single "original intention" that they all shared. Quite the contrary: The Great Compromise that these men finally settled on and placed at the center of the nation's life, far from taking an uncomplicated stand with one or the other of these two impulses, chose both. It declared that, henceforth, neither order nor liberty could be sacrificed in the name of the other, no matter how excruciating the tension between them might become. And it embraced the two aspirations under a more general and grander principle that rose naturally from the political culture they shared: that each individual is safest when power is most widely dispersed throughout the polity, when there are no unchecked concentrations of power, when, in fact, power and responsibility come closest to residing equally in the hands of all citizens.

APPENDIX 1.
CONSTITUTION OF THE UNITED
STATES

[Preamble]

WE, THE PEOPLE of the United States, in Order to form a more perfect Union, establish Justice, insure domestic Tranquility, provide for the common defence, promote the general Welfare, and secure the Blessings of Liberty to ourselves and our Posterity, do ordain and establish this Constitution for the United States of America.

Article I

Section 1. All legislative powers herein granted shall be vested in a Congress of the United States, which shall consist of a Senate and House of Representatives.

Section 2. [1] The House of Representatives shall be composed of members chosen every second year by the people of the several States, and the Electors in each State shall have the qualifications requisite for Electors of the most numerous branch of the State legislature.

[2] No person shall be a Representative who shall not have attained to the age of twenty-five years, and been seven years a citizen of the United States, and who shall not, when elected, be an inhabitant of that State in which he shall be chosen.

[3] Representatives and direct taxes shall be apportioned among the several States which may be included within this Union, according to their respective numbers, which shall be determined by adding to the whole number of free persons, including those bound to service for a term of years, and excluding Indians not taxed, three-fifths of all other persons. The actual enumeration shall be made within three years after the first meeting of the Congress of the United States, and within every subsequent term of ten years, in such manner as they shall by law direct. The number of Representatives shall not exceed one for every thirty

thousand, but each State shall have at least one Representative; and until such enumeration shall be made, the State of New-Hampshire shall be entitled to chuse three, Massachusetts eight, Rhode-Island and Providence Plantations one, Connecticut five, New-York six, New-Jersey four, Pennsylvania eight, Delaware one, Maryland six, Virginia ten, North-Carolina five, South-Carolina five, and Georgia three.

[4] When vacancies happen in the representation from any State, the Executive authority thereof shall issue writs of election to fill such vacancies.

[5] The House of Representatives shall chuse their Speaker and other officers; and shall have the sole power of impeachment.

Section 3. [1] The Senate of the United States shall be composed of two Senators from each State, chosen by the legislature thereof, for six years; and each Senator shall have one vote.

[2] Immediately after they shall be assembled in consequence of the first election, they shall be divided as equally as may be into three classes. The seats of the Senators of the first class shall be vacated at the expiration of the second year, of the second class at the expiration of the fourth year, and of the third class at the expiration of the sixth year, so that one-third may be chosen every second year; and if vacancies happen by resignations, or otherwise, during the recess of the Legislature of any State, the Executive thereof may make temporary appointments until the next meeting of the Legislature, which shall then fill such vacancies.

[3] No person shall be a Senator who shall not have attained to the age of thirty years, and been nine years a citizen of the United States, and who shall not, when elected, be an inhabitant of that State for which he shall be chosen.

[4] The Vice-President of the United States shall be President of the Senate, but shall have no vote, unless they be equally divided.

[5] The Senate shall chuse their other officers, and also a President pro tempore, in the absence of the Vice-President, or when he shall exercise the office of President of the United States.

[6] The Senate shall have the sole power to try all empeachments. When sitting for that purpose, they shall be an oath or affirmation. When the President of the United States is tried, the Chief Justice shall preside: And no person shall be convicted without the concurrence of two-thirds of the members present.

[7] Judgment in cases of impeachment shall not extend further than to removal from office, and disqualification to hold and enjoy any office of honor, trust or profit under the United States; but the party convicted shall nevertheless be liable and subject to indictment, trial, judgment and punishment, according to law.

Section 4. [1] The times, places and manner of holding elections for Senators and Representatives, shall be prescribed in each State by the legislature thereof; but the Congress may at any time by law make or alter such regulations, except as to the places of chusing Senators.

[2] The Congress shall assemble at least once in every year, and such

meeting shall be on the first Monday in December, unless they shall by law appoint a different day.

Section 5. [1] Each House shall be the judge of the elections, returns and qualifications of its own members, and a majority of each shall constitute a quorum to do business; but a small number may adjourn from day to day, and may be authorized to compel the attendance of absent members, in such manner, and under such penalties as each House may provide.

[2] Each House may determine the rules of its proceedings, punish its members for disorderly behaviour, and, with the concurrence of two-thirds, expel a member.

[3] Each House shall keep a journal of its proceedings, and from time to time publish the same, excepting such parts as may in their judgment require secrecy; and the yeas and nays of the members of either House on any question shall, at the desire of one-fifth of those present, be entered in the journal.

[4] Neither House, during the session of Congress, shall, without the consent of the other, adjourn for more than three days, nor to any other place than that in which the two Houses shall be sitting.

Section 6. [1] The Senators and Representatives shall receive a compensation for their services, to be ascertained by law, and paid out of the Treasury of the United States. They shall in all cases, except treason, felony and breach of the peace, be privileged from arrest during their attendance at the session of their respective Houses, and in going to and returning from the same; and for any speech or debate in either House, they shall not be questioned in any other place.

[2] No Senator or Representative shall, during the time for which he was elected, be appointed to any civil office under the authority of the United States, which shall have been created, or the emoluments whereof shall have been encreased during such time; and no person holding any office under the United States, shall be a member of either House during his continuance in office.

Section 7. [1] All Bills for raising revenue shall originate in the House of Representatives; but the Senate may propose or concur with amendments as on other bills.

[2] Every bill which shall have passed the House of Representatives and the Senate, shall, before it become a law, be presented to the President of the United States; if he approve he shall sign it, but if not he shall return it, with his objections to that House in which it shall have originated, who shall enter the objections at large on their journal, and proceed to reconsider it. If after such reconsideration two-thirds of that House shall agree to pass the bill, it shall be sent, together with the objections, to the other House, by which it shall likewise be reconsidered, and if approved by two-thirds of that House, it shall become a law. But in all such cases the votes of both Houses shall be determined by yeas and nays, and the names of the persons voting for and against the bill shall be entered on the journal of each House respectively. If any bill

shall not be returned by the President within ten days (Sundays excepted) after it shall have been presented to him, the same shall be a law, in like manner as if he had signed it, unless the Congress by their adjournment prevent its return, in which case it shall not be a law.

[3] Every order, resolution, or vote to which the concurrence of the Senate and House of Representatives may be necessary (except on a question of adjournment) shall be presented to the President of the United States; and before the same shall take effect, shall be approved by him, or, being disapproved by him, shall be repassed by two-thirds of the Senate and House of Representatives, according to the rules and limitations prescribed in the case of a bill.

Section 8. [1] The Congress shall have power to lay and collect taxes, duties, imposts and excises, to pay the debts and provide for the common defence and general welfare of the United States; but all duties, imposts and excises shall be uniform throughout the United States;

[2] To borrow money on the credit of the United States;

[3] To regulate commerce with foreign nations, and among the several States, and with the Indian tribes;

[4] To establish an uniform rule of naturalization, and uniform laws on the subject of bankruptcies throughout the United States;

[5] To coin money, regulate the value thereof, and of foreign coin, and fix the standard of weights and measures;

[6] To provide for the punishment of counterfeiting the securities and current coin of the United States;

[7] To establish post offices and post roads;

[8] To promote the progress of science and useful arts, by securing for limited times to authors and inventors the exclusive right to their respective writings and discoveries;

[9] To constitute tribunals inferior to the Supreme Court;

[10] To define and punish piracies and felonies committed on the high seas, and offences against the law of nations;

[11] To declare war, grant letters of marque and reprisal, and make rules concerning captures on land and water;

[12] To raise and support armies, but no appropriation of money to that use shall be for a longer term than two years;

[13] To provide and maintain a navy;

[14] To make rules for the government and regulation of the land and naval forces;

[15] To provide for calling forth the militia to execute the laws of the union, suppress insurrections and repel invasions;

[16] To provide for organizing, arming, and disciplining, the militia, and for governing such part of them as may be employed in the service of the United States, reserving to the States respectively, the appointment of the officers, and the authority of training the militia according to the discipline prescribed by Congress;

[17] To exercise exclusive legislation in all cases whatsoever, over such district (not exceeding ten miles square) as may, by cession of par-

ticular States, and the acceptance of Congress, become the seat of the government of the United States, and to exercise like authority over all places purchased by the consent of the legislature of the State in which the same shall be, for the erection of forts, magazines, arsenals, dock-yards, and other needful buildings;— And

[18] To make all laws which shall be necessary and proper for car-rying into execution the foregoing powers, and all other powers vested by this Constitution United States, or in any department or officer thereof.

Section 9. [1] The migration or importation of such persons as any of the States now existing shall think proper to admit, shall not be pro-hibited by the Congress prior to the year one thousand eight hundred and eight, but a tax or duty may be imposed on such importation, not exceeding ten dollars for each person.

[2] The privilege of the writ of habeas corpus shall not be suspended unless when in cases of rebellion or invasion the public safety may re-quire it.

[3] No bill of attainder or ex post facto law shall be passed.

[4] No capitation, or other direct, tax shall be laid, unless in propor-tion to the census or enumeration herein before directed to be taken.

[5] No tax or duty shall be laid on articles exported from any State.

[6] No preference shall be given by any regulation of commerce or revenue to the ports of one State over those of another: nor shall vessels bound to, or from, one State, be obliged to enter, or pay duties in an-other.

[7] No money shall be drawn from the Treasury, but in consequence of appropriations made by law; and a regular Statement and account of the receipts and expenditures of all public money shall be published from time to time.

[8] No title of nobility shall be granted by the United States:- And no person holding any office of profit or trust under them, shall, without the consent of the Congress, accept of any present, emolument, office, or title, of any kind whatever, from any king, prince, or foreign State.

Section 10. [1] No State shall enter into any treaty, alliance, or con-federation; grant letters of marque and reprisal; coin money; emit bills of credit; make any thing but gold and silver coin a tender in payment of debts; pass any bill of attainder, ex post facto law, or law impairing the obligation of contracts, or grant any title of nobility.

[2] No State shall, without the consent of the Congress, lay any im-posts or duties on imports or exports, except what may be absolutely necessary for executing its inspection laws; and the net produce of all duties and imposts, laid by any State on imports or exports, shall be for the use of the Treasury of the United States; and all such laws shall be subject to the revision and controul of the Congress.

[3] No State shall, without the consent of congress, lay any duty of tonnage, keep troops, or ships of war in time of peace, enter into any agreement or compact with another State, or with a foreign power, or

engage in war, unless actually invaded, or in such imminent danger as will not admit of delay.

Article II

Section 1. [1] The executive power shall be vested in a President of the United States of America. He shall hold his office during the term of four years, and, together with the Vice-President, chosen for the same term, be elected as follows:

[2] Each State shall appoint, in such manner as the legislature thereof may direct, a number of Electors, equal to the whole number of Senators and Representatives to which the State may be entitled in the Congress: but no Senator or Representative, or person holding an office of trust or profit under the United States, shall be appointed an Elector.

[3] The Electors shall meet in their respective States, and vote by ballot for two persons, of whom one at least shall not be an inhabitant of the same State with themselves. And they shall make a list of all the persons voted for, and of the number of votes for each; which list they shall sign and certify, and transmit sealed to the seat of the government of the United States, directed to the President of the Senate. The President of the Senate shall, in the presence of the Senate and House of Representatives, open all the certificates, and the votes shall then be counted. The person having the greatest number of votes shall be the President, if such number be a majority of the whole number of Electors appointed; and if there be more than one who have such majority, and have an equal number of votes, the House of Representatives shall immediately chuse by ballot one of them for President; and if no person have a majority, then from the five highest on the list the said House shall in like manner chuse the President. But in chusing the President, the votes shall be taken by States, the representation from each State having one vote; a quorum for this purpose shall consist of a member or members from two-thirds of the States, and a majority of all the States shall be necessary to a choice. In every case, after the choice of the President, the person having the greatest number of votes of the Electors shall be the Vice-President. But if there should remain two or more who have equal votes, the Senate shall chuse from them by ballot the Vice-President.

[4] The Congress may determine the time of chusing the Electors, and the day on which they shall give their votes; which day shall be the same throughout the United States.

[5] No person except a natural born citizen, or a citizen of the United States, at the time of the adoption of this Constitution shall be eligible to the office of President; neither shall any person be eligible to that office who shall not have attained to the age of thirty-five years, and been fourteen years a resident within the United States.

[6] In case of the removal of the President from office, or of his death, resignation, or inability to discharge the powers and duties of the said

office, the same shall devolve on the Vice-President, and the Congress may by law provide for the case of removal, death, resignation or inability, both of the President and Vice-President, declaring what officer shall then act as President, and such officer shall act accordingly, until the disability be removed, or a President shall be elected.

[7] The President shall, at stated times, receive for his services, a compensation, which shall neither be encreased nor diminished during the period for which he shall have been elected, and he shall not receive within that period any other emolument from the United States, or any of them.

[8] Before he enter on the execution of his office, he shall take the following oath or affirmation:

"I do solemnly swear (or affirm) that I will faithfully execute the office of President of the United States, and will to the best of my ability, preserve, protect and defend the Constitution of the United States."

Section 2. [1] The President shall be commander in chief of the army and navy of the United States, and of the militia of the several States, when called into the actual service of the United States; he may require the opinion, in writing, of the principal officer in each of the executive departments, upon any subject relating to the duties of their respective offices, and he shall have power to grant reprieves and pardons for offences against the United States, except in cases of impeachment.

[2] He shall have power, by and with the advice and consent of the Senate, to make treaties, provided two-thirds of the Senators present concur; and he shall nominate, and by and with the advice and consent of the Senate, shall appoint ambassadors, other public ministers and consuls, judges of the Supreme Court, and all other officers of the United States, whose appointments are not herein otherwise provided for, and which shall be established by law. But the Congress may by law vest the appointment of such inferior officers, as they think proper, in the President alone, in the courts of law, or in the heads of departments.

[3] The President shall have power to fill up all vacancies that may happen during the recess of the Senate, by granting commissions which shall expire at the end of their next session.

Section 3. He shall from time to time give to the Congress information of the State of the union, and recommend to their consideration such measures as he shall judge necessary and expedient; he may, on extraordinary occasions, convene with House, or either of them, and in case of disagreement between them, with respect to the time of adjournment, he may adjourn them to such time as he shall think proper; he shall receive ambassadors and other public ministers; he shall take care that the laws be faithfully executed, and shall commission all the officers of the United States.

Section 4. The President, Vice-President and all civil officers of the United States, shall be removed from office on impeachment for, and conviction of, treason, bribery, or other high crimes and misdemeanors.

Article III

Section 1. The judicial power of the United States, shall be vested in one Supreme Court, and in such inferior courts as the Congress may from time to time ordain and establish. The judges, both of the supreme and inferior courts, shall hold their offices during good behaviour, and shall, at stated times, receive for their services, a compensation, which shall not be diminished during their continuance in office.

Section 2. [1] The judicial power shall extend to all cases, in law and equity, arising under this Constitution United States, and treaties made, or which shall be made, under their authority; to all cases affecting ambassadors, other public ministers and consuls; to all cases of admiralty and maritime jurisdiction; to controversies to which the United States shall be a party; to controversies between two or more States, between a State and citizens of the same State claiming lands under grants of different States, and between a State, or the citizens thereof, and foreign States, citizens or subjects.

[2] In all cases affecting ambassadors, other public ministers and consuls, and those in which a State shall be party, the Supreme Court shall have original jurisdiction. In all the other cases before mentioned, the Supreme Court shall have appellate jurisdiction, both as to law and fact, with such exceptions, and under such regulations as the Congress shall make.

[3] The trial of all crimes, except in cases of impeachment, shall be by jury; and such trial shall be held in the State where the said crimes shall have been committed; but when not committed within any State, the trial shall be at such place or places as the Congress may by law have directed.

Section 3. [1] Treason against the United States, shall consist only in levying war against them, or in adhering to their enemies, giving them aid and comfort. No person shall be convicted of treason unless on the testimony of two witnesses to the same overt act, or on confession in open court.

[2] The Congress shall have power to declare the punishment of treason, but no attainder of treason shall work corruption of blood, or forfeiture except during the life of the person attainted.

Article IV

Section 1. Full faith and credit shall be given in each State to the public acts, records, and judicial proceedings of every other State. And the Congress may by general laws prescribe the manner in which such acts, records and proceedings shall be proved, and the effect thereof.

Section 2. [1] The citizens of each State shall be entitled to all privileges and immunities of citizens in the several States.

[2] A person charged in any State with treason, felony, or other crime, who shall flee from justice, and be found in another State, shall, on de-

mand of the executive authority of the State from which he fled, be delivered up, to be removed to the State having jurisdiction of the crime.

[3] No person held to service or labour in one State, under the laws thereof, escaping into another, shall, in consequence of any law or regulation therein, be discharged from such service or labour, but shall be delivered up on claim of the party to whom such service or labour may be due.

Section 3, [1] New States may be admitted by the Congress into this union; but no new State shall be formed or erected within the jurisdiction of any other State; nor any State be formed by the junction of two or more States, or parts of States, without the consent of the legislatures of the States concerned as well as of the Congress.

[2] The Congress shall have power to dispose of and make all needful rules and regulations respecting the territory or other property belonging to the United States; and nothing in this Constitution the United States, or of any particular State.

Section 4. The United States will guarantee to every State in this union a Republican form of government, and shall protect each of them against invasion; and on application of the legislature, or of the executive (when the legislature cannot be convened) against domestic violence.

Article V

The Congress, whenever two-thirds of both Houses shall deem it necessary, shall propose amendments to this Constitution on the application of the legislatures of two-thirds of the several States, shall call a convention for proposing amendments, which, in either case, shall be valid to all intents and purposes, as part of this Constitution three-fourths of the several States, or by conventions in three-fourths thereof, as the one or the other mode of ratification may be proposed by the Congress; Provided, that no amendment which may be made prior to the year one thousand eight hundred and eight shall in any manner affect the first and fourth clauses in the Ninth Section of the First Article; and that no State, without its consent, shall be deprived of its equal suffrage in the Senate.

Article VI

[1] All debts contracted and engagements entered into, before the adoption of this Constitution, shall be as valid against the United States under this Constitution as under the Confederation.

[2] This Constitution shall be made in pursuance thereof; and all treaties made, or which shall be made, under the authority of the United States, shall be the supreme law of the land; and the judges in every State shall be bound thereby, any thing in the Constitution notwithstanding.

[3] The Senators and Representatives before mentioned, and the members of the several State legislatures, and all executive and judicial officers, both of the United States and of the several States, shall be bound by oath or affirmation, to support this Constitution qualification to any office or public trust under the United States.

Article VII

The ratification of the conventions of nine States shall be sufficient for the establishment of this Constitution between the States so ratifying the same.

Done in Convention, by the unanimous consent of the States present, the seventeenth day of September, in the year of our Lord one thousand seven hundred and eighty-seven, and of the Independence of the United States of America the twelfth. In witness whereof we have hereunto subscribed our Names.

APPENDIX 2.
AMENDMENTS TO THE CONSTITUTION
(BILL OF RIGHTS)

First Amendment (1791)

CONGRESS SHALL MAKE no law respecting an establishment of religion, or prohibiting the free exercise thereof; or abridging the freedom of speech, or of the press; or the right of the people peaceably to assemble, and to petition the Government for a redress of grievances.

Second Amendment (1791)

A well regulated militia being necessary to the security of a free State, the right of the people to keep and bear Arms shall not be infringed.

Third Amendment (1791)

No Soldier shall, in time of peace, be quartered in any house without the consent of the Owner, nor in time of war, but in a manner to be prescribed by law.

Fourth Amendment (1791)

The right of the people to be secure in their persons, houses, papers, and effects, against unreasonable searches and seizures, shall not be violated, and no warrants shall issue, but upon probable cause, supported by oath or affirmation, and particularly describing the place to be searched, and the persons or things to be seized.

Fifth Amendment (1791)

No person shall be held to answer for a capital, or otherwise infamous crime, unless on a presentment or indictment of a grand jury, except in cases arising in the land or naval forces, or in the militia, when in actual service in time of war or public danger; nor shall any person be subject for the same offence to be twice put in jeopardy of life or limb; nor shall be compelled in any criminal case to be a witness against himself, nor be deprived of life, liberty, or property, without due process of law; nor shall private property be taken for public use without just compensation.

Sixth Amendment (1791)

In all criminal prosecutions, the accused shall enjoy the right to a speedy and public trial, by an impartial jury of the State and district wherein the crime shall have been committed, which district shall have been previously ascertained by law, and to be informed of the nature and cause of the accusation; to be confronted with the witness against him; to have compulsory process for obtaining witnesses in his favor, and to have the assistance of counsel for his defence.

Seventh Amendment (1791)

In suits at common law, where the value in controversy shall exceed twenty dollars, the right of trial by jury shall be preserved, and no fact tried by a jury, shall be otherwise reexamined in any court of the United States, than according to the rules of the common law.

Eighth Amendment (1791)

Excessive bail shall not be required, nor excessive fines imposed, nor cruel and unusual punishments inflicted.

Ninth Amendment (1791)

The enumeration in the Constitution of certain rights shall not be construed to deny or disparage others retained by the people.

Tenth Amendment (1791)

The powers not delegated to the United States by the Constitution, nor prohibited by it to the States, are reserved to the States respectively, or to the people.

APPENDIX 3.
DELEGATES TO THE CONSTITUTIONAL
CONVENTION BY STATE

Connecticut

Oliver Ellsworthy*
William Samuel Johnson
Roger Sherman

Delaware

Richard Bassett
Gunning Bedford, Jr.
Jacob Broom
John Dickinson
George Read

Georgia

Abraham Baldwin
William Few
William Houston*
William L. Pierce*

Maryland

Daniel Carroll
Daniel of St. Thomas Jenifer
James McHenry
Luther Martin*
John Francis Mercer*

Massachusetts

Elbridge Gerry*
Nathaniel Gorham
Rufus King
Caleb Strong*

New Hampshire

Nicholas Gilman
John Langdon

New Jersey

David Brearly
Jonathan Dayton
William Churchill Houston*
William Livingston
William Paterson

New York

Alexander Hamilton
John Lansing, Jr.*
Robert Yates*

North Carolina

William Blount
William R. Davie*

Alexander Martin*
Richard Dobbs Spaight, Sr.
Hugh Williamson

Pennsylvania

George Clymer
Thomas Fitzsimons
Benjamin Franklin
Jared Ingersoll
Thomas Mifflin
Gouverneur Morris
Robert Morris
James Wilson

*Nonsigner

South Carolina

Pierce Butler
Charles Pinckney
Charles Cotesworth Pinckney
John Rutledge

Virginia

John Blair
James McClurg*
James Madison
George Mason*
Edmund J. Randolph*
George Washington
George Wythe*

A NOTE ON THE SOURCES

THE PRINCIPAL SOURCES for this book are the notes and journals of the delegates to the convention, particularly the notes of Madison, which are to be found along with the other delegates' notes in Farrand's *The Records*. . . . I drew heavily, too, on Elliot, Force, Jensen, and Kaminski for original documents. For orientation on the essential dispute between centrists and localists, James Hutson's "Country, Court, and Constitution" was extremely helpful. Among recent books, I found Rossiter's *The Grand Convention* very useful, even though (or because) I usually disagreed with his interpretations. I have not tried to list all the secondary sources on which I've drawn, or to give sources in the notes for all the material that has long been familiar. I have tried, rather, to acknowledge my debts to those sources on which I most often leaned, and to identify specifically any material that is new. In preparation for the bicentennial celebration of the framing of the constitution, a number of people and organizations scoured the country for previously unknown original documents. David Kimball and Robert Sutton at Independence National Historical Park and James Hutson at the Library of Congress turned up some interesting material. When I have drawn on any of this, I have identified it in the notes that follow the bibliography. The references below, by author, are to works listed in the bibliography which follows the notes.

NOTES

Chapter 1. The Man of History

For Madison's character and appearance, see Brant passim and Wills 10. For the journey to Philadelphia, see Saint-Méry 96 and Brissot de Warville 152. For the background on the oyster war, see Morison 79ff. For the Annapolis meeting, see Rossiter's *Convention* 54ff and Smith's *The Constitution* 84ff. For a sense of Philadelphia as it was when Madison arrived, see Saint-Méry passim. Brissot's quote is in Brissot 253. The westward movement is recounted in Jensen 112ff., among other places. For general remarks on the political climate of America, see Jensen 85ff. and Rossiter 24ff. Barbé-Marbois's remarks about Boston appear in Barbé-Marbois (ed. Roberts) 76. The scathing remarks about Adams are in Kaminski 89ff., and Madison's letter to Jefferson is quoted in Kaminski 84. For life at Mrs. House's, see Ketcham 88. For boardinghouses and taverns, see Rice 41ff. For observations on Witherspoon and Princeton, see Wills 15ff. For impressions of Madison, see Ketcham 107ff. For Eliza Trist's letter to Jefferson, see Ketcham 138. For Madison's habits, see Ketcham 149ff. For his relationship with Jefferson, see Ketcham 183ff. For the background of American colonial history, see Morison 132ff., Page Smith 19ff., Jensen 129ff., Morgan 95ff., Rossiter 24ff., among others. On state constitutions, see Morison 273ff., Morgan 88ff., Page Smith 56ff., Rossiter 60ff., and Main 17ff.,

Chapter 2. The Man of Order

For Washington's character and appearance, see Flexner passim. For his trip from Mount Vernon to Philadelphia, and his concerns and correspondence just before his trip, see Washington's own diary and letters for May. For his relationship with the Cincinnati, see Wills's article in *American Heritage*. For the route of his trip, see Saint-Méry 84ff. For Shays's

Rebellion, see Morison 301ff. and Main 55ff. For Washington's views of the country's troubles, see Rossiter 42ff. and Main 177ff., in addition to Washington's own correspondence. For Morris, see Oberholzer passim. For Morris's house, see Eberlein. For Shippen's letter to his son, see his correspondence for May 20, 1787, in the Letters of Thomas Lee Shippen, vol. 4, Shippen Papers, Manuscript Division, Library of Congress.

Chapter 3. The Man of Liberty

For Franklin's character and appearance, see Van Doren and Wright passim. The details of his building activities can be found in his papers; see particularly the Franklin Papers, Box F85.X60, 1787, May 14–July 5, Sebastian Sybert. Bill to Franklin, American Philosophical Society. For his thoughts at just this time, see, inter alia, his letter to M. L'Abbé de la Roche of April 22, 1787, in the New York Public Library Manuscript Collection, B. Franklin Letters, 1723–1789, and for other writings of this period, vol. 9 of Smyth. For a good summation of the antifederalist position, see Main 119ff. and Herbert Storing passim. For observations on the histories of the states, see Morison 64ff. and Main 55ff., among others. For Virginia, see especially Boorstin 103ff.

Chapter 4. Early Arrivals

On the Virginia delegation as a whole, see Rossiter 118ff. For Mason, see especially Helen Hill and Kate Rowland passim. Mason's letter to his son is quoted in Rowland, vol. 2, 103ff. The description of the Indian Queen comes from Cutler 253. For Washington's activities, see his diary for these days in Philadelphia. For general observations on Madison's understanding of the background of the convention, see Farrand's The Framing 4ff. and 42ff., and Wills 14ff. See also Rossiter 50ff. The essential documents outlining Madison's ideas (his manuscript on the "Vices of the Political System of the United States," and his briefing letter to George Washington) can all be found in Gaillard Hunt's edition of Madison's Writings but also, more conveniently, in Meyers.

Chapter 5. The Opening Session

For Independence Hall, see Kimball, Quinn, and Bowen 23. The archives of Independence National Historical Park also include a great number of other highly detailed studies done for purposes of the restoration of the building (note especially a staff report of August 1959 on the furnishing plan of the first floor of Independence Hall), which were extremely useful. For Rutledge, the Richard Barry biography must be treated with some skepticism for both its details and its overall assessment of Rutledge—though a better biography remains to be done. The account of the opening session comes from Farrand's records, vol. 1, 1ff. Washington's weekend is recounted in his own diary for May 25–27. The

Monday session is from Farrand, vol. 1, 7ff. Mason's letter to his son is from Farrand, vol. 3, 33.

Chapter 6. First Principles

The debate in the convention is from Farrand, vol. 1, 18ff. The biographer who suggested Pinckney stole Madison's plan is Brant. For American dining habits, see Saint-Méry 265. Jay's letter to Gouverneur Morris is quoted in Mintz 141. Sherman is not usually treated as the opposition leader in the convention, since he seemed, from the outset, ready to take a middle position rather than the more extreme position of Paterson. It is Paterson and his New Jersey plan that are most often treated as the "other" side in the convention. But clear lines cannot be drawn in this, and even though Sherman's position was "compromised" from the beginning, I have given him more weight than he is usually accorded: He arrived early, and he had the prestige that Paterson did not to draw colleagues around him. Brant called Sherman "the captain of the opposition" (p. 34); and although that may go too far, he was certainly one of the captains.

Chapter 7. The Question of Democracy

For the debates, see Farrand, vol. 1, 45ff. Franklin's remark to Rush comes from a letter Rush wrote to a friend of his, and is quoted in Farrand, vol. 3, 33. For a general discussion of the understanding of principles of republicanism and democracy at the time, I found Gordon Wood especially helpful.

Chapter 8. The Executive

For the debates, see Farrand, vol. 1, 62ff. One of the few significant exceptions to the observation above that little new material has come to light about the convention is the discovery and publication (see Hutson) of John Dickinson's notes on the debates. His own thoughts for an executive are extravagantly complicated but interesting. In addition to Madison's record, the notes of the other delegates are interesting on this debate too, especially those of King and Hamilton for June 1, and of Yates and King for June 2. Mason's notes record his own speech for June 4 in detail.

Chapter 9. The Keystone of the Constitution

For the debates, see Farrand, vol. 1, 115ff. Adams's sentiments about Sherman are quoted in Boyd 226. Hamilton's notes for June 6 (Farrand, vol, 145ff.) contain his remark that Madison's principles do not "conclude so strongly as he supposes."

Chapter 10. The Opposition in Place

I counted heavily on Hutson ("Country, Court . . .") for his general understanding of the split in the convention and on Rossiter (138ff.) for categorizing the delegates. Storing gives a good exposition of the basic position of the antifederalists. For Johnson, see McCaughey and also Greene passim. The remark about whether Philadelphia is on the coast of Sumatra comes from McCaughey 75. For Paterson, see O'Connor.

Chapter 11. The Localists Attack

For the debates, see Farrand, vol. 1, 148ff. For Dickinson in particular, see Hutson ("John Dickinson").

Chapter 12. The Localists Attack Again

For the extremes of Philadelphia weather—the story of the hornet's nest, and the stench of the open sewer—see Simon. For the debates, see Farrand, vol. 1, 241ff. For Wilson's comparison of the Virginia and New Jersey plans, see Farrand, vol. 1, 276ff. The presentation of the New Jersey Plan caused a flurry of notetaking by the delegates. The notes for June 16 by Yates, King, Hamilton, Paterson, and Wilson are all superb. William Pierce's thumbnail sketch of Lansing (and of some of the other delegates) are in Farrand, vol. 3, 87ff. Hamilton has inspired (or provoked) a great deal of wonderful writing; and some of the best is collected in Jacob Cooke. Both Yates and King took good notes of his speech in the convention, but Hamilton's own outline of his speech gives the best insight into the logic of its argument. Johnson's eloquent one-word comment on Hamilton's speech (pointed out to me by David Kimball) comes from the Johnson Papers in the Connecticut Historical Society, Diary of William Samuel Johnson 1787–1791.

Chapter 13. The Localists Attack Yet Again

For the debates, Farrand, vol. 1, 336ff. Ellsworth's letter to his wife is quoted in Brown 237. Other letters to his wife that contain interesting material on the convention are to be found in his papers in the Connecticut Historical Society (microfilm 81899). Saint-Méry's remarks on the heat and flies are to be found in Saint-Méry 324. For Luther Martin, see Goddard passim.

Chapter 14. Anarchy, and the Turning Point

For the debates, Farrand, vol. 1, 450ff. The biographer of Rutledge who records this meeting with Sherman is Barry.

Chapter 15. The Fourth of July

Washington's activities are recorded in his diary and letters. Some of the details of the day come from the *Pennsylvania Herald*, July 7, p. 191. The Fourth of July oration is in Kaminski 163ff. The Cutler story comes primarily from Cutler himself. I've taken some liberties with chronological sequence here to keep Cutler from interrupting the flow of debate. In New Haven on July 4, he arrived in Philadelphia ten days later—in the midst of the debate that follows. For Peale, see Sellars, especially 13ff. For Bartram, see Campbell.

Chapter 16. The Great Compromise

For the debates, see Farrand, vol. 1, 524ff. Madison's own account of the caucus witnessed by the small states is in Farrand, vol. 2, 19ff. See also Brant 100.

Chapter 17. The President

For the eagerness of the small-state men now to give great powers to the central government, see Brant 103ff., Rossiter 196ff., and the debates themselves, Farrand, vol. 2, 21ff. Farrand's narrative *The Framing*, 115–23, is good on the executive too.

Chapter 18. Details

For the work of the committee, see Farrand's *The Framing* 115ff., Rossiter 200ff., and Brant 116. For the ensuing debates, see Farrand, vol. 2, 176ff. Gerry's letters to his wife are from the Elsie O. and Philip D. Sang Collection at Southern Illinois University (dated August 9–September 1)

Chapter 19. Slavery

The debate on slavery erupts several times in the convention: on August 8, again on August 21, and again on August 25. See Farrand, vol. 2, 213ff., 352ff., and 408ff. The letter of August 29 from Gerry to his wife, in which he says he suspects spies may be opening his letters, is in the Manuscripts Department of the Lilly Library at Indiana University. The argument is customarily made that one should not judge eighteenth-century attitudes toward slavery anachronistically, that these men were creatures of their time, not ours. While this is true, it is also true that not everything ought to be overlooked on that account: The eighteenth-century did not possess a uniform pro-slavery attitude. The horrors of the system were apparent to Brissot de Warville and Barbé-Marbois as well as Gouverneur Morris and Colonel Mason. One still hears that one ought not judge the racism of *Gone With the Wind* too harshly, since it was the product of another era, the 1930s—although that era came 150 years after Mason and Madison had seen the light.

Chapter 20. The Powers of Congress

For the debates, see Farrand, vol 2., 303ff. See also Rossiter 207ff. and Brant 132ff.

Chapter 21. The President Again

For the debates, see Farrand, vol. 2, 396ff. On the difficulties the delegates were having over the presidency, see John Dickinson's letter to Senator George Logan of November 4, 1802, in the Dickinson papers at the Delaware State Archives. The rumor about the bishop of Osnaburgh is in Kaminski 168ff.

Chapter 22. Finishing Touches and Final Objections

See Rossiter 224ff. on the Committee of Style. For the debates, see Farrand, vol. 2, 565ff. Mason's objections are in Farrand, vol. 2, 637ff.

Chapter 23. The Signing

For the last speeches of the convention, see Farrand, vol. 2, 641ff. For Washington's trip home, see his diary of September 18 and 19.

Epilogue. Ratification

For the ratification debates in general, see Elliot. For newspaper accounts of the time and other contemporary writings in general, see Jensen's *Documentary History* and Kaminski. Main's *The Antifederalists* is also good on ratification. For details on the state ratifying convention in Pennsylvania, see McMaster and Stone; for Massachusetts, see Harding; for Virginia, see Grigsby; for New York, see Miner. See also Rossiter 274ff.

BIBLIOGRAPHY

Documents

Burnett, E. C., ed. *Letters of the Members of the Continental Congress.* 8 vols. Washington, 1921–36.

Elliot, Jonathan, ed. *The Debates in the Several State Conventions, on the Adoption of the Federal Constitution.* 5 vols. Washington, 1854.

Farrand, Max, ed. *The Records of the Federal Convention of 1787.* 4 vols. New Haven, 1911, 1937.

Force, Peter, ed. *American Archives.* 9 vols. Washington, 1837–53.

Ford, W. C., et al., eds. *Journals of the Continental Congress 1774–1789.* 34 vols. Washington, 1904–37.

Jensen, Merrill. *The Documentary History of the Ratification of the Constitution.* Vols. 1–3. Madison, Wis., 1976–78.

Kaminski, John P., and Gaspare Saladino. *Commentaries on the Constitution, Public and Private.* Vol. 1. Madison, Wis., 1981.

Strayer, J. R., ed. *The Delegate from New York, or Proceedings of the Federal Convention of 1787 from the Notes of John Lansing, Jr.* Princeton, 1939.

Tansill, C. C., ed. *Documents of the Formation of the Union of the American States.* House Doc. 398, 69th Cong.

Unpublished Letters and Other Papers

Most of the essential letters and papers have been collected and published. In those instances where letters and other papers from manuscript collections have been used, they are cited in the preceding notes.

McGuire, Robert, and Robert Ohsfeldt. "Economic Interests and the American Constitution: A Quantitative Rehabilitation of Charles A.

Beard." Economic History Association meeting, Washington, D.C., 1983.

Other Contemporary Writings

Armes, Ethel, ed. *Nancy Shippen, Her Journal Book*. Philadelphia, 1935.

Ballagh, J. C., ed. *The Letters of Richard Henry Lee*. 2 vols. New York, 1911–14.

Biddle, Henry D. *Extracts from the Journals of Elizabeth Drinker from 1759 to 1807*. Philadelphia, 1889.

Brissot de Warville, Jacques Pierre. *New Travels in the United States of America, 1788*. Edited by Durand Echeverria. Cambridge, Mass., 1964.

Butterfield, L. J., ed. *The Letters of Benjamin Rush*. 2 vols. Princeton, 1951.

Chastellux, François Jean, Marquis. *Travels in North America in the Years 1780, 1781, and 1782*. 2 vols. London, 1787.

Crèvecoeur, J. Hector St. John. *Letters from an American Farmer*. New York, 1904.

Cutler, William Parker, and Julia Perkins, eds. *Life, Journals and Correspondence of Rev. Manasseh Cutler*. Cincinnati, 1888.

Dickinson, John. Letters to his family. Dickinson Papers, Delaware State Archives.

Ellsworth, Oliver. Letters to his wife. Ellsworth Papers, Connecticut Historical Society.

Fitzpatrick, J. C., ed. *The Diaries of George Washington*. 4 vols. Boston, 1925.

———. *The Writings of George Washington*. 39 vols. Washington, 1931–44.

———. *The Writings of John Dickinson*. Philadelphia, 1895.

Ford, Paul Leicester, ed. *Essays on the Constitution of the United States*. Brooklyn, 1892.

———. *Pamphlets on the Constitution of the United States*. Brooklyn, 1888.

François, Marquis de Barbé-Marbois. *Our Revolutionary Forefathers*. New York, 1929.

Gerry, Elbridge. Letters to his wife. Elsie O. and Philip D. Sang Collection, Southern Illinois University.

Henry W. W. *Patrick Henry: Life, Correspondence, and Speeches*. 3 vols. New York, 1891.

Hunt, Gaillard, ed. *The Writings of James Madison*. 9 vols. New York, 1910.

Hunter, Robert, Jr. *Quebec to Carolina in 1785–1786, Being the Travel Diary and Observations* . . . Edited by L. B. Wright and Marian Tinling. New York, 1943.

Hutchinson, William T., Robert A. Rutland, and William M. E. Rachal, eds. *The James Madison Papers*. 7 vols. to date. Chicago, 1962–.

Kenyon, Cecilia, ed. *The Antifederalists*. Indianapolis, 1966.

King, C. R. *The Life and Correspondence of Rufus King*. 6 vols. New York, 1894–1900.

Lodge, H. C. *The Works of Alexander Hamilton.* 12 vols. New York, 1904.
———. *Letters and Other Writings of James Madison.* 4 vols. Philadelphia, 1867.
McDonald, T. H., ed. *Exploring the Northwest Territory: Sir Alexander Mackenzie's Journal . . . in 1789.* Norman, Okla., 1966.
Madison, James, Alexander Hamilton, and John Day. *The Federalist Papers.* Edited by Willmoore Kendall and George W. Carey. New Rochelle, N.Y., n.d.
Moore, Charles. *George Washington's Rules of Civility and Decent Behaviour in Company and Conversation.* Boston, 1926.
Morris, Anne C., ed. *The Diary and Letters of Gouverneur Morris.* 2 vols. New York, 1888.
Parsons, James Cox, ed. *Extracts from the Diary of Jacob Hiltzheimer.* Philadelphia, 1893.
Read, W. T. *The Life and Correspondence of George Read.* Philadelphia, 1870.
Roberts, Kenneth, and Anna M. Roberts, eds. *Moreau de Saint-Méry's American Journey.* New York, 1947.
Smyth, A. H., ed. *The Writings of Benjamin Franklin.* 10 vols. New York, 1906.

Unpublished Essays and Dissertations

Campbell, William M. "Bernard McMahon's The American Gardener's Calendar and the Eighteenth Century Garden." Independence National Historical Park, April 1966.
Cody, William Bermond. "An Analysis of the Issues of Democracy and Nationalism at the Constitutional Convention of 1787." PhD, New School for Social Research, 1980.
Dorman, Charles G. "The Furnishings of Franklin Court 1765–1790." Independence National Historical Park, July 1969.
Dutcher, David C. "A Study of the Theatre in Philadelphia, 1790–1800." Independence National Historical Park, April 1973.
Graham, Robert E. "Philadelphia Inns and Taverns." Independence National Historical Park, 1950.
Kimball, David A. "Historical Research Report on Cobblestone Paving." Independence National Historical Park, July 1960.
Naroll, Raoul Soskin. "Clio and the Constitution: The Influence of the Study of History on the Federal Convention of 1787." PhD, University of California, Los Angeles, 1953.
Platt, John. "Franklin's Home." Historic Data Section, Independence National Historical Park, November 1969.
Quinn, Miriam. "Paving of the Footways Around the State House Yard." Independence National Historical Park, June 1961.

Articles

Boyd, Julian P. "Roger Sherman: Portrait of a Cordwainer Statesman." *New England Quarterly,* April 1932, 221.

Colbourn, H. Trevor. "John Dickinson, Historical Revolutionary." *Pennsylvania Magazine of History and Biography* 83, no. 3 (January 1959): 271.

Corwin, Edward S. "The Progress of Constitutional Theory Between the Declaration of Independence and the Meeting of the Philadelphia Convention." *American Historical Review* 30 (1924–25): 511–36.

Crowl, Philip A. "Anti-Federalism in Maryland, 1787–1788." *The William and Mary Quarterly*, 3rd. ser., 4 (1947): 463.

Eberlein, Harold Donaldson. "190, High Street." *American Philosophical Society Transactions*, 1953, 161.

Evans, William B. "John Adams' Opinion of Benjamin Franklin." *The Pennsylvania Magazine of History and Biography*, April 1968, 220.

Gardiner, A. B. "General James M. Varnum of the Continental Army." *Magazine of American History* 18, no. 3 (September 1887): 185.

Gould, Ashley M. "Luther Martin and the Trials of Chase and Burr." *Georgetown Law Journal* 1 (1912–13).

Graham, Robert Earle. "The Taverns of Colonial Philadelphia." *American Philosophical Society Transactions*, 1953, 318.

Greene, Evarts Boutell. "William Samuel Johnson and the American Revolution." *Columbia University Quarterly* 22, no. 2 (June 30): 157.

Hermens, Ferdinand A. "The Choice of the Framers." *Presidential Studies Quarterly* 9, no. 1 (1981): 9.

Hutson, James H. "Country, Court, and Constitution: Antifederalism and the Historians." *The William and Mary Quarterly*, 3rd ser., 38 (July 1981): 337.

―――. "John Dickinson at the Federal Constitutional Convention." *The William and Mary Quarterly*, 3rd ser., 40 (April 1983): 256.

―――. "Pierce Butler's Records of the Federal Constitutional Convention." *Quarterly Journal of the Library of Congress* 37 (1980): 64.

―――. "Robert Yates' Notes on the Constitutional Convention of 1787: Citizen Genet's Edition." *Quarterly Journal of the Library of Congress* 35 no. 3 (1978): 173.

Jensen, Merrill. "Democracy and the American Revolution." *Huntington Library Quarterly* 20 (1957): 321.

Jillson, Calvin. "Constitution-Making: Alignment and Realignment in the Federal Convention." *The American Political Science Review* 75 (September 1981): 598.

―――, and Thornton Anderson. "Realignment in the Convention of 1787, The Slave Trade Compromise." *Journal of Politics* 40 (August 1977): 712.

―――. "Voting Bloc Analysis in the Constitutional Convention: Implications for an Interpretation of the Connecticut Compromise." *Western Political Quarterly*, December 1978, 535.

Kenyon, Cecilia. "Men of Little Faith: The Anti-Federalists on the Nature of Representative Government." *The William and Mary Quarterly*, 3rd. ser., 12 (1955): 3.

McKeon, Richard. "The Development of the Concept of Property in Polit-

ical Philosophy: A Study of the Background of the Constitution."
Ethics 48 (1938): 297.

McLaughlin, Andrew C. "James Wilson in the Philadelphia Convention."
Political Science Quarterly 12, no. 1 (1897): 1.

Morey, William C. "The Genesis of a Written Constitution." *Annals* 1 (1891):
529.

Morison, Samuel E. "Elbridge Gerry, Gentleman-Democrat." *New England Quarterly*, January 1929, 6.

Morris, Richard B. "Insurrection in Massachusetts," in Daniel Aaron, ed.,
American in Crisis (New York, 1952).

———. "John Jay and the Adoption of the Federal Constitution in New
York: A New Reading of Persons and Events." *New-York Historical
Society* 62, no. 2 (1982): 133.

Powell, J. H. "John Dickinson and the Constitution." *The Pennsylvania
Magazine of History and Biography* 60, no. 1 (January 1937): 1.

Riley, Edward M. "Franklin's Home." *American Philosophical Society
Transactions*, 1953, 148.

Simon, Grant Miles. "Houses and Early Life in Philadelphia." *American
Philosophical Society Transactions*, 1953, 280.

Smith, W. L. "Journal 1790–91." *Massachusetts Historical Proceedings* 51
(1917): 35.

Swindler, William F. "The Selling of the Constitution." *Supreme Court
Historical Society*, 1980, 49.

Ulmer, S. Sidney. "Sub-group Formation in the Constitutional Convention." *Midwest Journal of Political Science* 10 (August 1966): 288.

Wills, Garry. "George Washington and 'The Guilty, Dangerous & Vulgar
Honor.'" *American Heritage*, February/March 1980, 4.

Books

Austin, James T. *The Life of Elbridge Gerry*. 2 vols. Boston, 1827–29.

Bailyn, Bernard. *Ideological Origins of the American Revolution*. Cambridge, Mass., 1967.

Bancroft, George. *History of the Formation of the Constitution of the United
States of America*. New York, 1882.

Barry, Richard H. *Mr. Rutledge of South Carolina*. New York, 1942.

Beard, Charles A. *An Economic Interpretation of the Constitution of the
United States*. New York, 1935.

Billias, George. *Elbridge Gerry*. New York, 1976.

Binney, Horace. *The Leaders of the Old Bar of Philadelphia*. Philadelphia,
1859.

Boardman, Roger S. *Roger Sherman, Signer and Statesman*. Philadelphia,
1938.

Boorstein, Daniel J. *The Americans: The Colonial Experience*. New York,
1958.

Bowen, Catherine Drinker. *Miracle at Philadelphia: The Story of the Constitutional Convention, May to September 1787*. Boston, 1966.

Brant, Irving. *James Madison, The Nationalist, 1780–1787.* New York, 1948.

Bridenbaugh, Carl, and J. Bridenbaugh. *Rebels and Gentlemen: Philadelphia in the Age of Franklin.* New York, 1942.

Brown, Robert E. *Charles Beard and the Constitution.* Princeton, 1956.

Brown, Wallace. *The King's Friends: The Composition and Motives of the American Loyalist Claimants.* Providence, 1965.

Brown, William G. *The Life of Oliver Ellsworth.* New York, 1905.

Cooke, Jacob E., ed. *Alexander Hamilton, A Profile.* New York, 1967.

Corwin, Edward S. *The "Higher Law" Background of American Constitutional Law.* Ithaca, 1955.

Crosskey, W. W. *Politics and the Constitution.* 2 vols. Chicago, 1953.

Cunliffe, Marcus. *George Washington, Man and Monument.* New York, 1960.

Dickerson. O. M. *American Colonial Government.* Cleveland, 1912.

Douglass, Elisha P. *Rebels and Democrats.* Chapel Hill, 1955.

Earle, Alice Morse. *Two Centuries of Costume in America.* New York, 1910.

Earnest, Ernest. *John and William Bartram.* Philadelphia, 1940.

Eidelberg, Paul. *The Philosophy of the American Constitution.* New York, 1968.

Ernst, Robert. *Rufus King, American Federalist.* Chapel Hill, 1968.

Farrand, Max. *The Framing of the Constitution of the United States.* New Haven, 1913.

Flexner, James Thomas. *George Washington.* 4 vols. Boston, 1965–72.

Flower, Milton E. *John Dickinson, Conservative Revolutionary.* Charlottesville, 1983.

Goddard, Henry P. *Luther Martin.* Baltimore, 1887.

Grigsby, H. B. *The History of the Virginia Federal Convention.* Richmond, 1890–91.

Groce, George C. *William Samuel Johnson.* New York, 1937.

Groennings, Sven, et al., eds. *The Study of Coalition Behavior.* New York 1970.

Hacker, Louis M. *Alexander Hamilton in the American Tradition.* New York, 1957.

Hall, John. *Memoirs of Matthew Clarkson.* Philadelphia, 1890.

Hamilton, Walton, and Douglas Adair. *The Power to Govern.* New York, 1937.

Harding, Samuel B. *The Contest over the Ratification of the Federal Constitution in the State of Massachusetts.* New York, 1896.

Hargrave, Catherine Perry. *A History of Playing Cards and a Bibliography of Cards and Gaming.* New York, 1966.

Hill, Helen. *George Mason, Constitutionalist.* Cambridge, 1938.

Jensen, Merrill. *The Articles of Confederation.* Madison, 1940.

———. *The New Nation: A History of the United States During the Confederation.* New York, 1950.

Johnson, Allen, and Dumas Malone. *Dictionary of American Biography.* 22 vols. New York, 1928–44.

Joseph, Charles. *The Origins of the American Party System.* Williamsburg, 1956.

Ketcham, Ralph. *James Madison.* New York, 1971.

Koch, Adrienne. *Jefferson and Madison.* New York, 1950.

——. *Power, Morals, and the Founding Fathers.* Ithaca, 1961.

Levy, Leonard W., ed. *Essays on the Making of the Constitution.* New York, 1969.

McCaughey, Elizabeth Peterken. *William Samuel Johnson.* New York, 1980.

McClellan, Elisabeth. *History of American Costume, 1607–1870.* New York, 1937.

McDonald, Forrest. *We the People: The Economic Origins of the Constitution.* Chicago, 1963.

McLaughlin, A. C. *The Confederation and the Constitution, 1783–1789.* New York, 1905.

——. *The Foundations of American Constitutionalism.* New York, 1932.

McMaster, J. B., and F. D. Stone. *Pennsylvania and the Federal Constitution, 1787–1788.* Philadelphia, 1942.

Main, Jackson T. *The Antifederalists.* Chapel Hill, 1961.

Meyers, Marvin. *The Mind of the Founder: Sources of the Political Thought of James Madison.* Hanover, 1981.

Miller, John C. *Alexander Hamilton.* New York, 1959.

Miner, C. E. *The Ratification of the Federal Constitution by the State of New York.* New York, 1921.

Mintz, Max M. *Gouverneur Morris and the American Revolution.* Norman, Okla. 1970.

Mitchell, Broadus. *Alexander Hamilton.* 2 vols. New York, 1957–62.

Morgan, Edmund S. *The Birth of the Republic, 1763–1789.* Chicago, 1956.

Morison, Samuel E. *The Oxford History of the American People.* New York, 1965.

Nevins, Allan. *The American States During and After the Revolution.* New York, 1924.

Oberholzer, E. P. *Robert Morris.* New York, 1903.

O'Connor, John E. *William Patterson.* New Brunswick, N.J. 1979.

Rice, Kym S. *Early American Taverns.* Chicago, 1983.

Rossiter, Clinton. *Alexander Hamilton and the Constitution.* New York, 1964.

——. *Seedtime of the Republic.* New York, 1953.

——. *1787, The Grand Convention.* New York, 1966.

Rowland, Kate Mason. *The Life of George Mason.* 2 vols. New York, 1892.

Rutland, Robert A. *The Ordeal of the Constitution: The Antifederalists and the Ratification Struggle of 1787–1788.* Norman, Okla. 1966.

Sellers, Charles Coleman. *Mr. Peale's Museum.* New York, 1980.

Selsam, J. Paul. *The Pennsylvania Constitution of 1776.* Philadelphia, 1936.

Smith, David G. *The Convention and the Constitution: The Political Ideas of the Founding Fathers.* New York, 1965.

Smith, Page. *The Constitution: A Documentary and Narrative History.* New York, 1980.

——. *James Wilson.* Chapel Hill, 1956.

Sparks, Jared, ed. *The Life of Gouverneur Morris.* 3 vols. Boston, 1832.

Storing, Herbert J. *What the Anti-Federalists Were For.* Chicago, 1981.

Swiggert, Howard. *The Extraordinary Mr. Morris.* Garden City, N.Y., 1952.

Thach, Charles C., Jr. *The Creation of the Presidency, 1775–1789.* Baltimore, 1923.

Van Doren, Carl. *Benjamin Franklin.* New York, 1938.

———. *The Great Rehearsal.* New York, 1948.

Ver Steeg, Clarence L. *Robert Morris: Revolutionary Financier.* Philadelphia, 1954.

Warren, Charles. *The Making of the Constitution.* Boston, 1928.

Wheeler, John N. *Richard Dobbs Spaight.* Baltimore, 1880.

Williams, Frances Leigh. *A Founding Family: The Pinckneys of South Carolina.* New York, 1978.

Willison, George F. *Patrick Henry and His World.* Garden City, N.Y., 1969.

Wills, Garry. *Explaining America: The Federalist.* New York, 1982.

Wood, Gertrude S. *william Paterson of New Jersey.* Fair Lawn, N.J., 1933.

Wood, Gordon S. *The Creation of the American Republic, 1776–1787.* New York, 1969.

Wright, Esmond. *Franklin of Philadelphia.* Cambridge, Mass., 1986.

INDEX